IMAGES
of America

SEMINOLE

I0806451

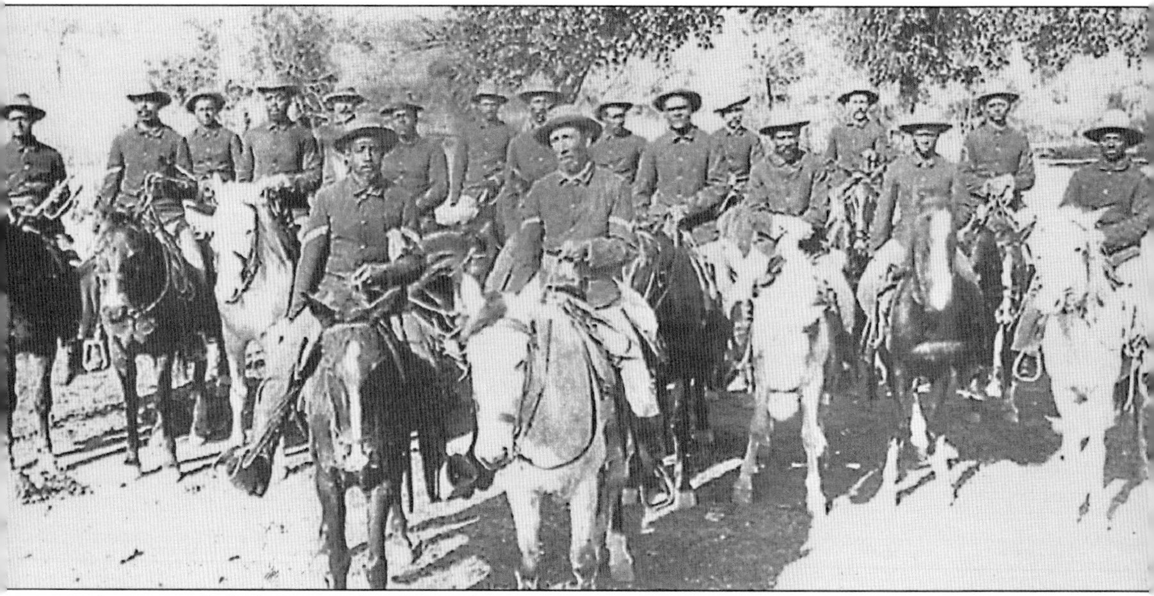

A group of Black Seminoles, descendants of runaway slaves who fled Georgia and lived among Seminole Indians in Florida swamps, left Florida in 1850 and were recruited by the US Cavalry as scouts in 1872. It was said that Black Seminoles could track a lizard across rock. In the 1870s, under the command of Lt. Col. W.R. "Pecos Bill" Shafter, the scouts explored an area of arid West Texas that was supposedly uninhabitable because it lacked water. They spotted a grove of trees in the bottom of a shallow draw and discovered hand-dug water wells. Shafter named them Seminole Wells in honor of the scouts. The discovery of water opened the area to settlement, and the town established north of the draw was named Seminole. (Gaines County Museum, Seminole Division.)

On the Cover: In Gaines County, Texas, the successful completion of the first oil wells in the 1930s led to an oil boom lasting decades. Hundreds of wells were drilled, and gangs of workers serviced wells, pipelines, storage tanks, and other oil facilities. In 1947, the gang pictured on the cover worked for Ohio Oil Company (later called Marathon Oil). In front of their gang truck are, from left to right, (first row) "Tater" Salmon (the pumper), Don Keller, Clarence Dewey (the gang pusher), "Slim" McNabb, John Warren, and Rex Foster; (second row) Charlie George (the coauthor's father), Bill Baldwin, and W.P. "Stan" Stanley. (George family.)

IMAGES
of America

SEMINOLE

Charles and Linda George

ARCADIA
PUBLISHING

Copyright © 2012 by Charles and Linda George
ISBN 978-0-7385-8539-0

Published by Arcadia Publishing
Charleston, South Carolina

Printed in the United States of America

Library of Congress Control Number: 2011939731

For all general information, please contact Arcadia Publishing:
Telephone 843-853-2070
Fax 843-853-0044
E-mail sales@arcadiapublishing.com
For customer service and orders:
Toll-Free 1-888-313-2665

Visit us on the Internet at www.arcadiapublishing.com

To the early pioneers of Seminole and Gaines County, whose determination, foresight, hard work, and sense of community and fair play created a place so many have called home.

Contents

Acknowledgments

The authors would like to extend heartfelt thanks to everyone who contributed photographs or information for this book and to all the residents of Seminole for making this city what it is today. Parenthetical notations are included with each photograph's caption to denote its source. Many thanks to the following for contributing their photographs to this book: Roy Lynn Barnes, director of the Gaines County Museum, Seminole Division, and museum employee Gene Bering (Museum); Shelby Crow Concotelli and the Seminole Chamber of Commerce (Chamber); *Seminole Sentinel* editor Dustin Wright and feature writer Leo Copeland (*Sentinel*); Alene, Charles, and Linda George (George family); Kathy Davis and Vicki Clark (Thompson family); Robert Jones and Mary Davis (Jones family); Jim and Barbara Culver (Culver family); Zach and Melissa Holbrooks (Holbrooks family); Hyle and Skeet Doss (Doss family), Tina Rempel Siemens (Rempel family); Linda Lawrence Liveley (Lawrence family); First Presbyterian Church; Lynn Whitaker (Whitaker family); Shirley Jameson (Jameson family); Dan Stark (Stark family); Tommie Roberts; Katy LaFollette Scroggins; Betty Moore Roberson; Cassandra Cobb Northcutt and Joyce Hargrove (Cobb family); Pat and Dink Aryain (Aryain family); Janie Butts and the Seminole Memorial Hospital Auxiliary (Auxiliary); Betty Hill (Hill family); David Walden and Judy Walden Henry (Walden family); Mary Maloney Hughes (Maloney family); Leo Copeland (Copeland family); Robbie Blount and the Western Peanut Growers' Association (Robbie Blount); Tommie Roberts, and Rich White, human resources director of Hess Corporation (Hess).

Special thanks also go to the First Presbyterian Adult Sunday School class members for helping identify people, places, and things in the photographs (Jim and Barbara Culver, David Shelton, Betty Golmon, Jerry and Margarett Malone, and Roy and Bea Barnes); to Dink and Pat Aryain, for similar help; to Ed Wegele and his friends for helping identify automobiles; to those at a Presbyterian luncheon and at the Great Comeback who took time to browse photographs and help us identify people; and to David Walden for helping format some of the photographs. We could not have provided the depth of historical information in this book without all of you. Thank you!

Introduction

Seminole, Texas, situated on the arid South Plains of West Texas, is today a thriving community of more than 6,000 people—the county seat of Gaines County. Just over 135 years ago, however, the area was an open, largely treeless plain inhabited only seasonally by Comanche Indians. In the 1870s, a military campaign of the US Army's 24th Infantry led by Cols. Ranald S. Mackenie and W.R. "Pecos Bill" Shafter arrived in what is now Gaines County. In October 1875, troops under the command of Lt. John L. "Whirlwind" Bullis, part of Shafter's force, encountered a large band of Indians camped along the shores of Cedar Lake, one of the largest playa lakes in the region, located approximately 20 miles northeast of present-day Seminole.

Bullis's command was unique, to say the least. His troops consisted of Black Seminoles (formerly called Seminole Negroes) from northern Mexico. They were descendants of runaway Alabama, Georgia, and Florida slaves who had intermarried with Seminole Indians in the swamps of Florida and northern Georgia, only to be captured by US forces and led on the infamous Trail of Tears to the Oklahoma Indian Territory in the 1830s. In 1849, a large group of Black Seminoles escaped Oklahoma and fled to northern Mexico, where they settled. In the 1870s, Black Seminoles were recruited as scouts for the Army on the frontier.

After the brief 1875 skirmish at Cedar Lake, Colonel Shafter established a camp there and sent scouting parties to explore the surrounding territory. In November of that year, Shafter's men reached a draw—a relatively shallow gully—two miles south of where the town of Seminole was later established. What they discovered in the bottom of the draw amazed them. Surrounded by miles and miles of relatively barren grassland stood a tall grove of healthy hackberry trees. Nearby, they found 50 hand-dug water wells, ranging in depth from four to 15 feet. Farther west, they found 20 more. The area apparently had served as a regular site for Comanche to meet and trade goods. The discovery of such an abundant water source made the area desirable for settlement. Because the wells were discovered by Bullis and his Black Seminole troops, the wells became known as the Seminole Wells.

In the mid-1890s, white settlers began to come to this corner of the South Plains. Among the first to arrive were W.B. Austin and his wife, Emma. They eventually constructed a two-story building near the draw, dubbing their fledgling community Caput. The Austins opened a store and post office on the lower floor of their new building while living on the second story. Emma Austin also ran a "free hotel" on the top floor for passing cowboys. More settlers moved into the area in the early 20th century when the State of Texas declared that settlers would be granted four sections of land after living on it for three years and "proving it up." Ranching became the county's first industry thanks to the abundant natural grass and water that could be pumped to the surface with windmills. Sandy, fertile soil later brought farmers to the area.

Named for James Gaines, one of the signers of the Texas Declaration of Independence, Gaines County had once been part of other Texas counties, including Martin County. On October 24, 1905, Gaines County was organized as a separate entity. Later in 1905, a group of nonresident landowners from New York donated 320 acres of land for a county seat to be named Seminole in honor of the water wells that made living in the area possible. In the spring of 1906, the Austins decided to move Caput to the site of the new town, two-story building and all. Faced with crossing the draw that lay between their current location and the new town site, they sawed the building in half and moved it by horse-drawn wagons in two pieces to Seminole. Other early merchants who set up shop in Seminole were W.H. Brennand and Guy Stark. Among early ranchers were M.S. Doss and his wife, Meek Lane, who decades later became philanthropists donating funds for numerous community projects.

In 1906, the Seminole post office opened, and a small wooden courthouse was constructed. The first floor of the courthouse building was completed by July 4, 1906, and its dedication included a

Fourth of July celebration picnic. People arrived mostly by wagon and camped on the courthouse grounds. Barbecue, speeches, and a dance rounded out the day. Established in 1906, Seminole's first church was the First Presbyterian Church, followed soon after by a Methodist church in 1908 and a Baptist church in 1922. The first permanent school building was constructed on the western edge of town near where the current elementary and primary schools are located. Erected by Dan Cobb in 1910, this building had four classrooms downstairs for younger students and two upstairs for high school students. The building also had an auditorium and was topped by a cupola with a large brass bell that could be heard for miles.

Seminole National Bank opened its doors in 1906, followed by First State Bank in 1907. In 1912, bank robbers stole more than $3,000 from Seminole National Bank. The two banks consolidated in 1914 as First State Bank. By this time, Seminole had about 300 residents. It also boasted telephone service and a movie theater. The weekly newspaper the *Seminole Sentinel* was established in 1907 by B.W. Cavender. The *Sentinel*, Seminole's oldest established business, still operates under its original name. From 1918 to 1923, Seminole enjoyed a railroad connection to Midland, but the route was not profitable enough to be maintained.

A severe drought in 1917–1918 left the area impoverished, and that was followed in 1929 by the Great Depression. Because of the economic crisis, First State Bank was forced to close in the 1930s. However, a growing oil industry protected the town from the Depression's worst effects. The oil industry had its beginnings in Gaines County in 1925 when an oil well was drilled south of Cedar Lake in the northeastern corner of the county. That same year, a group of oilmen from Oklahoma and Fort Worth leased large tracts of land southwest of Seminole for drilling. They paid 10¢ an acre for those leases. Soon after, Humble Oil (later Exxon) leased more than 100,000 acres west of town and began drilling. The first oil production in Gaines County occurred in 1935.

Seminole incorporated in 1936 with a commission form of city government. The town's first mayor was C.C. Cothes. The town's first bond issue financed a municipal water system. Another early vote was to determine whether alcohol could be sold in the county. That measure failed by a vote of 18-1. However, it was decided that local doctors could issue prescriptions for whiskey—to be taken for medicinal purposes only. Also in the 1930s, several rural schools around Gaines County were consolidated, making the Seminole school district one of the largest in the country. According to one source, the district covered 753 square miles, while serving only 370 students.

With the discovery of oil, Seminole's population grew dramatically. In 1940, there were 1,761 residents. By 1950, that number had doubled to 3,480, surpassing the neighboring Gaines County town of Seagraves (18 miles to the northeast) for the first time. In the 1950s, Seminole boomed. In 1953, a modern hospital was built; in 1954, the water system was expanded; in 1955, the courthouse was renovated and expanded; and in 1958, the Gaines County Library opened. By 1960, Seminole's population had increased to 5,737. By 2000, the city reached 5,910. Over the next 10 years, Seminole grew to 6,430 people, partially thanks to the influx of German-speaking families, many of them members of Mennonite churches who had begun arriving from Mexico and Canada in 1977, finding Seminole to be a friendly, welcoming community.

Seminole's centennial celebration occurred on October 24, 2005, with a daylong party that included an authentic chuckwagon meal of beans and corn bread. Entertainment included a cowboy poet and music provided by local musicians. A huge display at the Civic Building included memorabilia and an antique tractor and car show. A time capsule was also to be buried on the courthouse square.

Today, Seminole still boasts an excellent school system, a diverse economy, and some of the friendliest people in Texas. Cotton and peanuts are the most widely grown crops. In fact, Gaines County is consistently the number-one cotton-producing and the number-one peanut-producing county in Texas. Other crops raised in the area include pecans, peppers, potatoes, hay, and melons. Gaines County is also frequently the number-one oil-producing county in the state. Seminole's farmers, ranchers, oil producers, teachers, and merchants are always eager to greet and make welcome the 500–1,000 visitors who come to Seminole each year. The motto of the Seminole Chamber of Commerce—and a true indication of the welcoming spirit of the residents of Seminole—is, "When you're here, you're home!"

One

1900–1925

Echoes of the Past

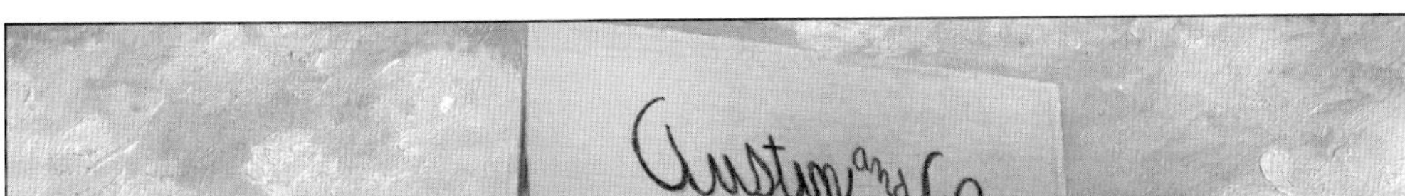

In 1904, William B. and Emma Austin settled south of present-day Seminole and built the area's first store—a 20-by-40-foot, two-story structure with living quarters, a general store, a free hotel, and a post office named Caput. In 1906, the building was cut into two parts and dragged by horses across the draw and over a mile north to Seminole's courthouse square, where it remained until 1936, when it was destroyed by fire. (Museum.)

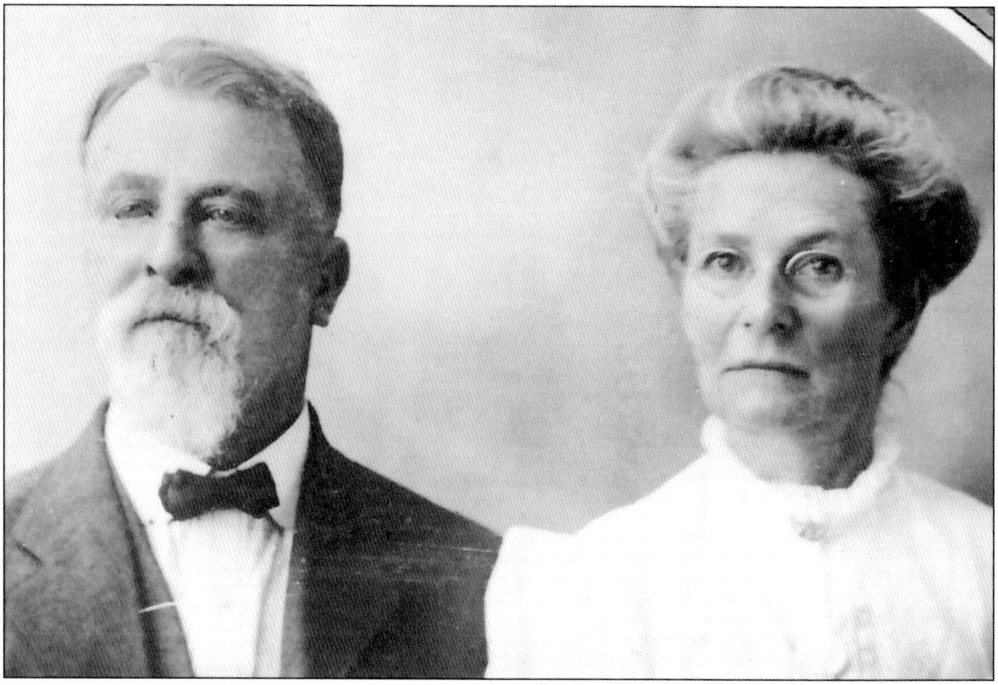

The first cattleman to bring his family to Seminole was C.C. Medlin. In 1880, the Medlins arrived at Cedar Lake, then in 1881, they moved to the draw south of present-day Seminole and built a modest home near Hackberry Grove, the site of the Seminole Wells. After only a few years, the Medlin family moved on to New Mexico. (Museum.)

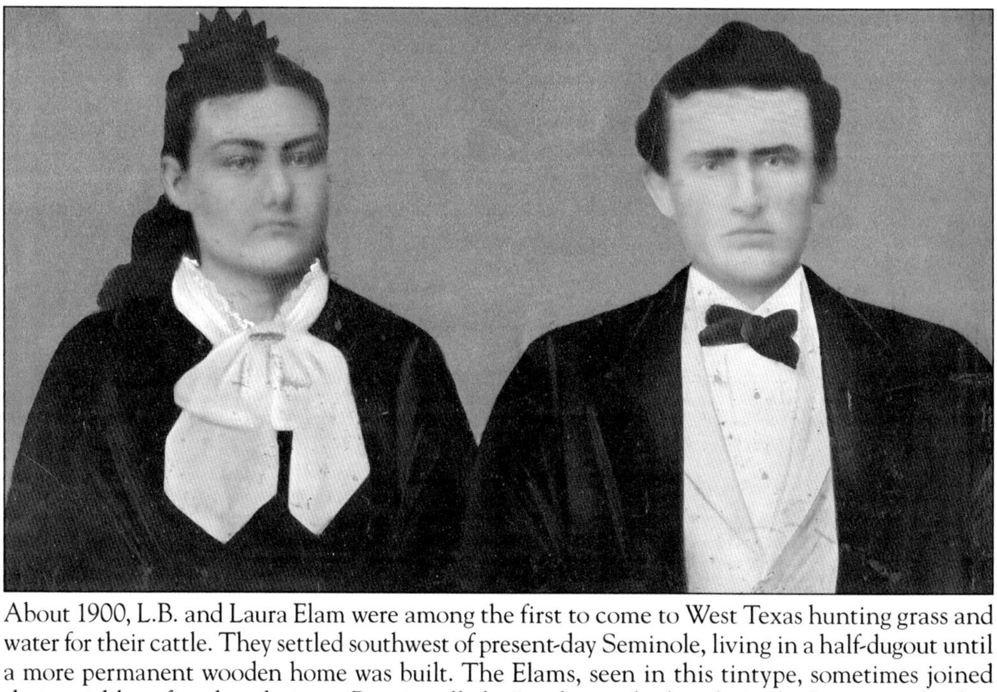

About 1900, L.B. and Laura Elam were among the first to come to West Texas hunting grass and water for their cattle. They settled southwest of present-day Seminole, living in a half-dugout until a more permanent wooden home was built. The Elams, seen in this tintype, sometimes joined their neighbors for what their son Barnie called a "wash-pot chicken fry." Chickens were fried in a wash pot and then doused with cream gravy. Delicious! (Museum.)

In 1903, a land rush brought several pioneer families to Seminole. These included the M.S. Doss, J.B. Thompson, C.H. Eubank, Guy Stark, J.R. Houston, J.W. Childers, W.B. Eubank, and W.H. "Bill" Birdwell families. Pictured from left to right are W.H. and Lettie Birdwell's children Gus, Robert, and Doll. Robert and Doll came to Seminole as children. Gus, born in 1905, was the second white child born in the county before it was organized. (Museum.)

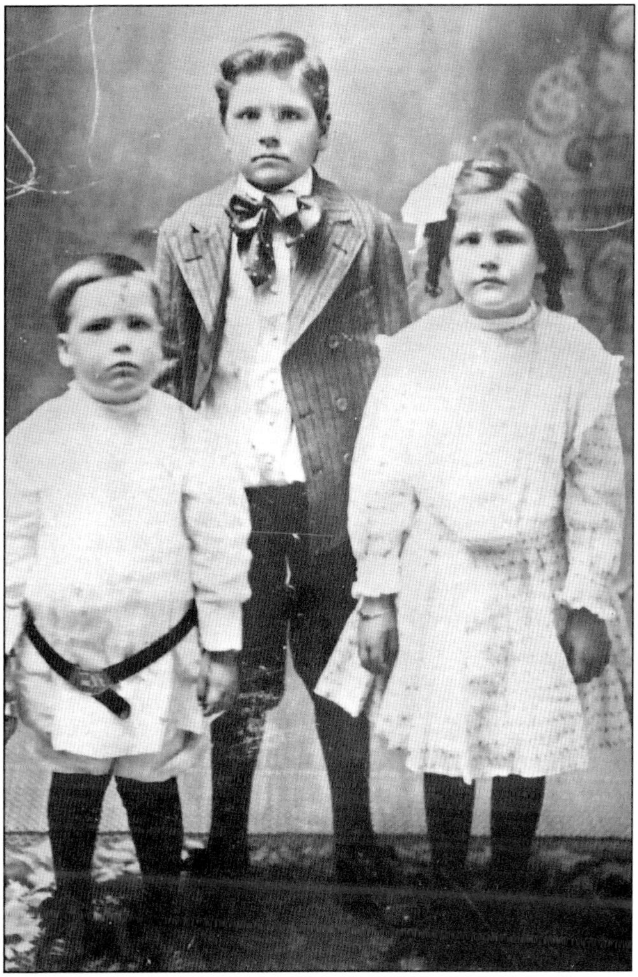

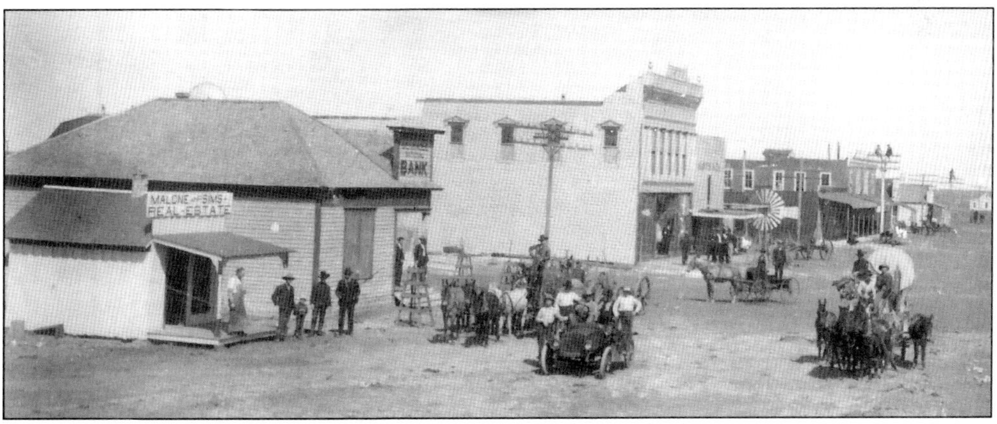

This photograph, taken between 1908 and 1910, looks north along Seminole's Main Street. Pictured are Malone and Sims Real Estate; Seminole National Bank; the Austin-Boyd building, which W.B. Austin constructed alongside his original general store and post office (the building with the flat awning) that he had moved into town in 1906; and, farther down the street, T.A. Robertson's Lone Star Hotel and Stark's Grocery. (Museum.)

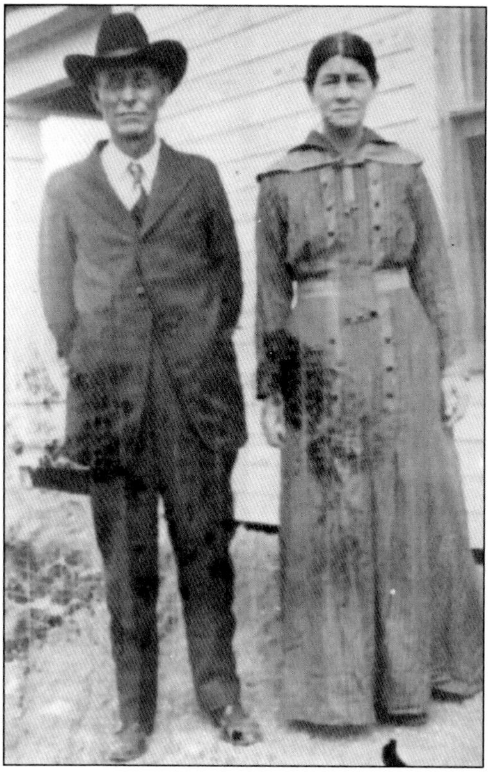

J.F. and Lula Wyatt came to Seminole by covered wagon in 1905. In 1906, county commissioners hired Wyatt and his son Lee—one of the best cowboys in the area—to dig a water well accessible to the community on the southwest corner of the courthouse square. Wyatt also built a wagon yard, started a freight business in Seminole, and eventually opened a feed store and grocery store. (Museum.)

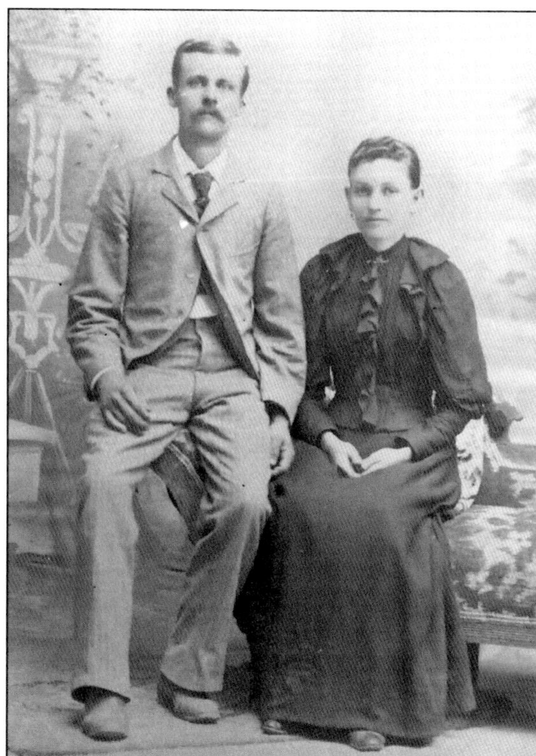

Guy Stark came to Seminole in 1904, filed on a piece of land north of town, and built a half-dugout. His wife, Betty, and their children followed in May 1905. In July, he attended the gathering at Hackberry Grove where local residents agreed to organize the county. Stark eventually opened a grocery store across from the northwest corner of the square, and the family operated a business at that location until 1945. (Museum.)

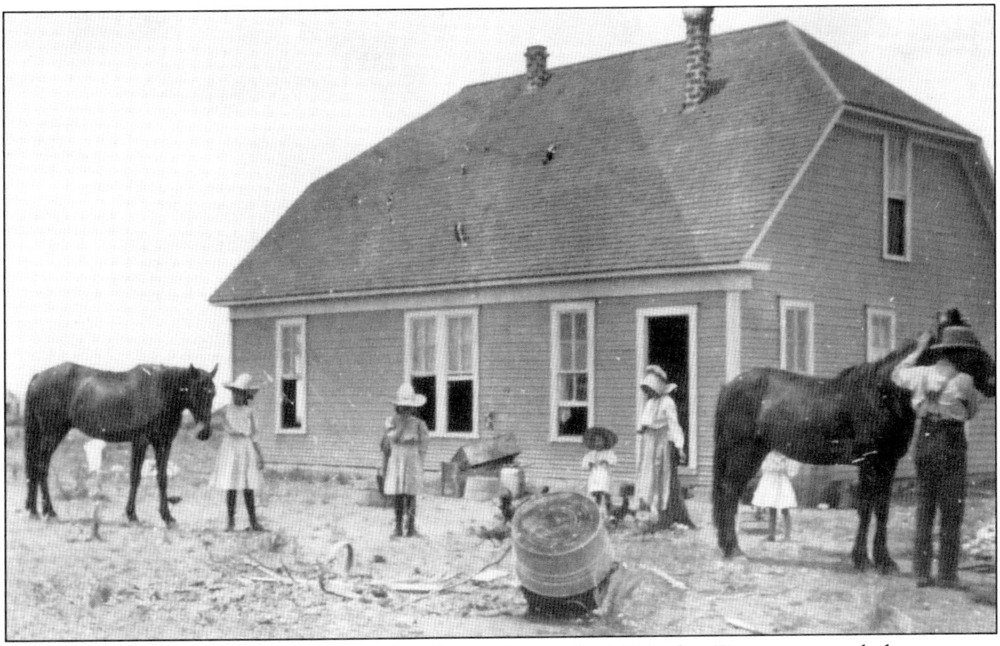

Dan and Aurelia Metcalf Cobb moved to Seminole in May 1906 after Dan was awarded a contract to build Gaines County's courthouse. The home he built for his family still stands in northwest Seminole, proudly bearing a Texas Historical Medallion as the oldest house in the county still occupied by family members. The Cobb family is seen behind their house. From left to right are Lois, Ora, Edna, Aurelia, Dorothy (behind the horse), and Dan. (Cobb family.)

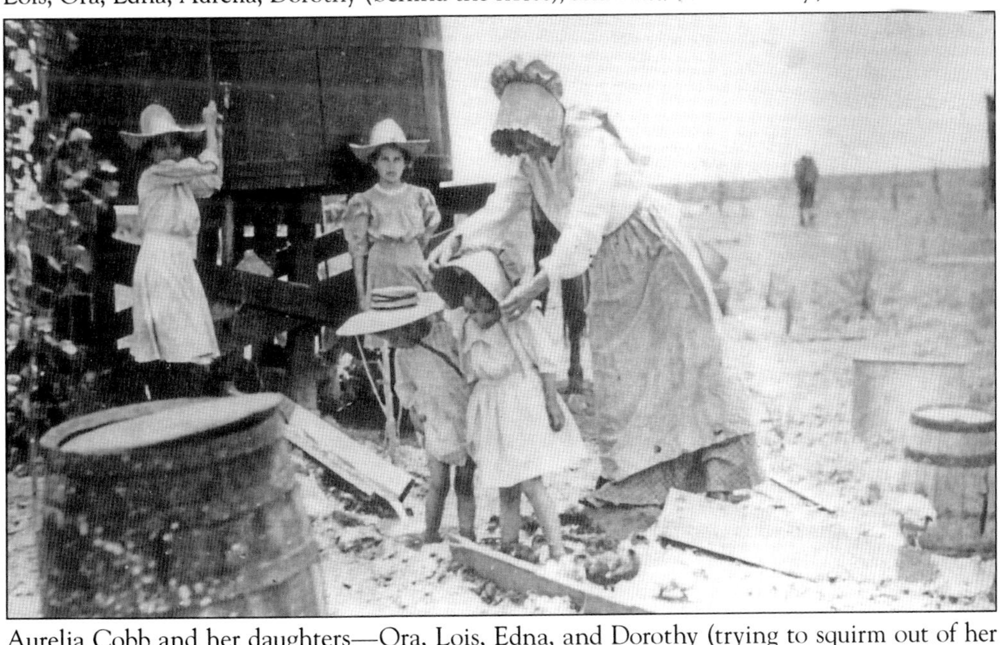

Aurelia Cobb and her daughters—Ora, Lois, Edna, and Dorothy (trying to squirm out of her bonnet)—stand by their elevated water tank constructed of cypress wood. Ora is opening the valve to allow Edna and Dorothy to wash their feet (as well as to provide water for the baby chicks and ducks scurrying around underfoot). Aurelia is trying to put Dorothy's bonnet on—again! (Cobb family.)

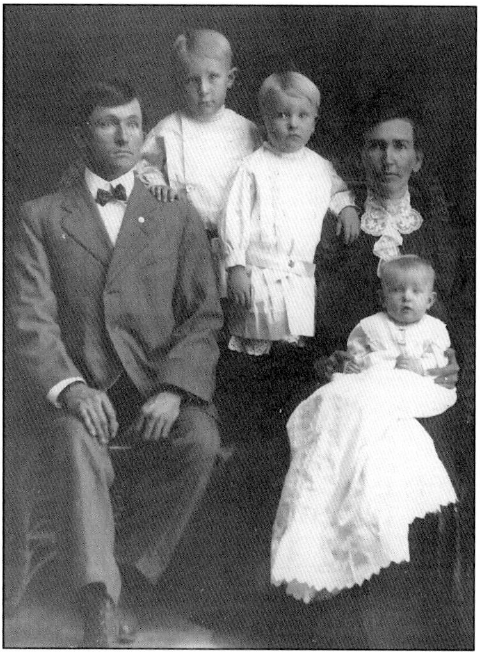

In 1905, Claude H. and Minerva "Jenny" Wescott arrived in Seminole, along with six-week-old C.T. Relatives had written that land was available for filing. After a couple of years, they returned to Erath County. In 1921, they came back to Seminole for good. Wescott raised cotton and broom corn, which the family made into brooms. According to C.T., "Papa traded brooms for anything you could wear, eat, or use in any way." (Museum.)

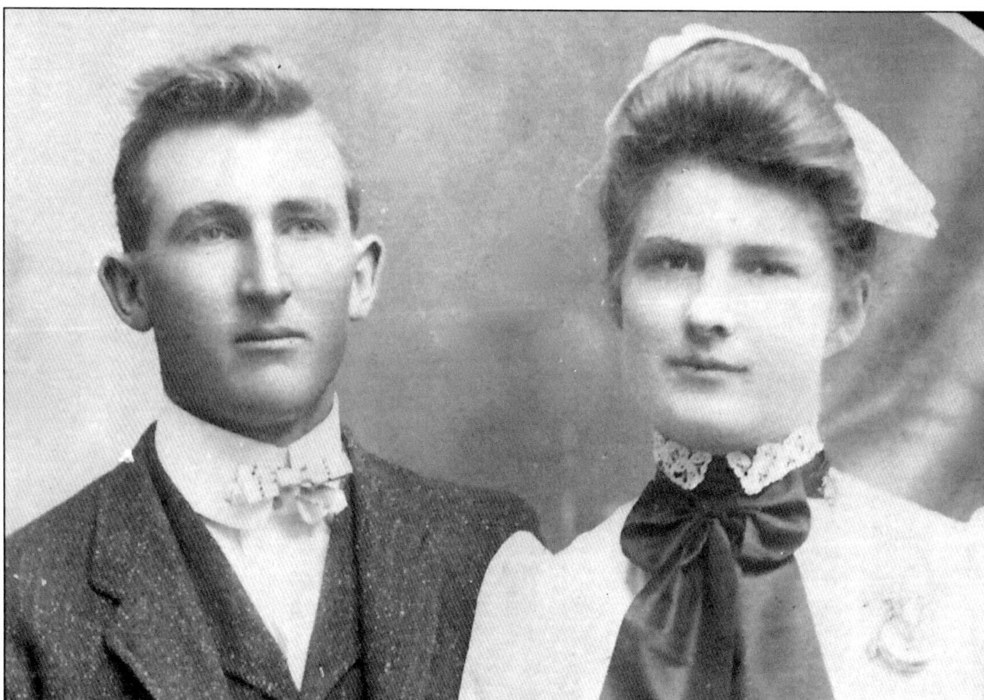

Edgar (C.E.) and Collie Rollins came to West Texas from Central Texas in 1907. Edgar, the first automobile dealer in Seminole, sold Hupmobiles. He also owned the first telephone company, was a charter member of the First Baptist Church and the Masonic lodge, served two terms each as sheriff and county commissioner, and taught many Seminole residents how to drive. After Collie died in childbirth, Edgar remarried, this time to Pauline Little, who came to Seminole and became a teacher in the local school. (Museum.)

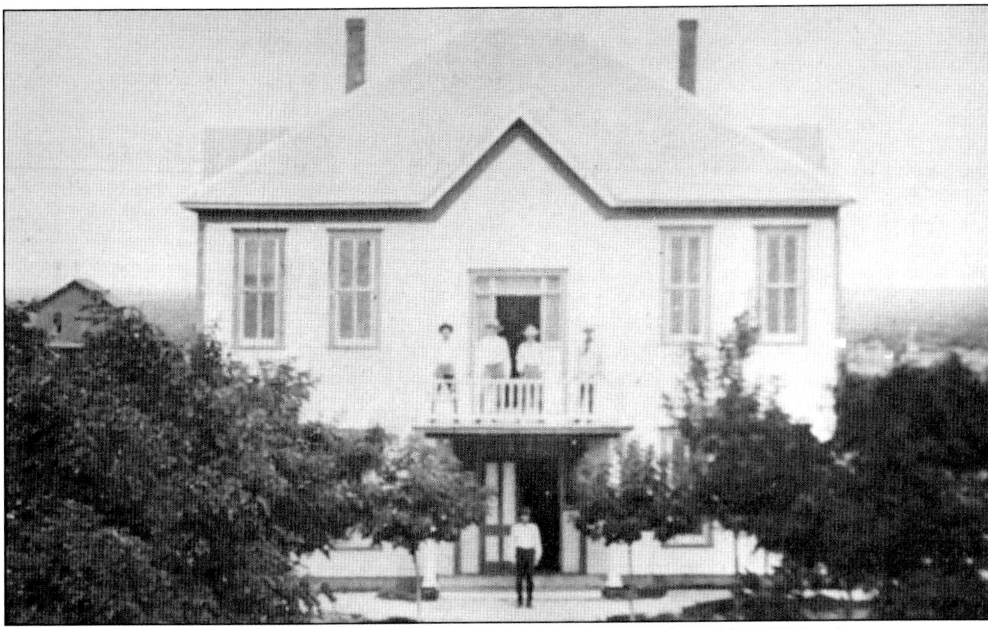

Early in 1906, county commissioners accepted a bid from Dan Cobb of $4,155 for the construction of a wooden courthouse. He began the building immediately, and the structure was complete enough for Seminole's first town barbecue and dance by July 4 of that year. People came from all over the county on July 3, camped out overnight, and enjoyed the festivities all the next day and into the night, including a dance on the completed floor of the courthouse. The building, pictured from the west, was completed in October. (Museum.)

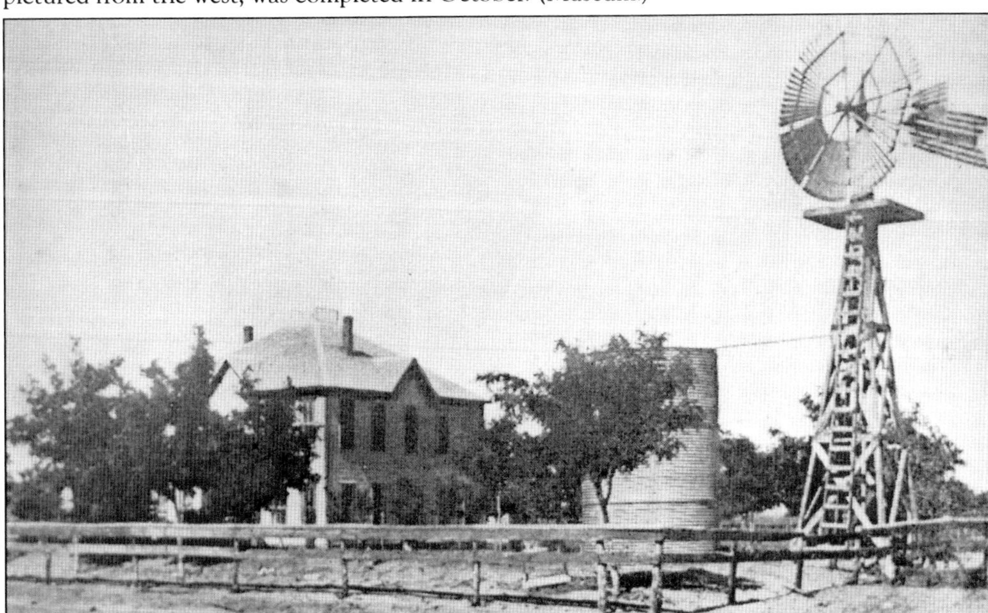

Seminole's first courthouse, this time photographed toward the northeast, shows the water well dug by J.F. and Lee Wyatt in 1906, which was used as a municipal water source. The Eclipse windmill, manufactured by Fairbanks Morse and Company of Chicago, pumped water into the storage tank to its left and supplied water to Seminole for many years. (Museum.)

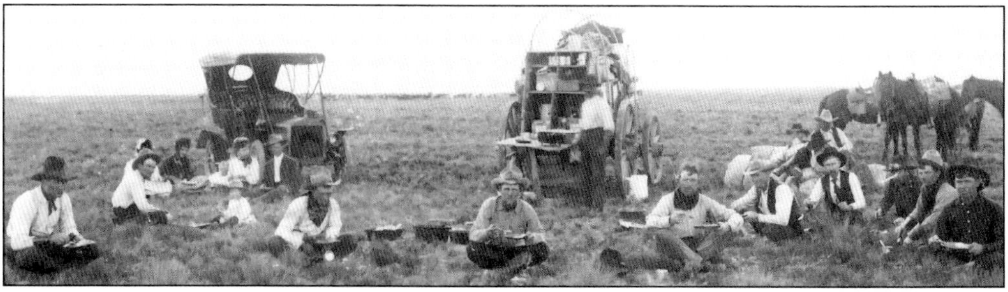

Ranch hands pause for a meal, "nooning" on the Brennand Ranch in this photograph, taken in 1905 or 1906. The chuckwagon in the center provided the grub, which was shared with members of the Brennand family who had driven to the site (labeled "Seminole Wells" on the photograph) in their automobile. (Museum.)

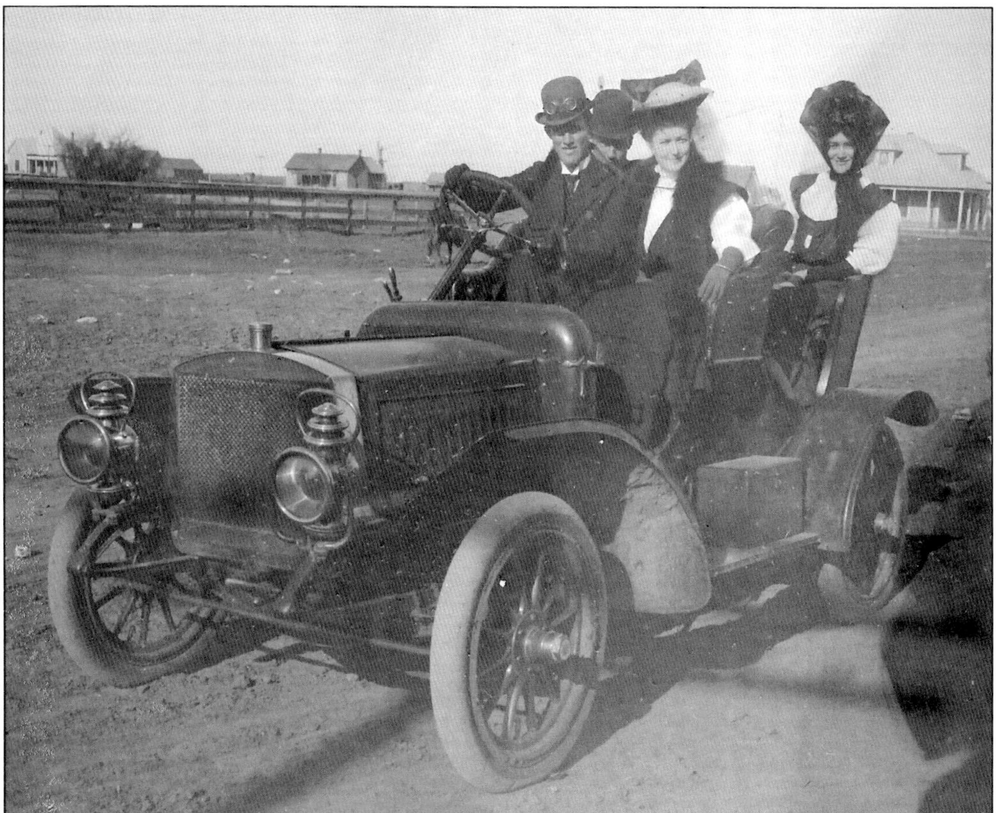

This photograph, taken in 1908, shows Myrtle Elam (in the front seat) and several friends riding in a Hupmobile (no doubt purchased from C.E. Rollins). Myrtle was the daughter of L.B. and Laura Elam. Sadly, an outbreak of typhoid fever in the fall of that year took Myrtle's life. She was 20. Four other members of the Elam family contracted the disease but survived. (Museum.)

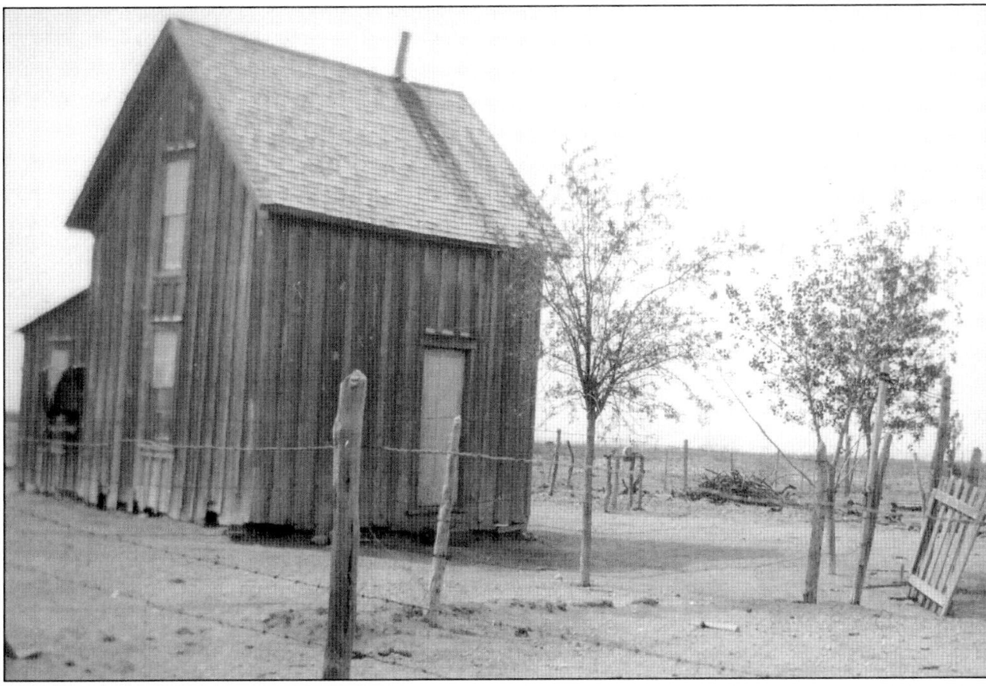

One Seminole family in particular became known for its generosity and community spirit—M.S. and Meek Lane Doss. When Monroe Scott Doss first came to the area in 1904, he was a poor cowhand striving to earn the love of Meek Lane. He obtained four sections of land about 15 miles southwest of Seminole that had the one-room rough plank house seen here and 100 head of cattle. M.S. and Meek Lane were married in December 1905 and moved into the house. (Doss family.)

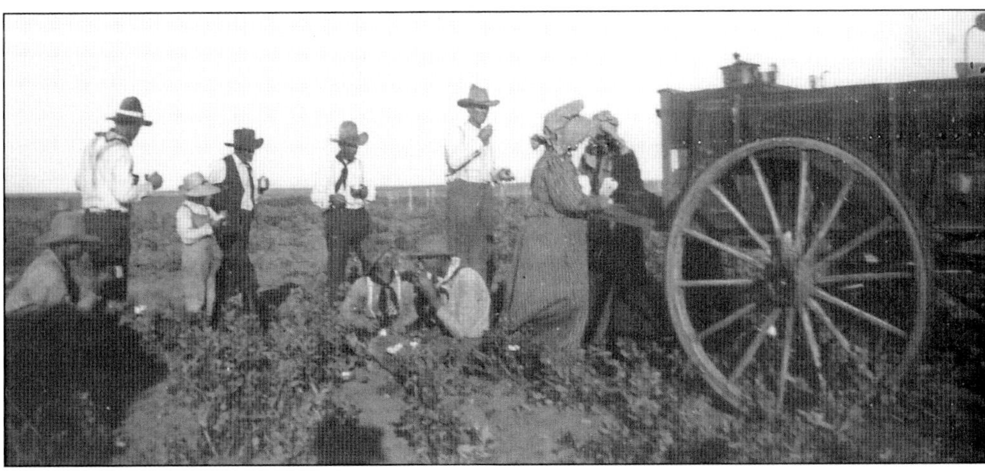

Around 1910, life on a farm or ranch was hard, and workers did not always go home for lunch. Instead, wives often accompanied their husbands to the fields and worked alongside them, stopping at noon to fix a meal in the back of the buckboard. This photograph of an unidentified family shows that children, when old enough, also contributed to the day's labor. (Museum.)

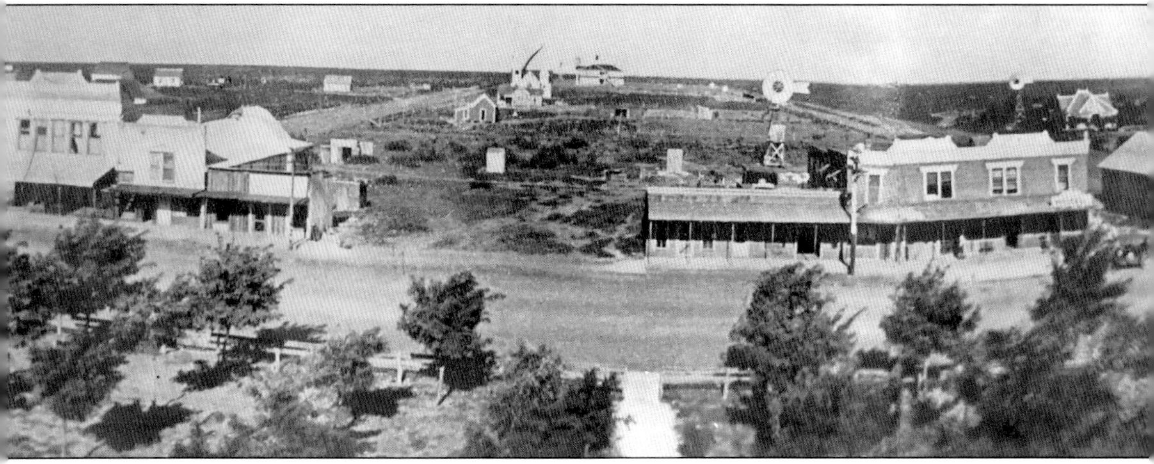

The three images on pages 18 and 19 are part of a panorama photograph taken around 1912 from the roof of the Gaines County Courthouse. The image above shows the view to the west. At the left end of the first block of South Main Street (visible here) is the two-story Austin-Boyd building. Next to it is the old Caput store and post office that had been moved into town by W.B. Austin several years earlier. Next to that is Ollie Haywood's barbershop. Just visible in the right side of the photograph—at the north end of the block—is Stark's Grocery. To its left are the two-story Lone Star Hotel and an unidentified building. On the horizon in the center of the photograph is the two-story Seminole school built by Dan Cobb. Slightly closer and to the left are the First Baptist Church and the First Methodist Church. Behind most buildings and homes are small structures. Most of those are outhouses—pit toilets with no running water and no heat! Also visible behind several structures are windmills. One other structure, seen on the far right just above the right corner of the Lone Star Hotel, is the W.H. Brennand family's home. (Museum.)

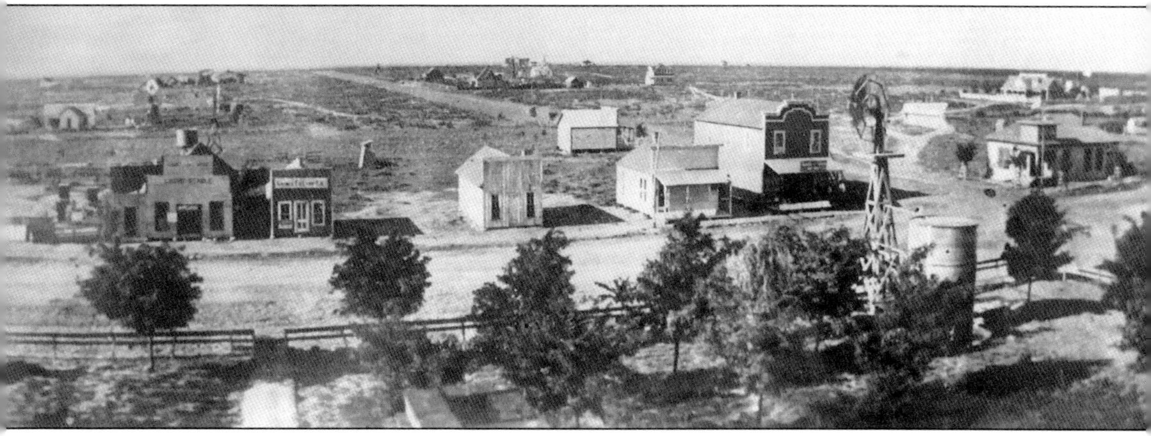

This portion of the 1912 panorama photograph looks toward the south and southwest. Many of the buildings on the left side of this image have not been identified. One structure near the center is a livery stable owned by Jimmy Wyatt. At the west end of this block—Avenue B—stands the two-story First State Bank building. In the distance, just above and to the left of the bank, is home of W.B. and Emma Austin. In front of the bank and across Avenue B is the municipal windmill and water storage tank. On the far right, across South Main Street from the First State Bank, is Seminole's other bank, Seminole National. In the distance above this structure is the Ramsey home, which still stands at the intersection of Southwest Second Street and Avenue C. (Museum.)

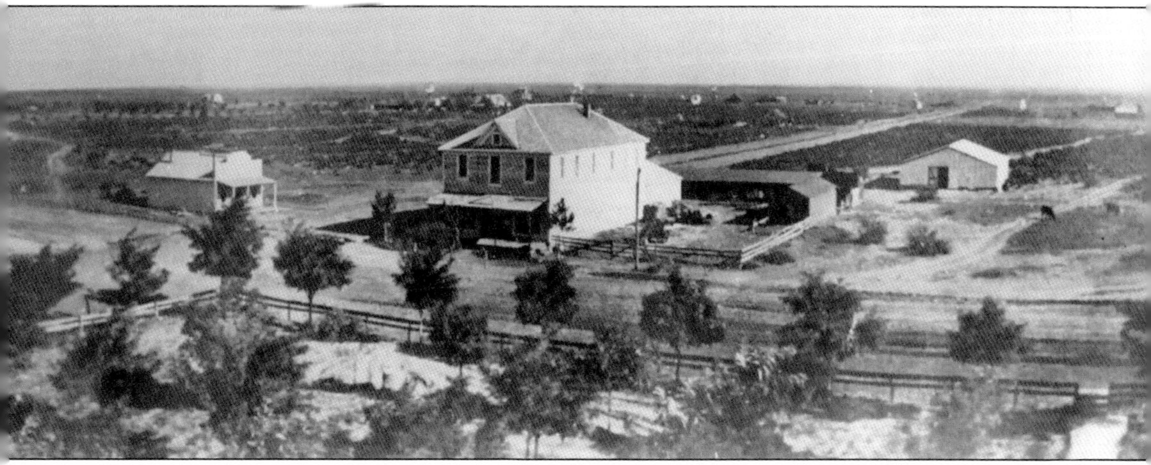

This last panorama section looks toward the north and northwest. The most prominent structures visible in the center of the photograph are the W.H. Brennand General Mercantile and Mitchel Wagon Yard. In the distance, barely visible, are the homes of the Dan Cobb family, the J.S. George family, and the T.O. Stark family. (Museum.)

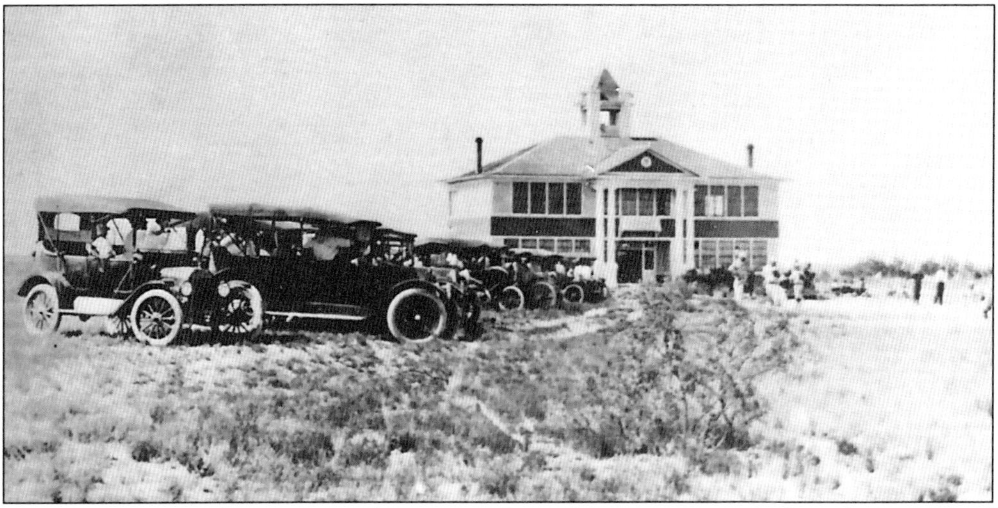

The first school building in Seminole was a small wood-frame structure built in the east part of town in 1906 that burned down two years later. In a location some six blocks west of downtown, Dan Cobb built the two-story school seen here in 1910. It featured six classrooms, an auditorium, and a bell tower. In this picture, cars parked nearby brought local residents to watch a baseball game being played on school grounds. (Museum.)

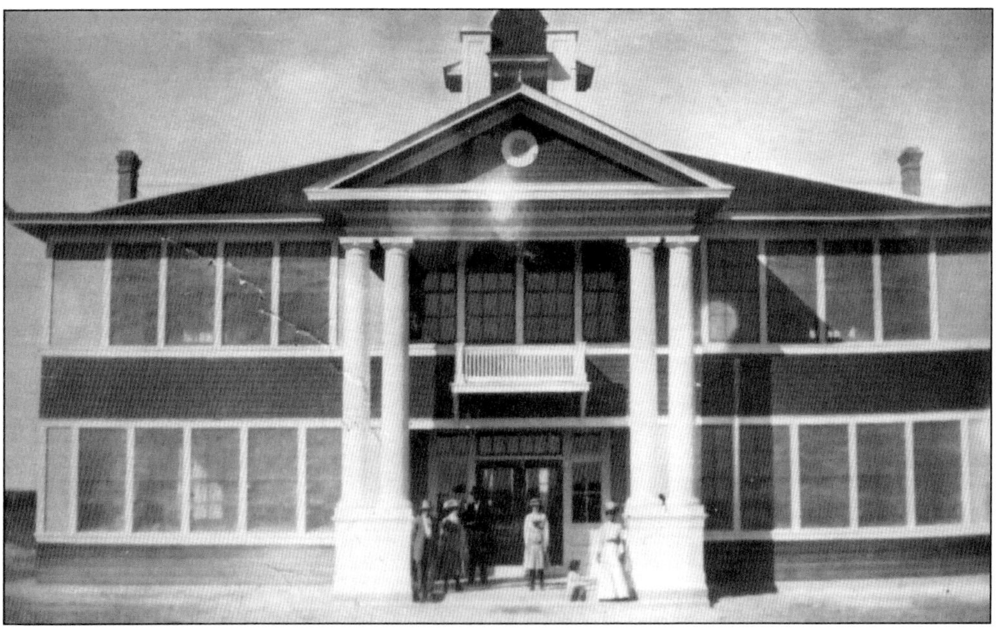

In all, there were 29 schools in Gaines County before most were consolidated into three districts: Seminole, Seagraves, and Loop. Pictured here is the same school building as seen above, constructed in 1910 on a site that today has the tennis courts and playground across from Seminole Elementary. This building served Seminole students until 1928. (Museum.)

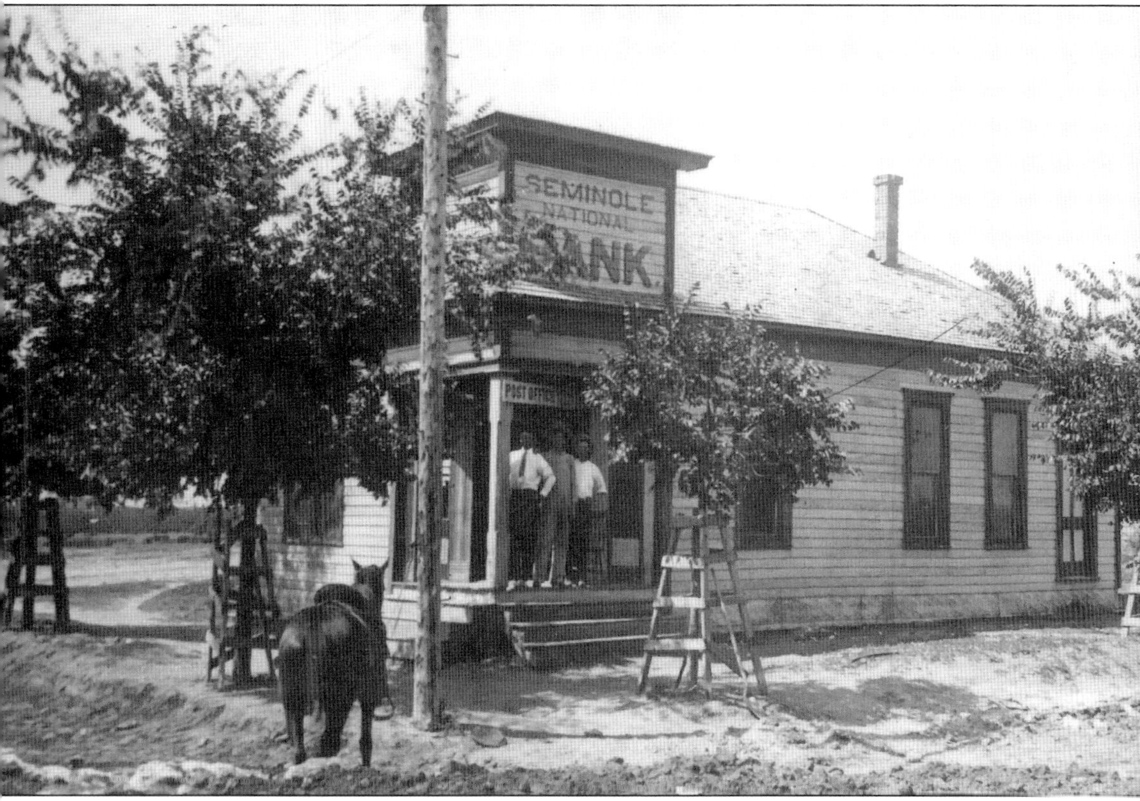

Pictured is Seminole National Bank, the town's first bank. Organized in 1906, it also served as Seminole's post office and stood across from the southwest corner of the courthouse square. The bank was robbed of $3,500 by two masked gunmen on February 12, 1912. Seminole National merged with First State Bank in May 1914. (Museum.)

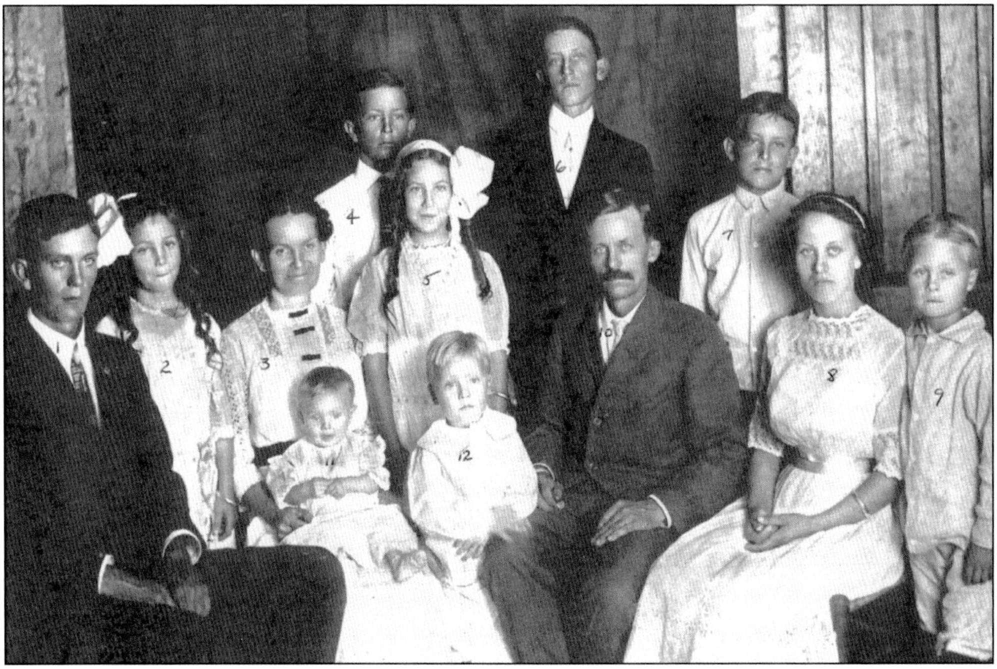

Mr. and Mrs. Guy Stark and 10 of their children pose for a family portrait in 1913. Pictured seated on the left side of the group (from left to right) are Floyd, Lou Mattie, and Mama Stark (Betty), holding one-year-old Gracie Lee in her lap. Standing in the center (from back to front) are Calvin, Ethel, and Terry, with his hand on his father's knee. Seated on the right side of the group (from left to right) are Papa Stark (Guy) and Gladys. Standing behind Papa is Glen, wearing a dark jacket, and behind Gladys is Homer. The young man standing on the far right is Guy, named for his father. Papa Stark's grocery store supplied farmers and ranchers all over Gaines County and into New Mexico. (Stark family.)

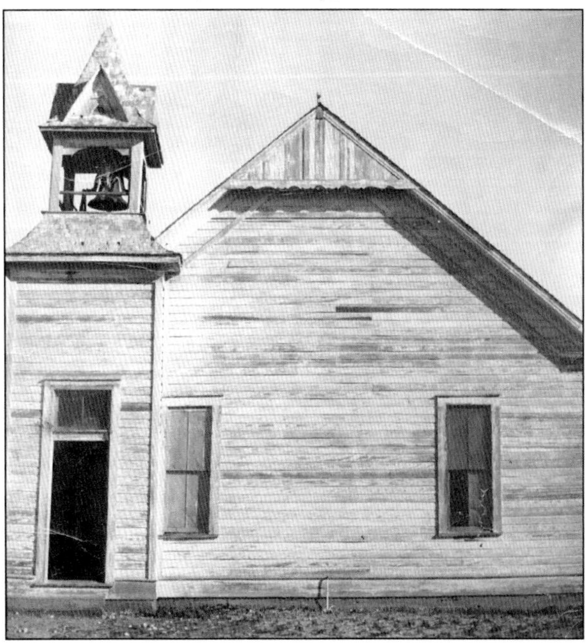

The first religious service held in Gaines County took place in 1904 at Hackberry Grove, just south of town. At another meeting held by itinerant preacher O.G. Jones in 1905, those in attendance organized the First Presbyterian Church. One year later, construction began on the first church building to be erected in Seminole. This wooden structure was completed in 1907 and stood on the northeast corner of the intersection of Southwest Third Street and Avenue C. Today's First Presbyterian Church stands across the street from this site, and the bell from that first church's belfry, now housed in its own tower outside on the grounds of the current church, still rings every Sunday. (First Presbyterian Church.)

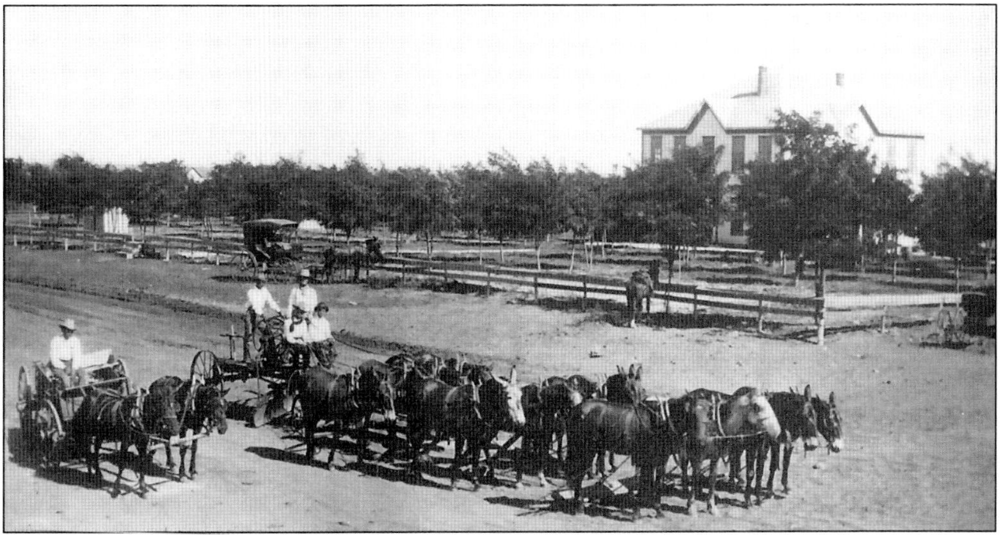

Roads in early Seminole were not paved. Periodically, the street and road crew had to blade the roads in town to keep them smooth. This image, taken around 1914, shows two teams of horses dragging blades—some called fresnos—along the north side of the courthouse. Pictured are Floyd Stark on the left and Albert O'Neal on the far right. (Museum.)

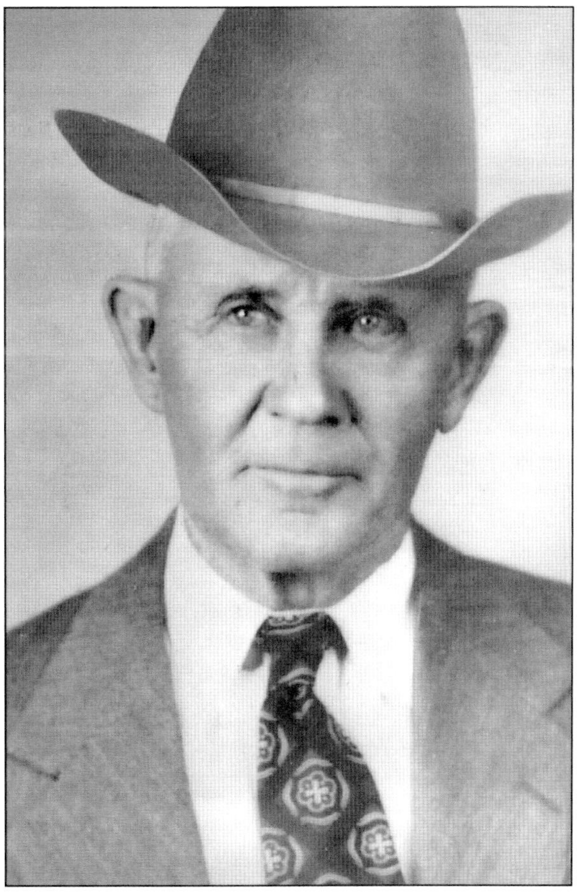

At his death in 1951, P.W. Dalmont held the distinction of having lived in Gaines County longer than anyone else. He first came to the area in 1889 to work for various ranching operations before starting his own ranch around the turn of the century. In 1910, he married Mary Hanna, who had come to Seminole in 1906 to teach at the Cedar Lake School, one of the county's first schools. (Museum.)

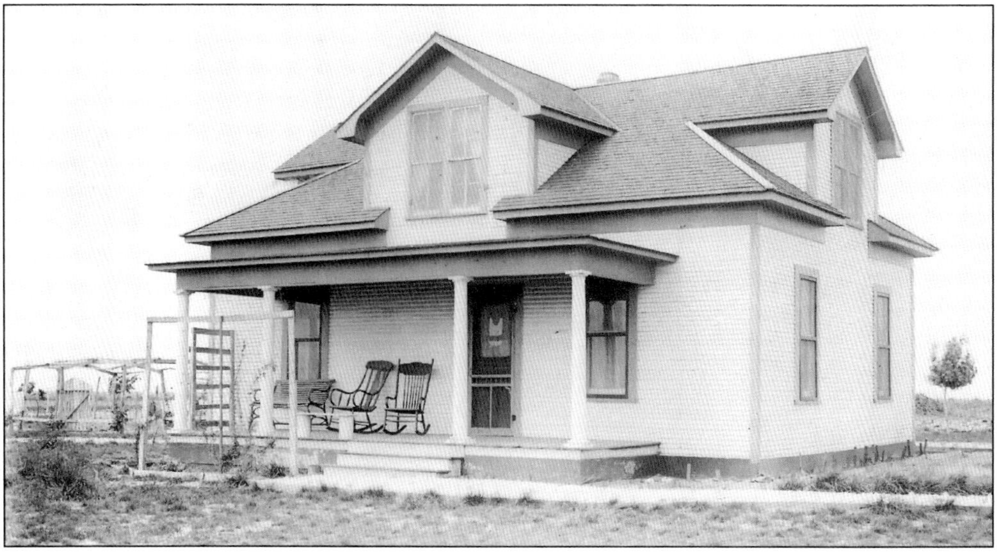

This two-story house was home to W.B. and Emma Austin. Located in the south part of Seminole, the Austin home provided a great place for social events during the town's early years. It was also where they raised their four children: Annie, Mary, Glen, and Velma. (Museum.)

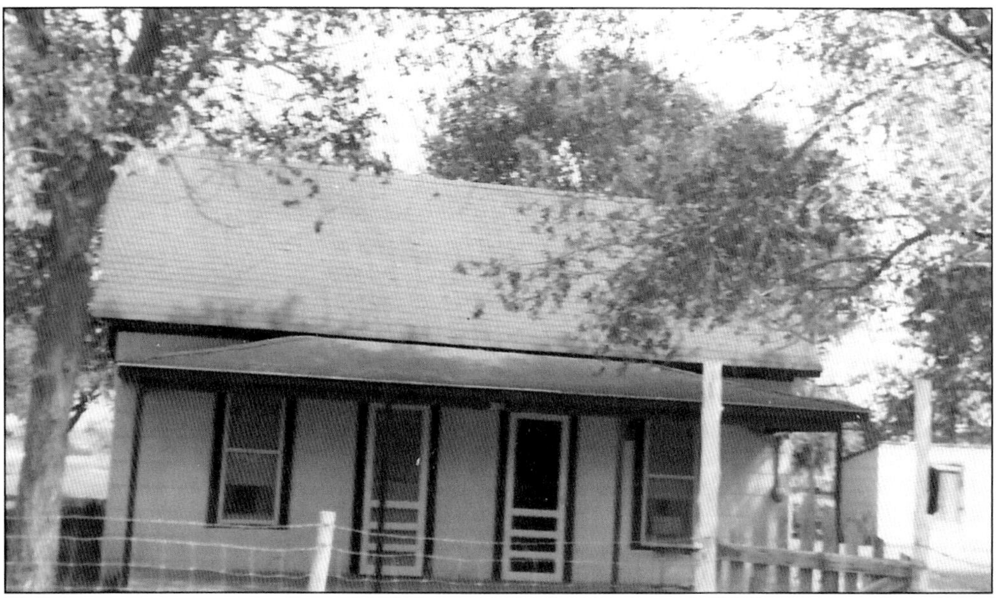

Located east of the Gaines County Courthouse, this modest house has been home to several pioneer families. It was built in 1908 by C.E. Rollins, whose family was first to reside there. Since that time, the R.W. Pittman family, the F.A. Marcus family, and several generations of the J.T.J. Jones family have called it home. (Museum.)

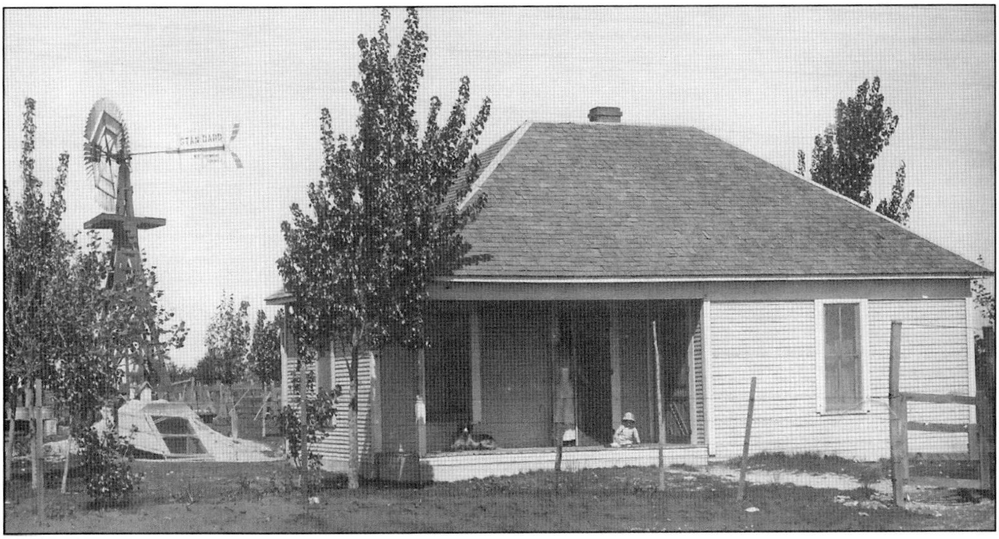

This photograph shows the home of J.S. and Cora Cordelia Marbut George in 1916. It stood at the intersection of North Main Street and Northwest Avenue C. Cora George can be seen standing on the front porch alongside her youngest son, Charles (the coauthor's father), and the family's dog. An Eclipse windmill and storm cellar are visible to the left of the house. Behind the house, the Georges also had a small vineyard. (George family.)

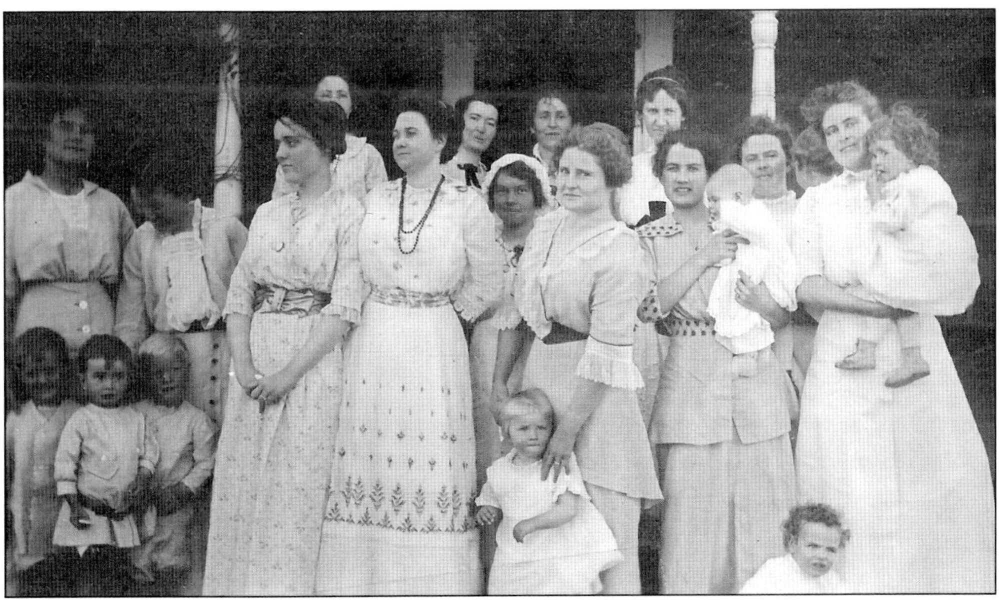

These ladies—members of the Ladies of Home Mission Society of the M.E. Church South (later called the Methodist Church)—posed for this photograph in 1913. On the back row at far left is Pauline Rollins. On the back row, fourth from the left, is Cora George. In front of Cora George is Ione Pittman. The woman in the front row with her hand on a child is Effie Dow, and the one holding a child on the far right is Mabel Curry. (George family.)

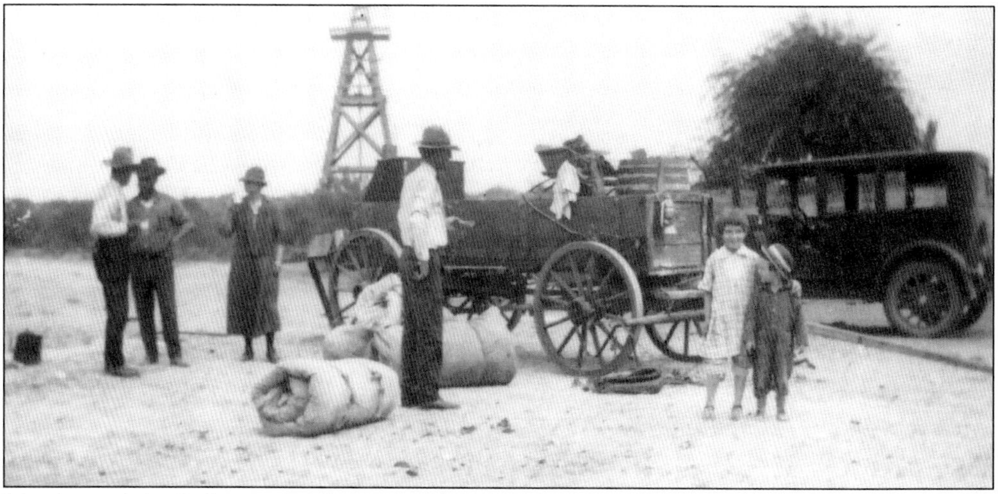

Members of the Dalmont family visit workers on their ranch some time around 1918 to 1920. Dalmont children Pauline and Hardy are standing to the right of the buckboard. P.W. Dalmont is in the center of the picture, and his wife, Mary, is to his left, drinking coffee with the ranch hands. (Museum.)

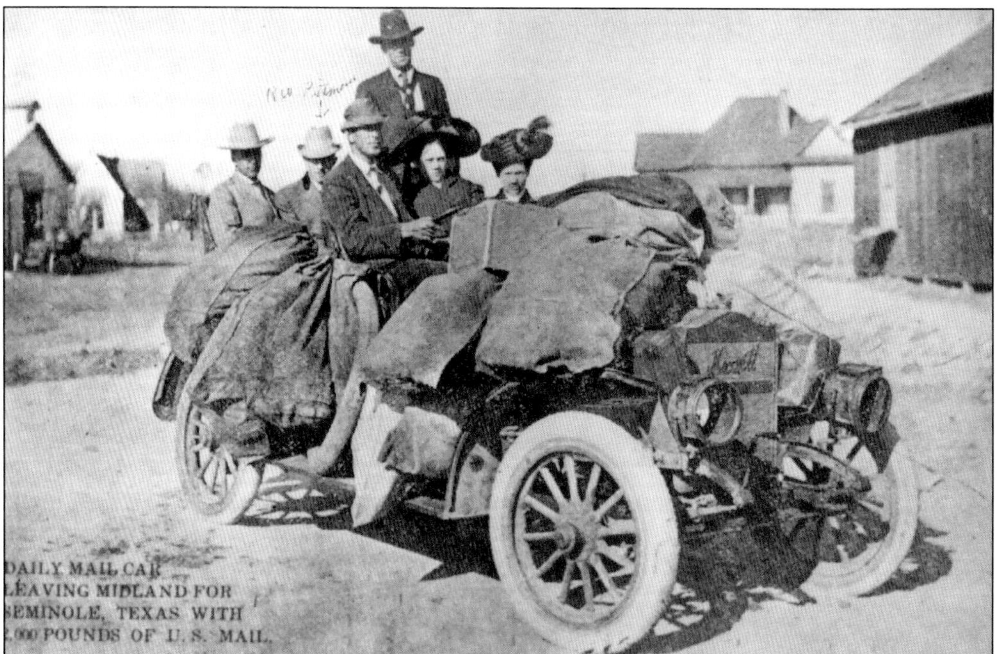

This 1910 Maxwell touring car carried mail and passengers once a week between Midland and Seminole. In this photograph, approximately 2,000 pounds of mail have been strapped onto the car in Midland to be taken to Seminole. The gentleman in the back seat with a dark coat collar has been identified as R.W. Pittman. (Museum.)

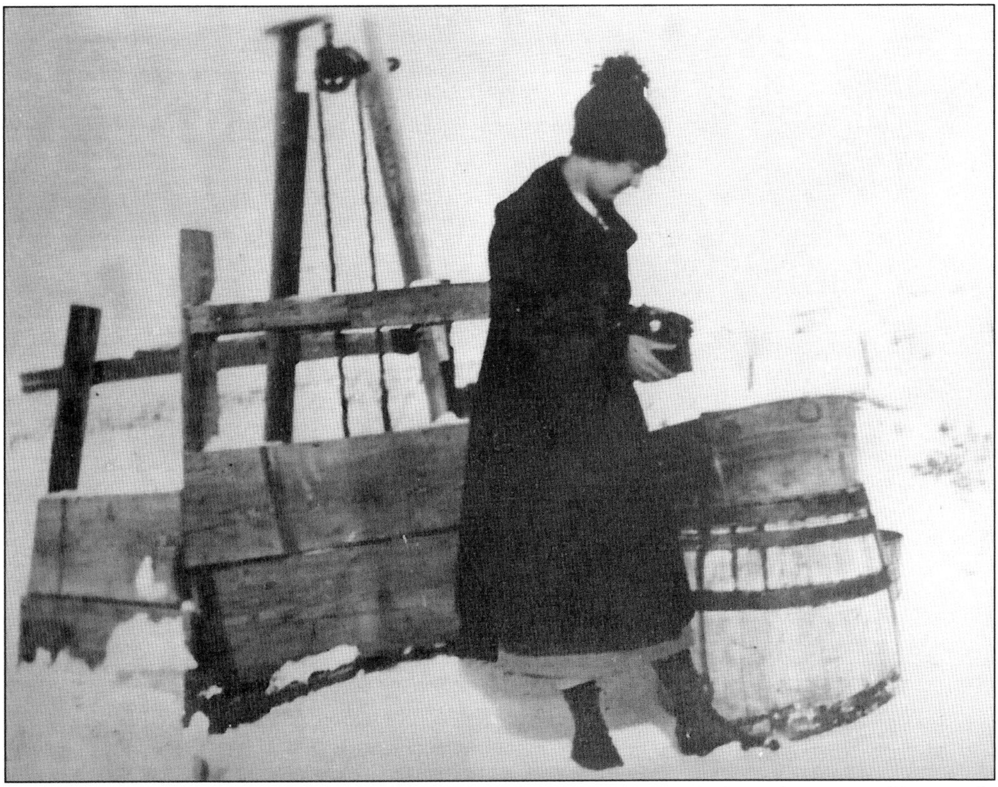

John Kuykendall and his wife, Eddie, arrived in Gaines County in 1916, settling west of Seminole and building a half-dugout. Because underground water was fairly close to the surface there, they were able to dig a well near their dugout using only a pick and shovel. Ila, one of their daughters, is seen here at the well during the harsh winter of 1918. (Museum.)

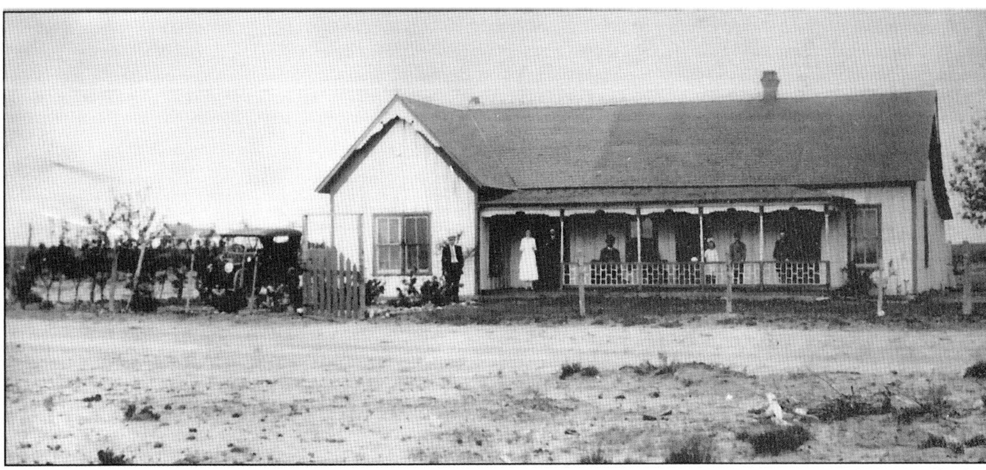

In 1902, J.B. and Ida Thompson staked their claim on land about eight miles southeast of what later became Seminole. They built a one-room lean-to cabin, dug a well, installed an Eclipse windmill, and built some fences. For supplies, they had to travel to Stanton by wagon, a round trip taking up to 10 days. Despite drought, harsh winters, and other hardships, they managed to build the ranch house seen here by 1914. (Museum.)

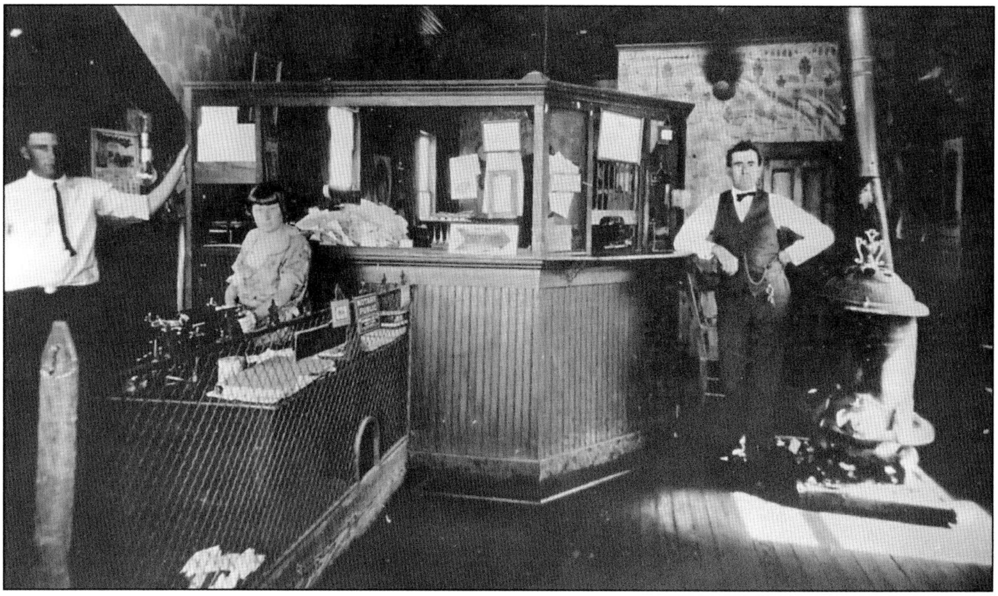

Organized in 1907, First State Bank was located across from the southwest corner of the courthouse square. This photograph of the interior of the bank shows, from left to right, Charley Thompson, Drucilla Lord, and B.B. "Buck" Curry next to the stove. In 1914, Seminole's two banks consolidated, keeping the name First State Bank. It served the community until the Great Depression forced its closing in 1933. (George family.)

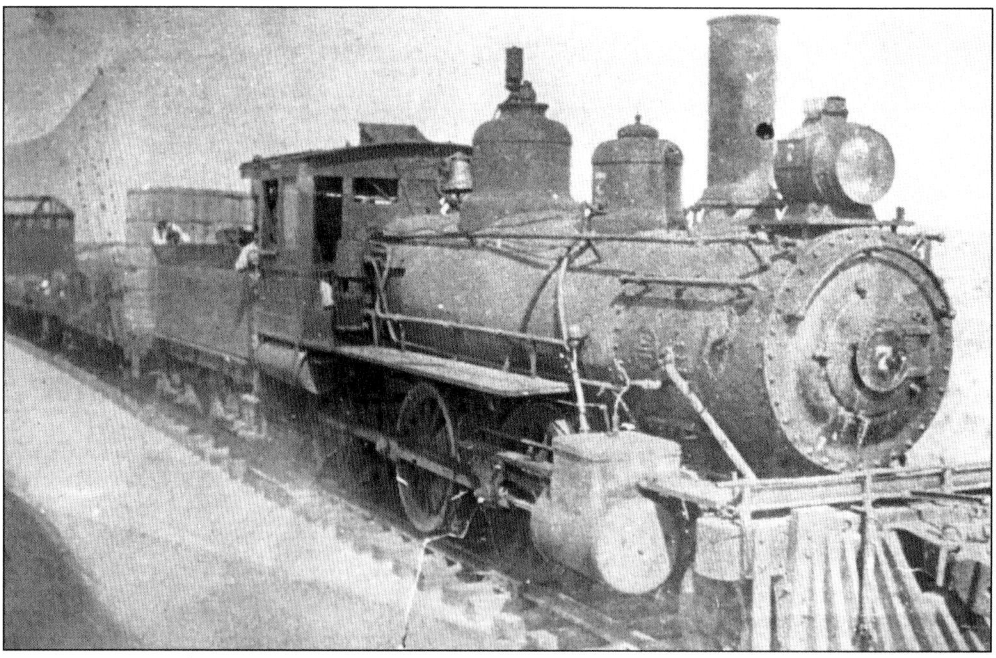

Prior to 1917, freight coming to Seminole arrived in Midland or Stanton by train and then came by wagon. In 1917, C.H. O'Donnell contracted to build tracks from Midland to Seminole. The project—the Midland Northwestern—was completed in 1918, with tracks coming into the southeast part of town. Pictured is one of the two locomotives that serviced the route. Unfortunately, extreme drought forced the company into bankruptcy that same year. (Museum.)

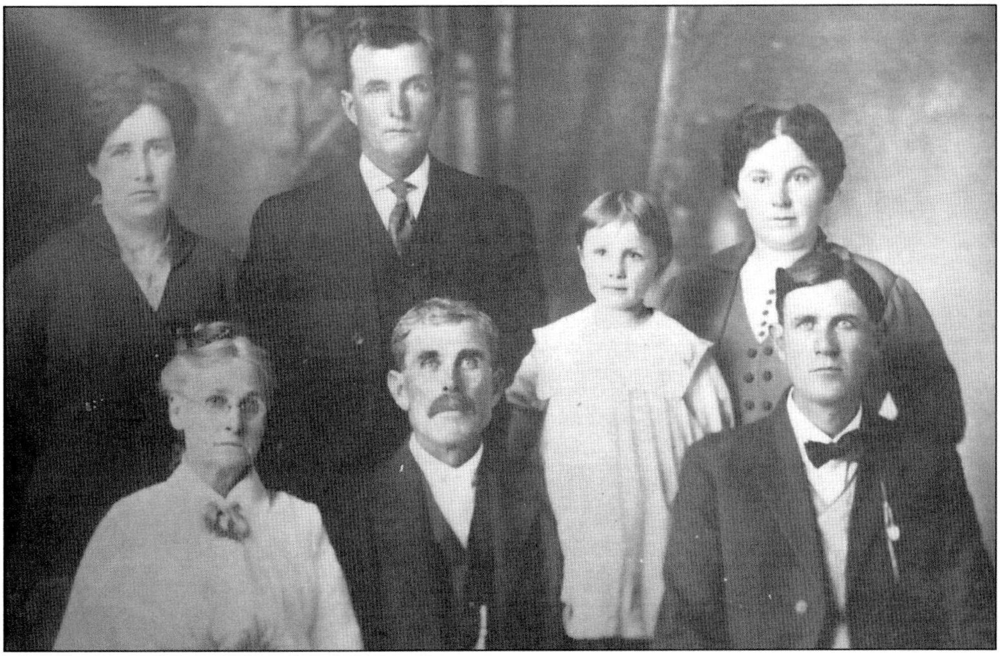

These three families came to Seminole in 1916. Will and Carrie Richards (in the back left) and Rufus and Mary Mitchell (on the right) operated a general mercantile store on the west side of the courthouse square until 1940. The older couple in the portrait (in the left front) is Mr. and Mrs. W.H. Mitchell (Mary), the parents of Carrie and Rufus and the grandparents of young Nuel Mitchell (standing between her grandfather and father). Nuel was the daughter of Rufus and Mary and was five years old when they moved to Seminole. Their store was called Richards and Mitchell. (Museum.)

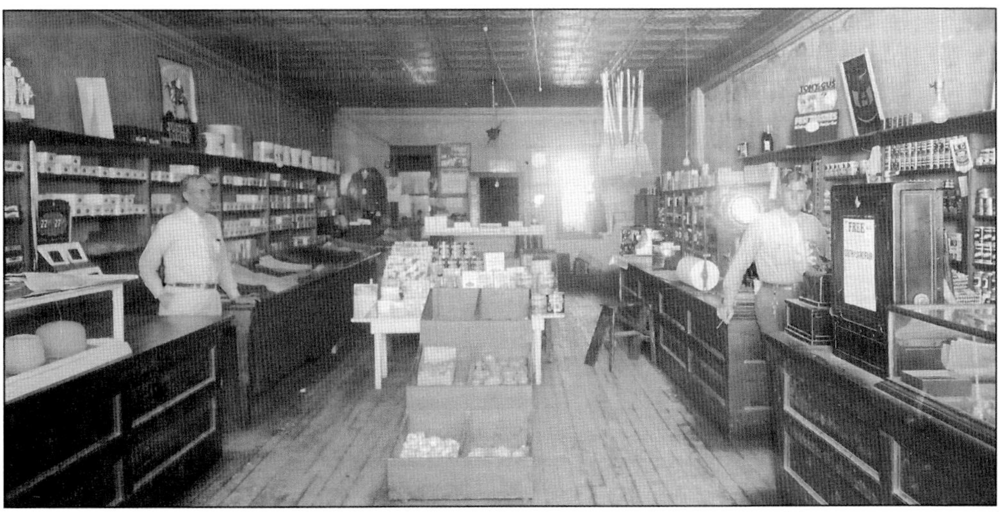

This is the interior of the Richards and Mitchell Store, located just south of the Lone Star Hotel on the west side of the courthouse square. Will Richards, on the left, sold general merchandise. Rufus Mitchell, on the right, sold groceries. When the Mitchell and Richards families first came to Seminole, they lived in the W.H. Brennand home, but they later built three homes on Southwest Third Street, the site of Seminole Independent School District's Success Center today. (George family.)

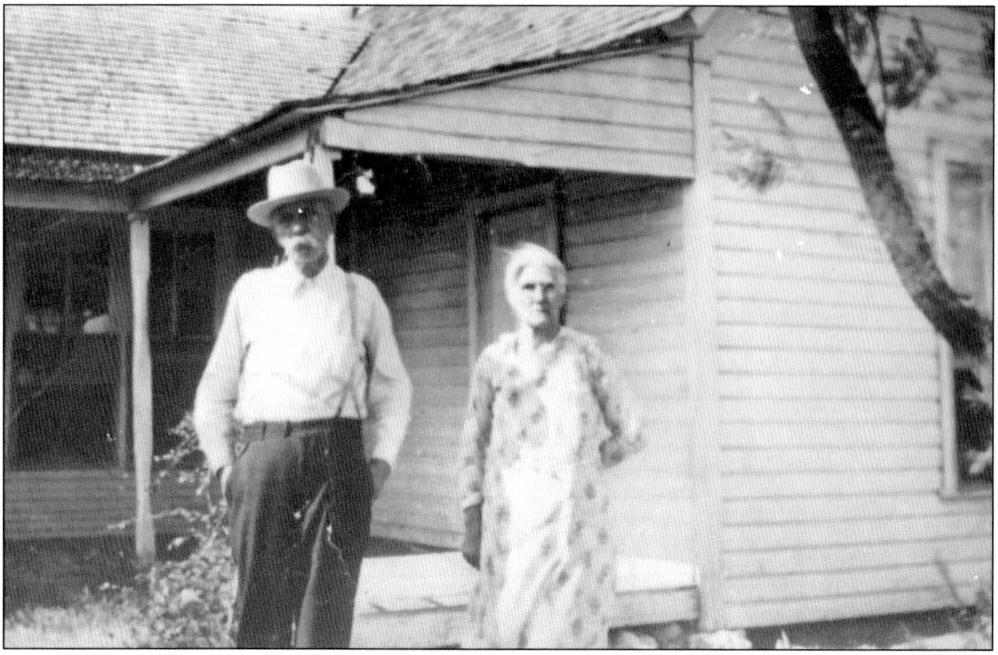

Robert Lee and Mary Frances (Molly) Turner came to Seminole by covered wagon in 1918, accompanied by their two youngest children, Maugie and Willie. From the Turner farm east of Seminole where the family raised cotton and corn, Willie rode horseback five miles to school each day at Fairview. In their later years, Robert and Mary moved into town and opened a flower shop—Flowerland—on the northwest corner of South Main Street and Avenue C. (Museum.)

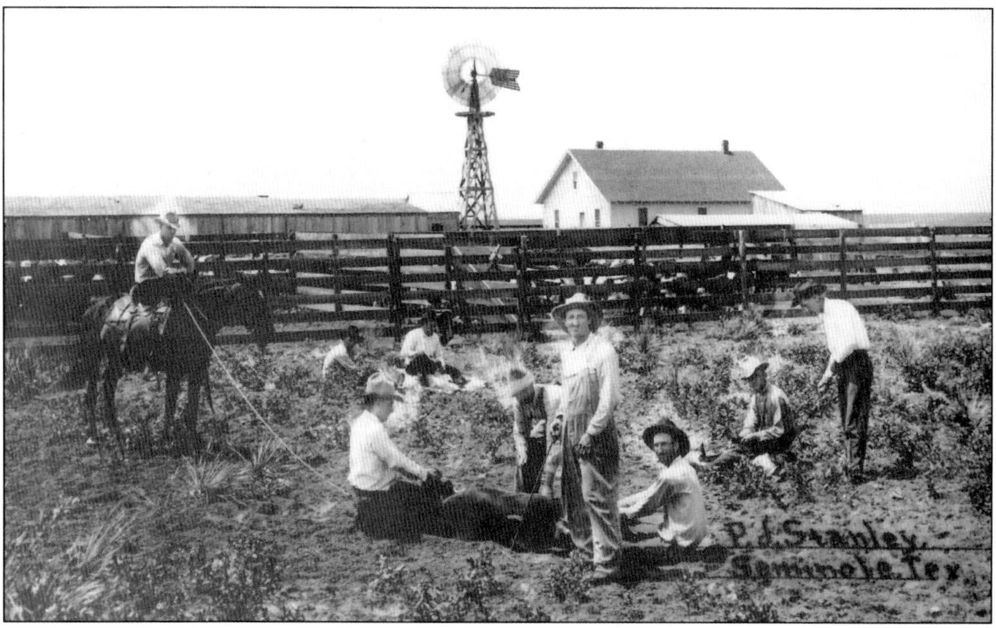

This photograph shows branding time on the Sam King Ranch, about eight miles southeast of Seminole, probably around 1920. On horseback is Lee Wyatt. Others helping are, from left to right, Ross Bowers, Boy Bowser, Barnie Elam, an unidentified hand, P.J. Stanley, James Stanley, Scott Doss, and Maugie Turner. An Eclipse windmill is visible in the background. (Museum.)

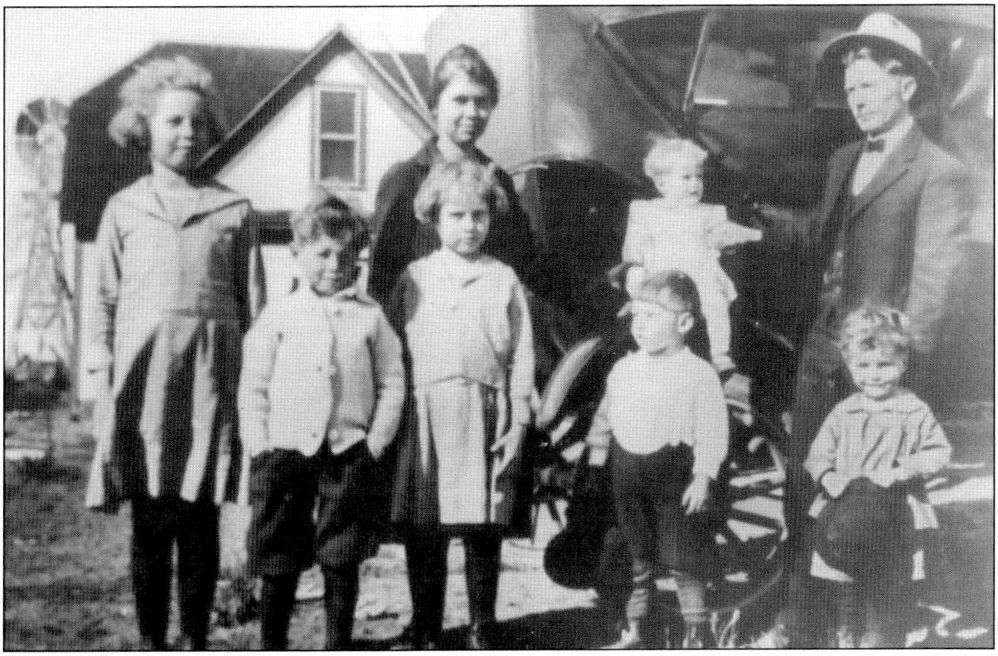

Rufus Willard Pittman came to Seminole in 1910, answering an advertisement in a Dallas newspaper. He roomed at the Lone Star Hotel and the Ramsey boardinghouse until he married Ione Miller in 1913. In 1919, they bought out "old man Rowsey" and opened their own general store on Main Street. R.W. served as Gaines County judge from 1927 to 1931. This photograph from the early 1920s shows the Pittman family in front of their first home. (Holbrooks family.)

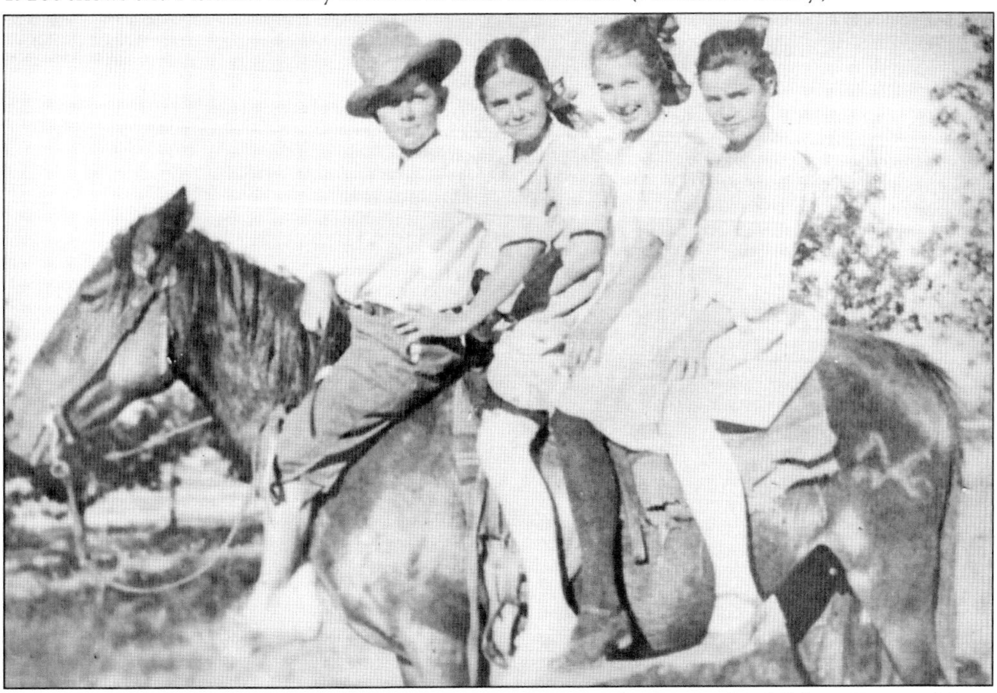

In the early years, horseback riding was a favorite pastime for Seminole children. Pictured from left to right are Gordon Cobb, Bess Ross, Leone Richards, and Dennise Cobb. (Museum.)

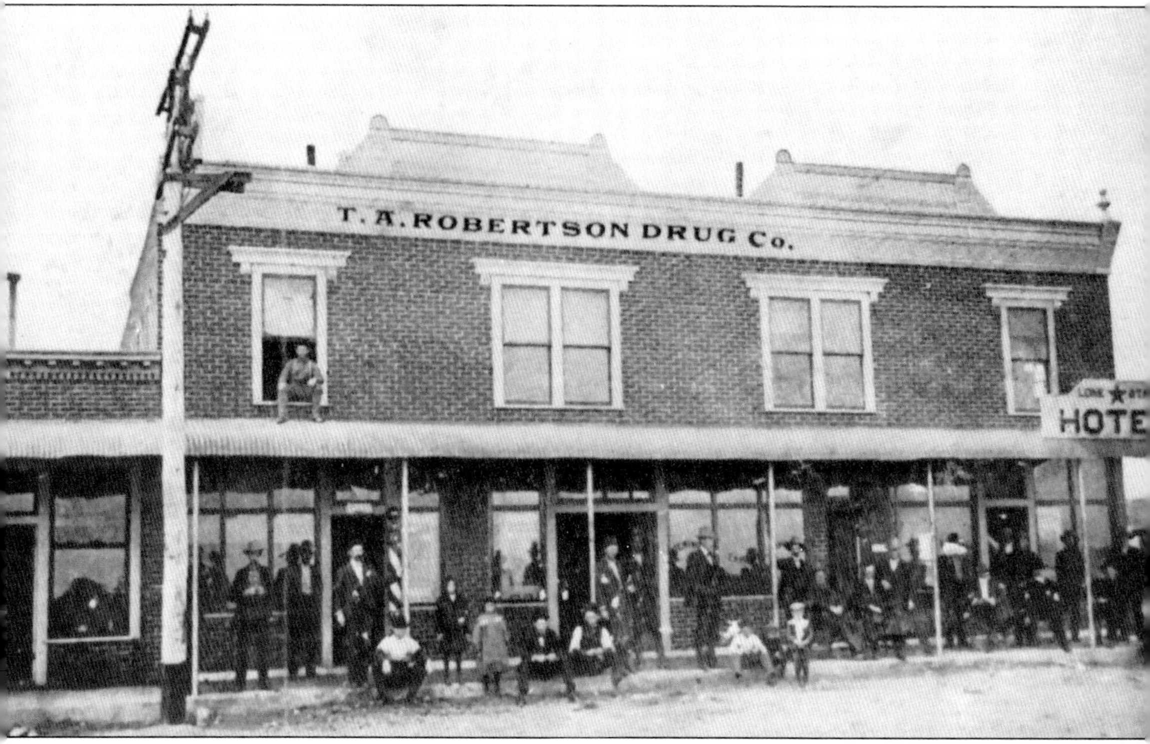

Seminole's first and finest hotel, the Lone Star Hotel, was built by T.A. "Bay" Robertson in 1907 on South Main Street facing the courthouse. The hotel featured Seminole's first drugstore as well. C.C. Cothes was hired to manage it, and he later bought it. Robertson also opened the area's first cotton gin but died in 1912 when his coat became tangled in the gin's machinery. The Lone Star Hotel burned down in 1923. (Museum.)

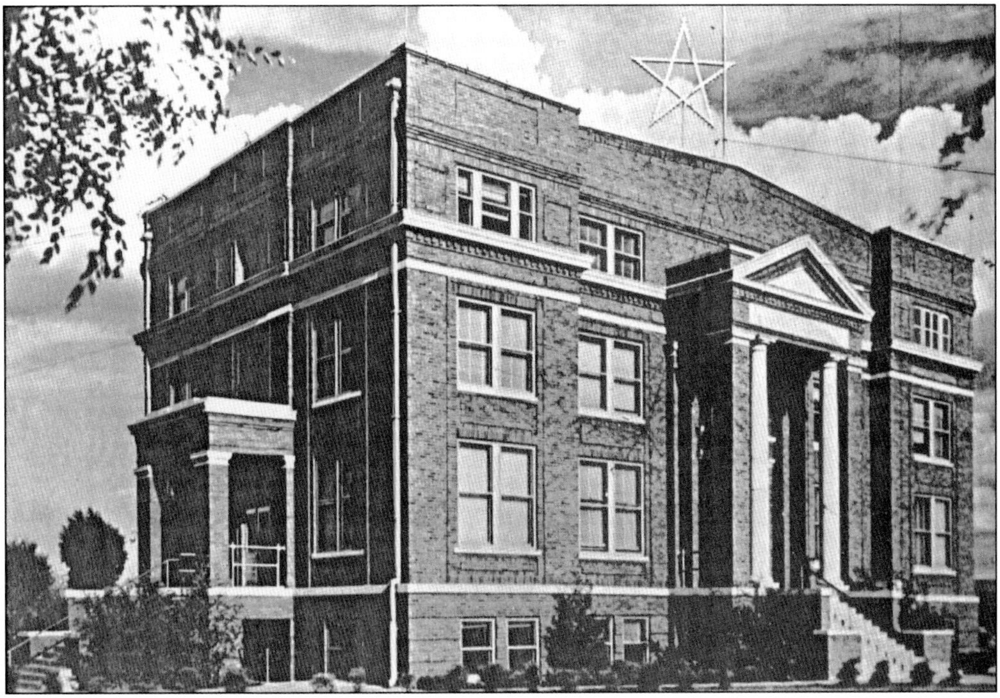

In 1919, Gaines County commissioners voted to issue a contract for the construction of a more permanent courthouse and jail. Dan Cobb was awarded the contract at a cost of $84,000. Materials were shipped in, and construction began immediately. Seen here, the new redbrick structure featured a full basement. (Museum.)

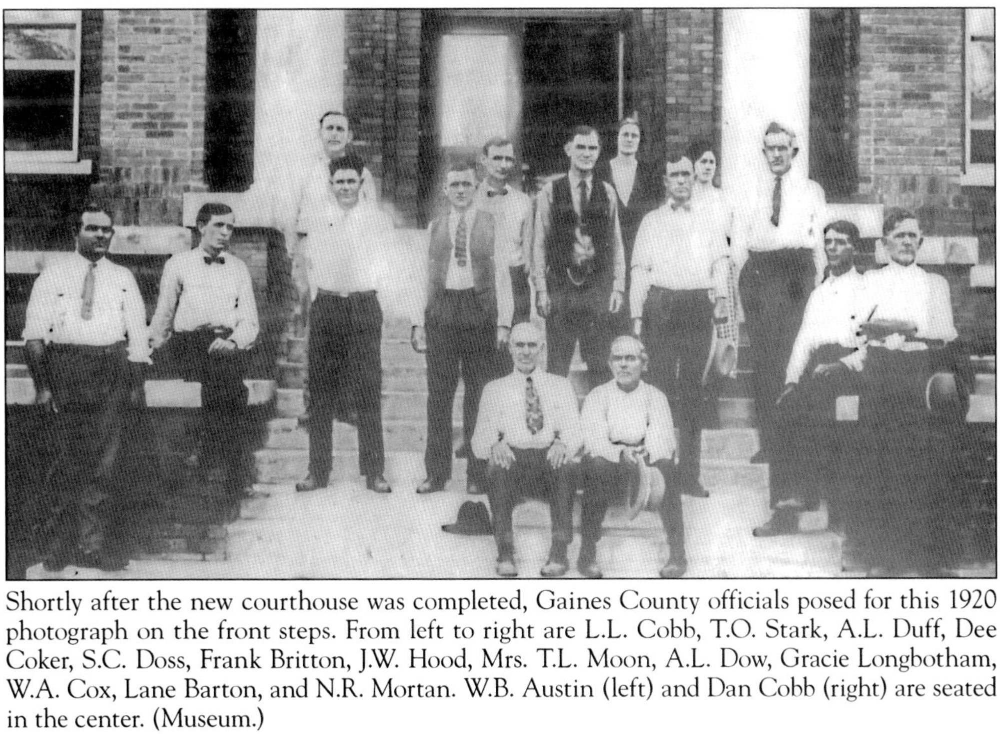

Shortly after the new courthouse was completed, Gaines County officials posed for this 1920 photograph on the front steps. From left to right are L.L. Cobb, T.O. Stark, A.L. Duff, Dee Coker, S.C. Doss, Frank Britton, J.W. Hood, Mrs. T.L. Moon, A.L. Dow, Gracie Longbotham, W.A. Cox, Lane Barton, and N.R. Mortan. W.B. Austin (left) and Dan Cobb (right) are seated in the center. (Museum.)

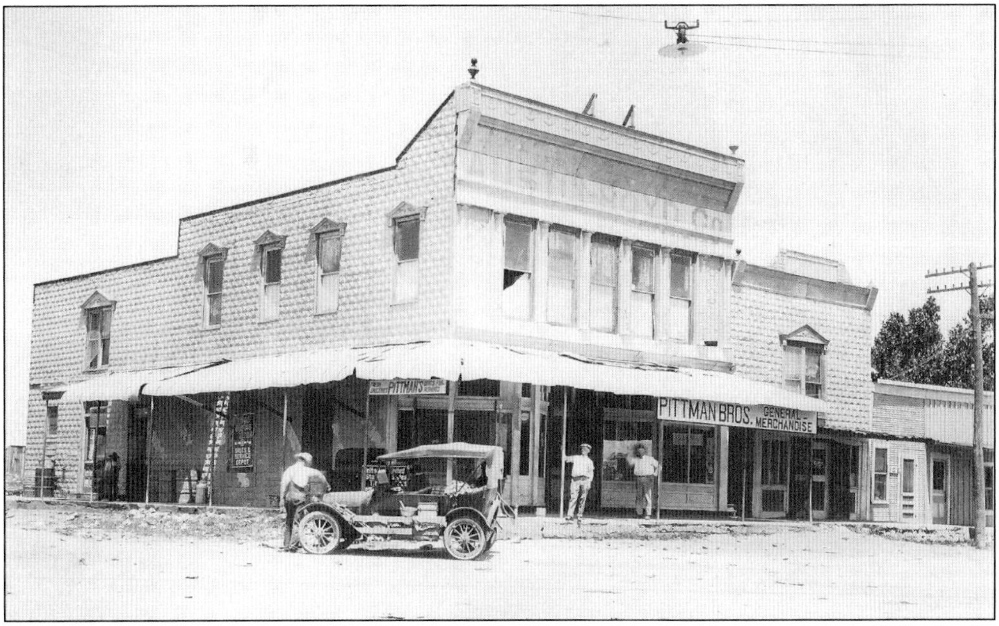

Across from the southwest corner of the square stood a two-story building that originally housed a general mercantile store owned by W.B. Austin. When the Austins sold out, that location became Williams Brothers Dry Goods, operated by J.J. and Andy Williams. In the mid-1920s, Pittman Brothers General Merchandise opened in the same building. Along the front of the upper floor is the faded name Austin-Boyd Co., and there is a streetlight suspended from overhead wires in front of the store. (Holbrooks family.)

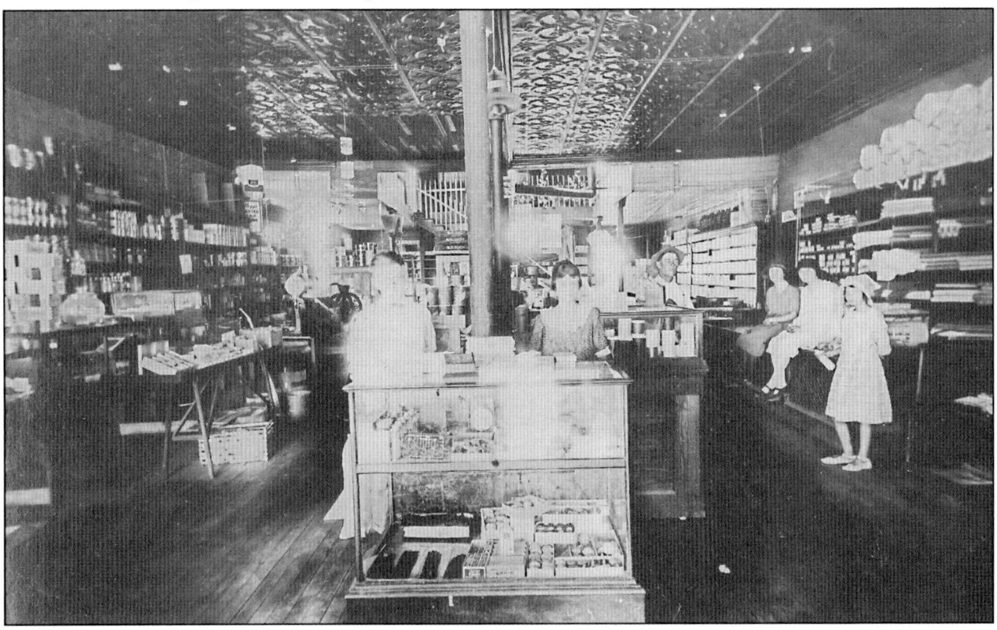

This is the interior of Pittman Brothers Department Store as it appeared in the mid-1920s. As with most stores in Seminole at the time, the ceiling was covered with pressed-tin panels. An example of such ceiling material has been preserved at the Gaines County Museum in Seminole. The people in this photograph are unidentified. (Museum.)

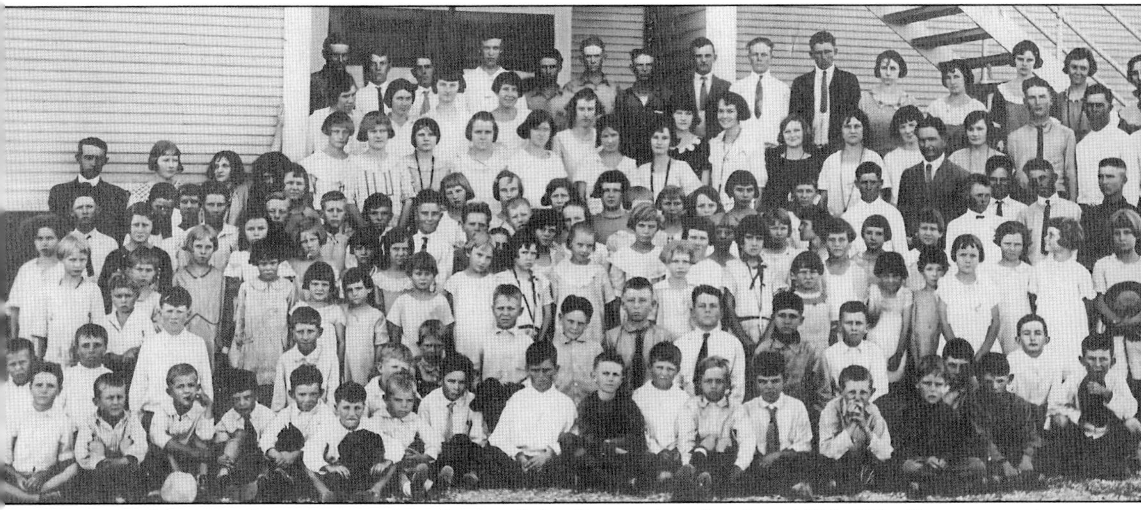

Pictured here is the entire student body of the Seminole school in 1923. G.L. Farrar was the superintendent at the time. Included in the picture are individuals who contributed to the expansion and success of Seminole throughout their lifetimes, like Reeves Cothes, Nuel Mitchell, Arzie Kirk, P.J. Stanley, Ben Birdwell, Ramsey Longbotham, Alma Heard, Charlie George, and Howard Mann, to name a few. (Museum.)

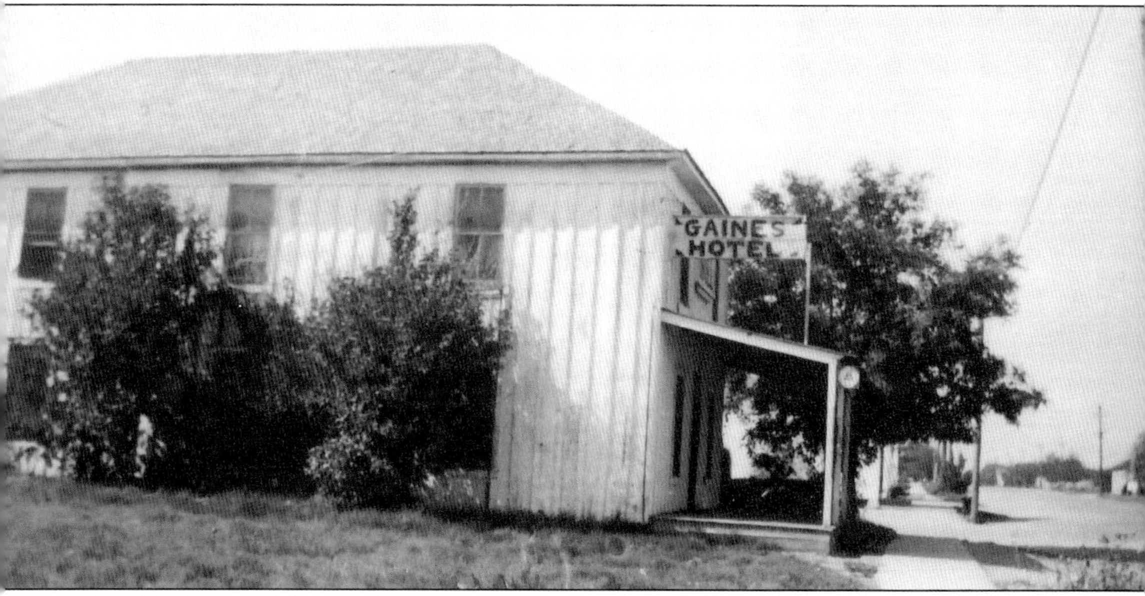

One block west of the courthouse on Southwest Avenue B stood the Gaines Hotel, a gathering place for locals. Food was served there "family style," and an old iron bell rang to announce mealtimes. The usually quiet hotel was the scene of one of Seminole's worst crimes. On the morning of April 9, 1923, cattle inspectors Dave Allison and H.L. Robertson were in the hotel's lobby when, without warning, they were gunned down. The perpetrators of this double murder were two Gaines County cattlemen—Tom Ross and Milt Goode—who were later tried and convicted for the killings. A piece of the wall of the Gaines Hotel with what looks like a bullet hole is on display at the Gaines County Museum, Seminole Division. (Museum.)

Two

1925–1950

Boom Times

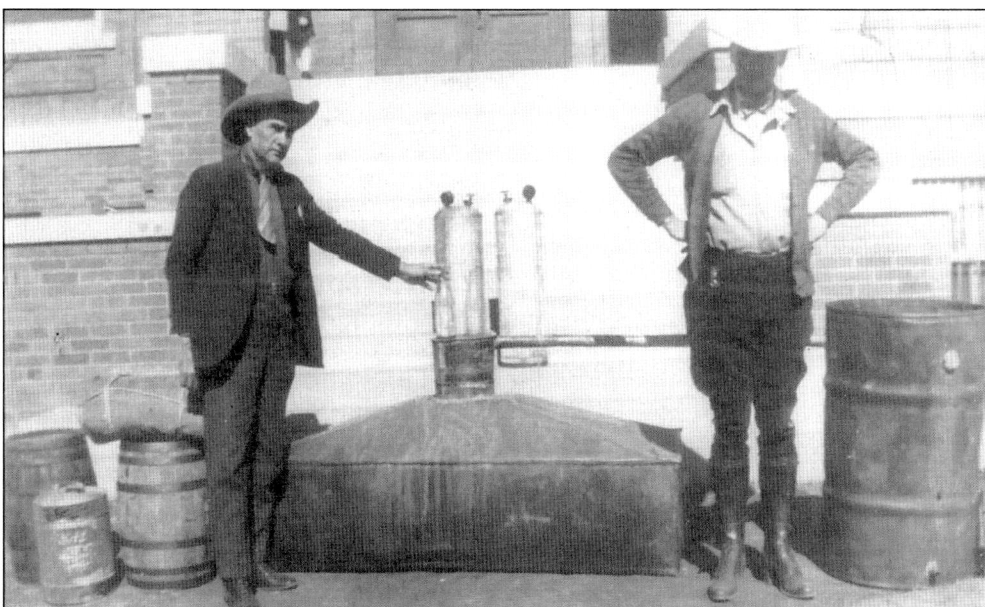

During the Prohibition era (1919–1933), it was illegal to manufacture, sell, or transport alcoholic beverages. Demand for liquor continued, however, and bootleggers in Gaines County did what they could to satisfy that demand. In this photograph, taken around 1928, Sheriff Newt McClesky (left) and Deputy A.R. Taylor pose at the courthouse next to the largest whiskey still that they had confiscated. McClesky later converted the copper boiler into a bathtub for his home. (Museum.)

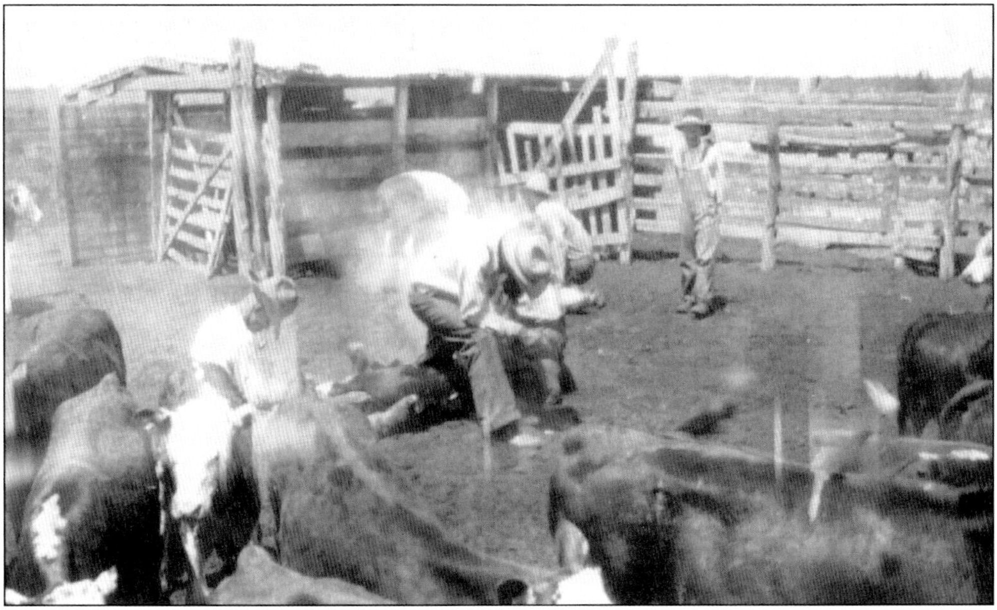

Cattle was king in Seminole in the 1920s. Ranches covered the county. In this 1928 photograph, it was branding time on the J.B. Thompson Ranch. Pictured hard at work are, from left to right, Lee Wyatt, J.B. Thompson, John Thompson, and Edd Thompson. (Museum.)

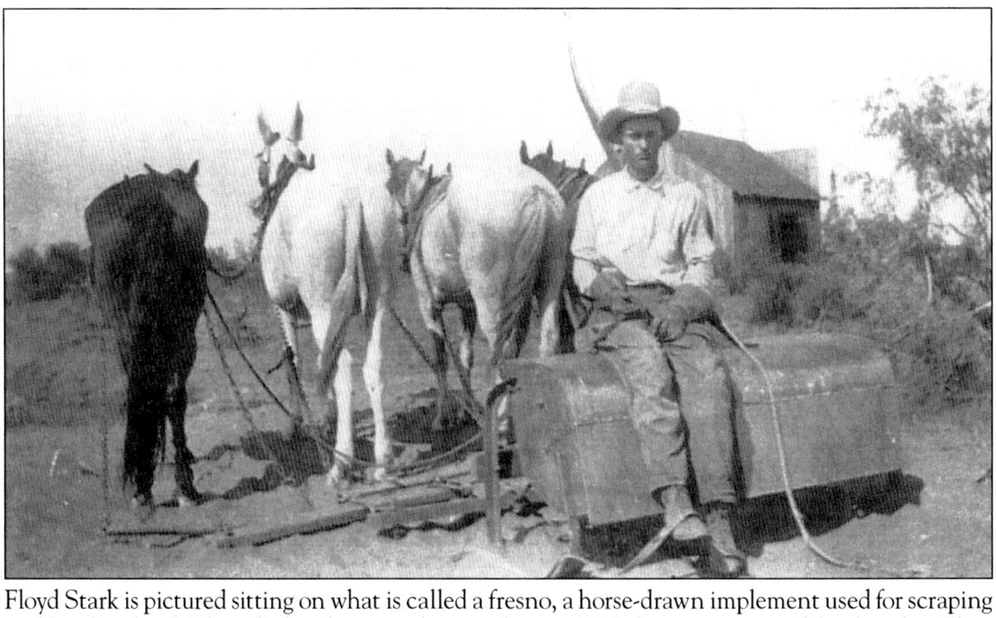

Floyd Stark is pictured sitting on what is called a fresno, a horse-drawn implement used for scraping and leveling land. Though the photograph was taken in 1915, fresnos were used for decades. They worked particularly well in the sandy West Texas soil. (Stark family.)

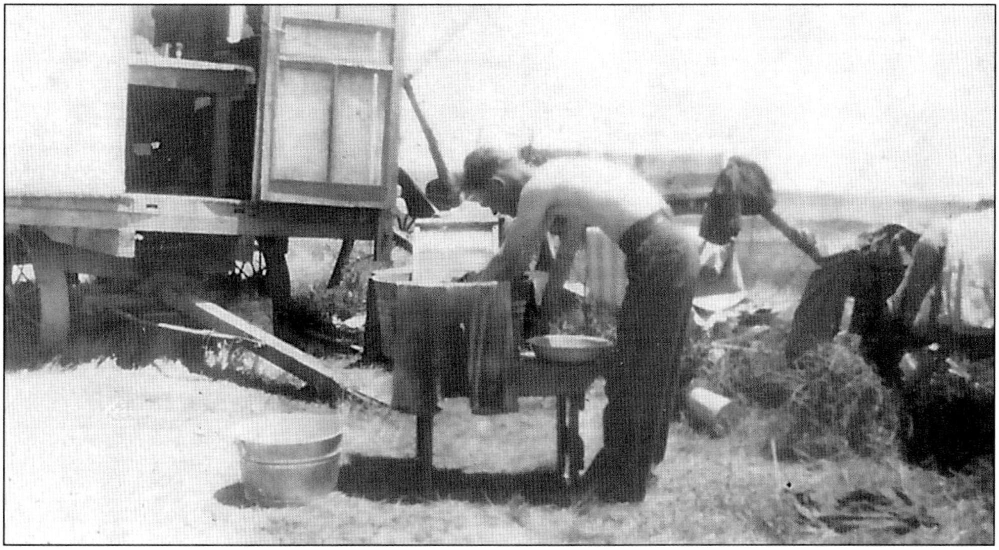

R.L. (Bob) Jones Sr. moved to Gaines County in 1905. Shortly thereafter, he married Lucille Irwin. Jones worked on various ranches, hauled freight and mail, and operated a road grader. Eldest son Robert Jr., seen at age 13, worked as a chuckwagon cook for one of the local ranches. This 1920s-vintage wagon even has a table and chairs inside. (Jones family.)

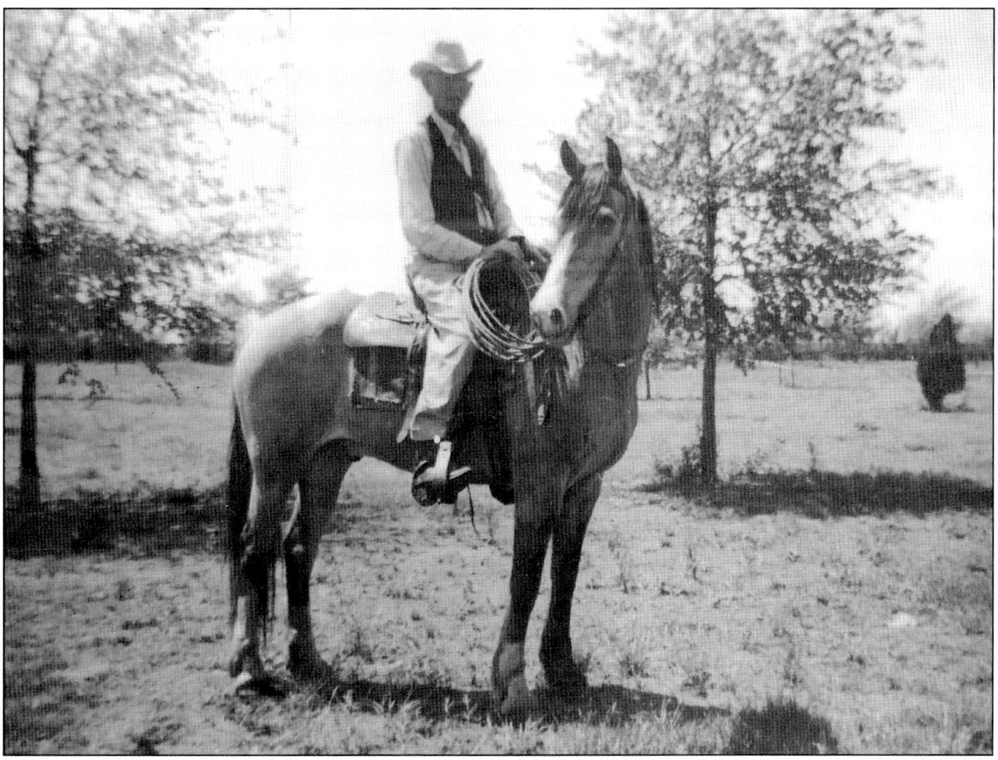

The Birdwell family first arrived in Seminole in 1904, but Soon Birdwell—pictured on one of his favorite horses, Kanuck—did not move here until 1909. During the 48 years he lived in Seminole, Soon served as deputy sheriff, sheriff, rancher, and animal and hide inspector. No rancher loved a good horse better than Soon Birdwell. (Museum.)

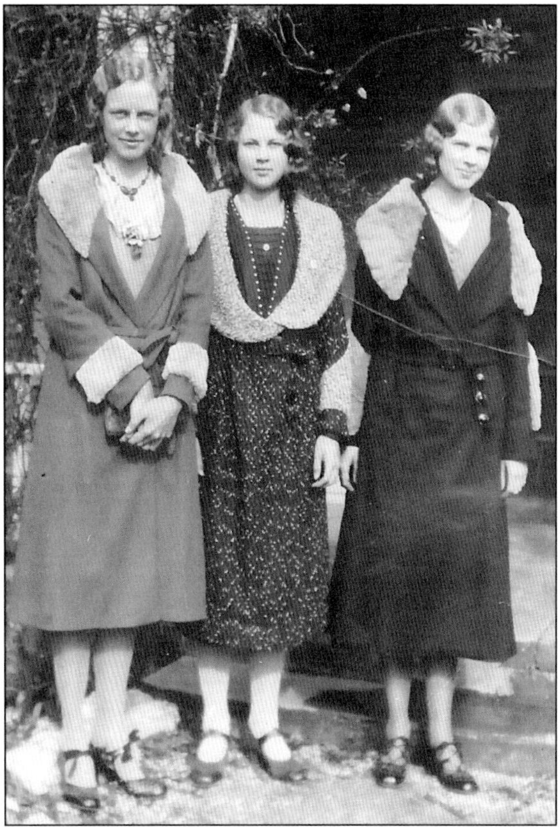

High fashion from the Roaring Twenties did not bypass the lovely young ladies of Seminole. Pictured in this photograph from the late 1920s are, from left to right, Lena Upton, Nancy Sawyer, and Lillie Kirk. Apparent are the latest hairstyles and dress lengths that actually show a young lady's ankles. (Jones family.)

Pictured here in 1924 are members of the S.C. (Scott) and Maggie Doss family in front of their home at 806 Southeast Third Street. Scott stands on the left, holding his youngest son, Hyle. Next are, from left to right, Cleo, Beth, Bobbie, Maggie Doss, Bernice, Scott Jr. (known as "Son"), and "Mother Cox" (Maggie's mother). Scott farmed, ranched, carried the mail, and worked as a carpenter, a clerk, and as tax assessor. From 1935 to 1950, he served as state cattle inspector. (Museum.)

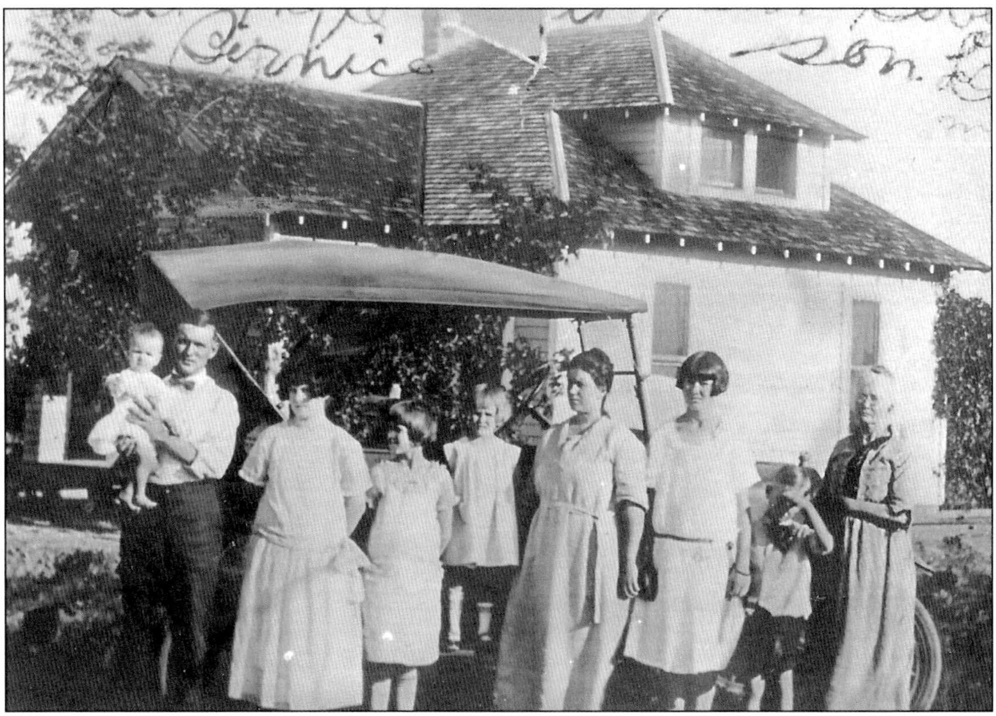

C.C. "Chunk" Cothes came to Seminole in 1907 to manage the drugstore in the Lone Star Hotel. When hotel and drugstore owner "Bay" Robertson died in 1912, Cothes purchased the pharmacy, changing its name to Cothes Drug. Cothes was a man of vision and seemingly limitless community spirit. When the city was incorporated, he was unanimously chosen its first mayor, and he was reelected several times before his death in 1937. (Museum.)

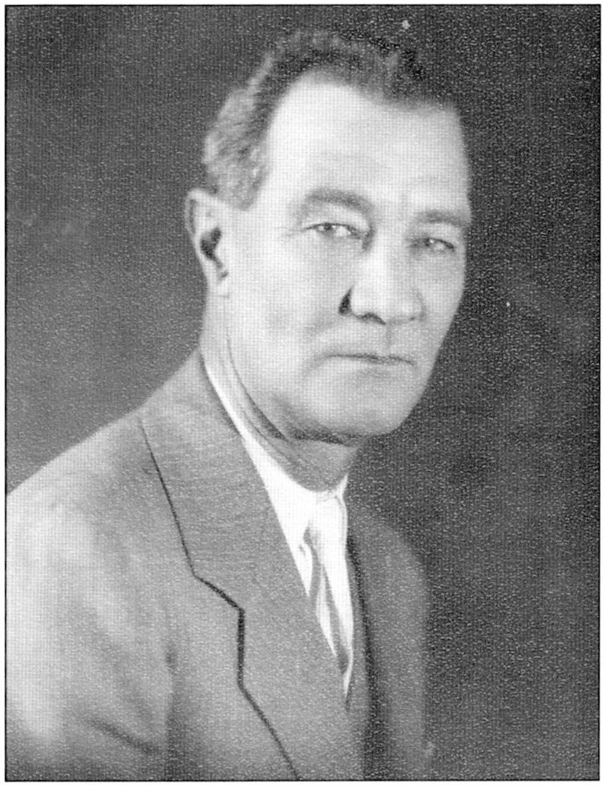

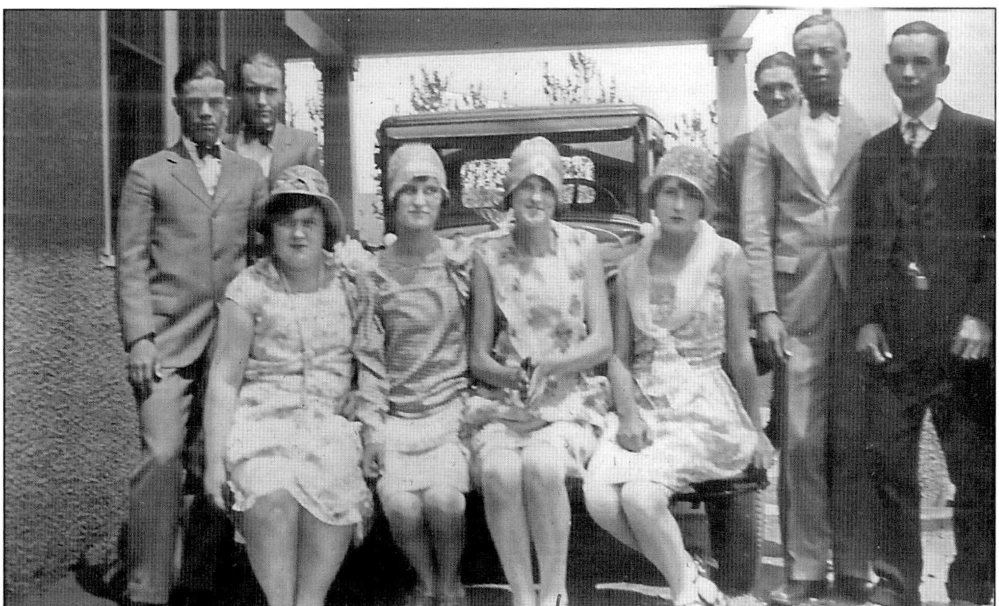

This photograph shows a group of some of Seminole's finest young adults—the graduating class of 1928. From left to right are Reeves Cothes, Maury Burrows, Nuel Mitchell, Alta Rollins, Birdie Lee Daniels, Evelyn Heard, O.J. Daniels, Terry Stark, and Marbut George. Not shown are graduates R.L. Jones Jr. and Ila Prindle. (Jones family.)

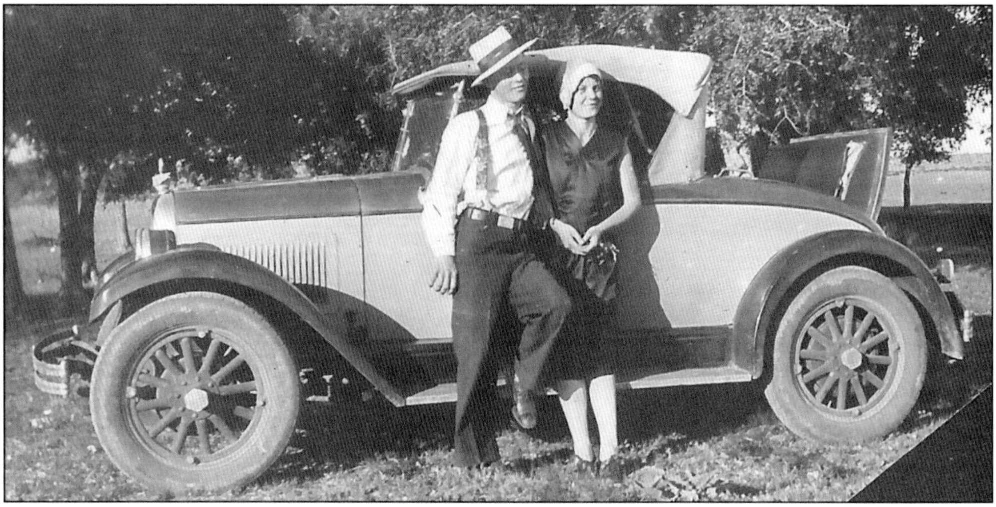

The height of fashion, R.L. Jones Jr. and Gracie Lee Stark pose in front of R.L.'s car—a mid- to late-1920s Model A coupe. The couple married on March 25, 1933, in Lovington, New Mexico, and raised four children in Seminole. (Jones family.)

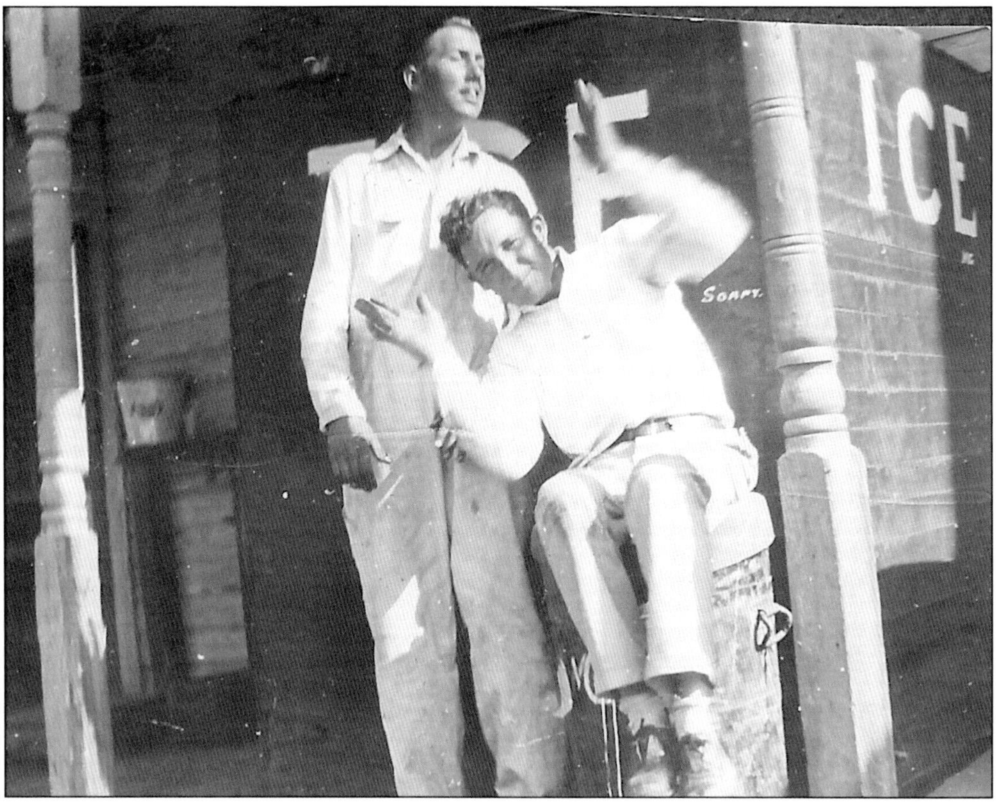

Ice was an important commodity in Gaines County and not easy to come by. When C.C. Cothes took over Seminole's first drugstore in 1912, ice had to be hauled by freight wagon from Midland. By the time it arrived in Seminole, a 300-pound block was usually only about 75 pounds. By the 1920s, a small icehouse had been built. Here, employees "Soapy" Walker (left) and William Bryant Jones mug for the camera on the front step. (Jones family.)

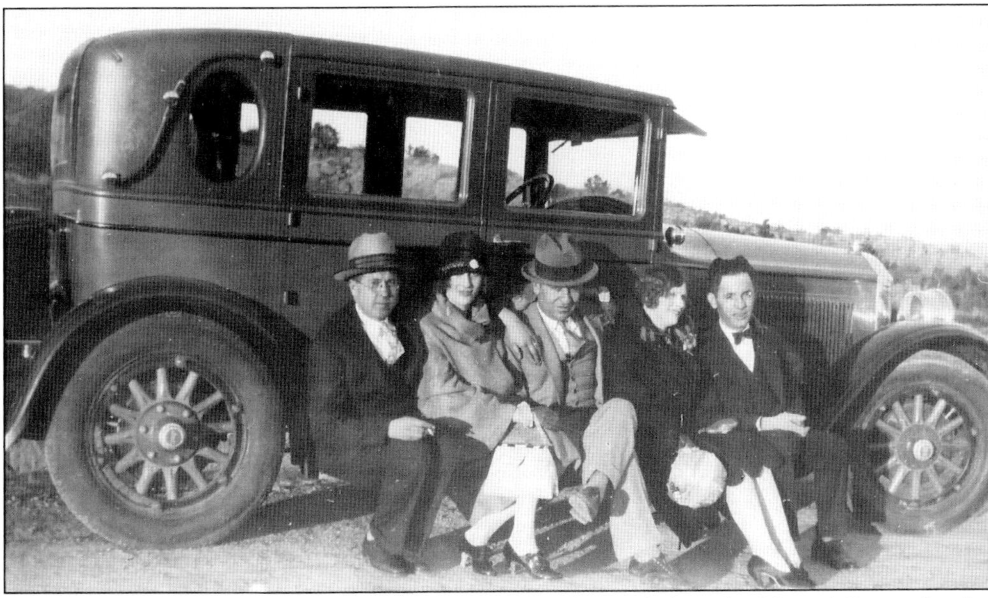

Ed Aryain left his native Syria when he was 15 and traveled to the United States. In this photograph, taken in Lamesa in 1927, from left to right are Ed's friend Fays Fandy, Etta Stone (Ed's future bride), Ed, and Etta's aunt and uncle Luma and Sam Hameed. The group is sitting on the running board of a Buick Brougham 51 Master Six. Ed and Etta opened a clothing store at 110 South Main Street in Seminole in 1939. (Aryain family.)

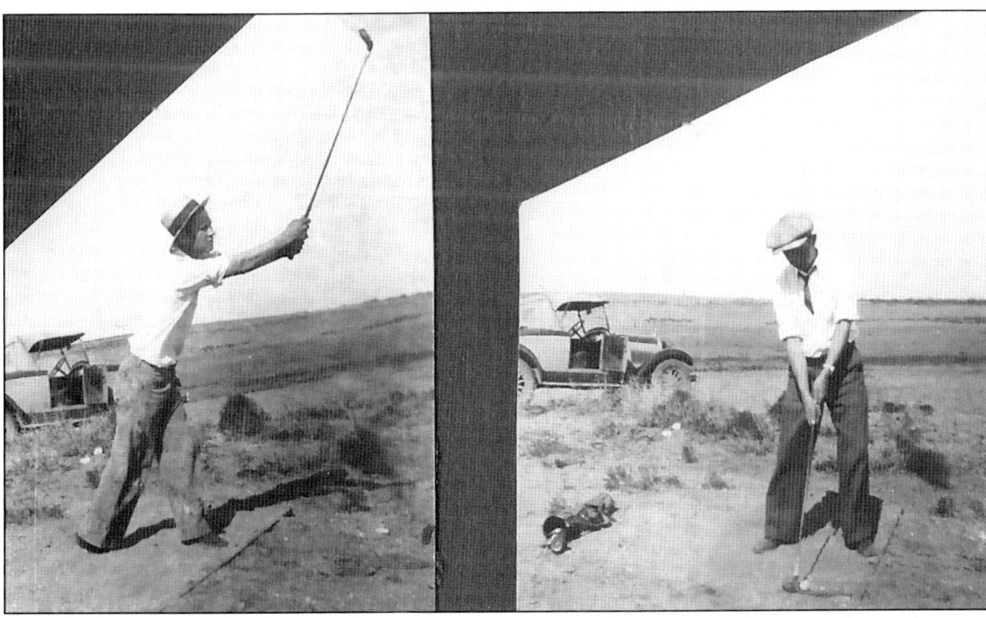

These two photographs taken from an old family album show a sport that gained popularity in Seminole in the 1920s—pasture golf. No one seems to know much about it, but the rules are assumed to be roughly the same as the more formal game. No doubt traps included rattlesnakes, prairie dog holes, cow patties, and plenty of sand dunes! (Jones family.)

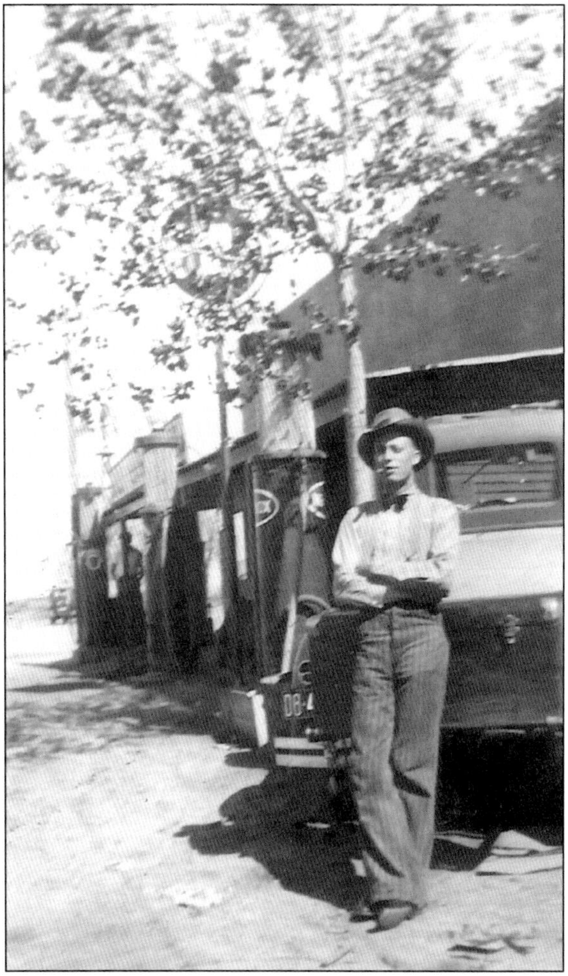

Driving into downtown Seminole today, eastbound in the right lane of US 180 is what was once a Gulf Oil station run by the Stark family. They added this lean-to structure onto the north side of their hardware store. This view looking east shows the three tall round gas pumps and Terry Stark, proudly standing beside his 1931 Ford. (Stark family.)

Below is the interior of Stark and Son Hardware and Furniture at the corner of South Main Street and the Hobbs Highway in the late 1920s–early 1930s. Guy Stark, co-owner with his eldest son, Floyd, stands amid his wares—potbellied stoves, cookware, tools, and hundreds of other items needed around the house, shop, or farm. (Stark family.)

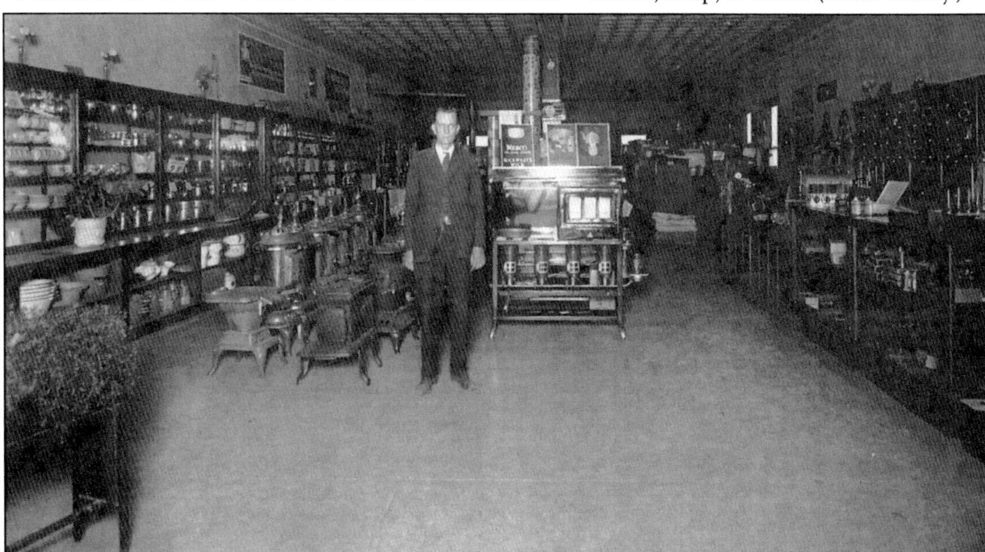

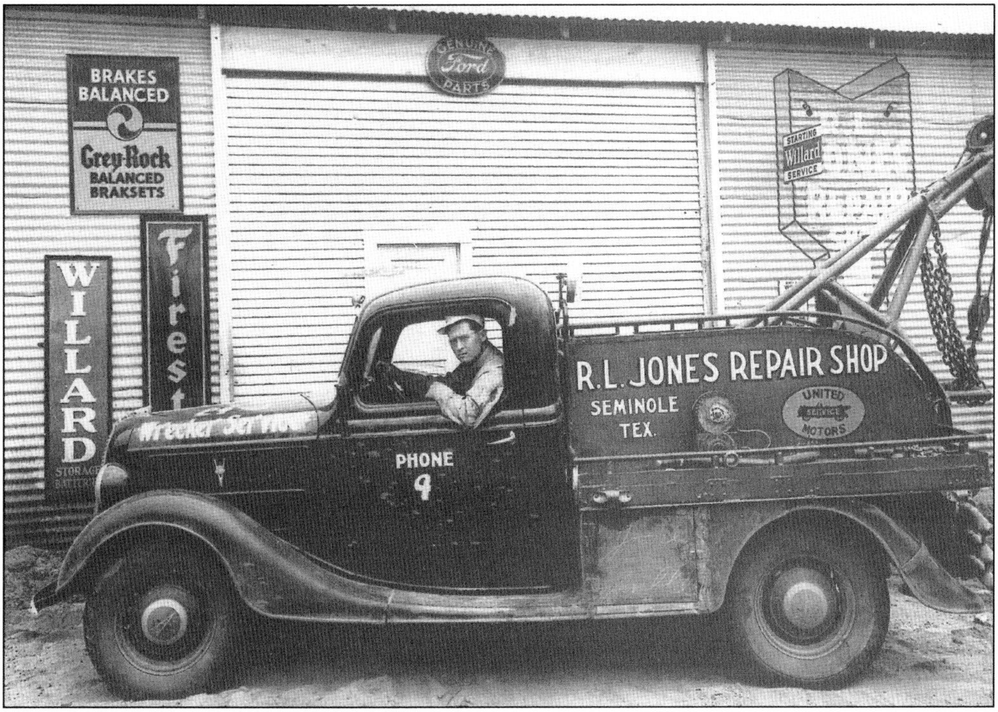

If someone needed work done on a car, tractor, or any other piece of machinery, chances are the guys at R.L. Jones Jr. Repair Shop could fix it. R.L., seen in his wrecker in 1938, began as a mechanic in 1929 at Rollins Motor Company. Two years later, he opened a service station and auto repair shop on Northwest Second Street. (Museum.)

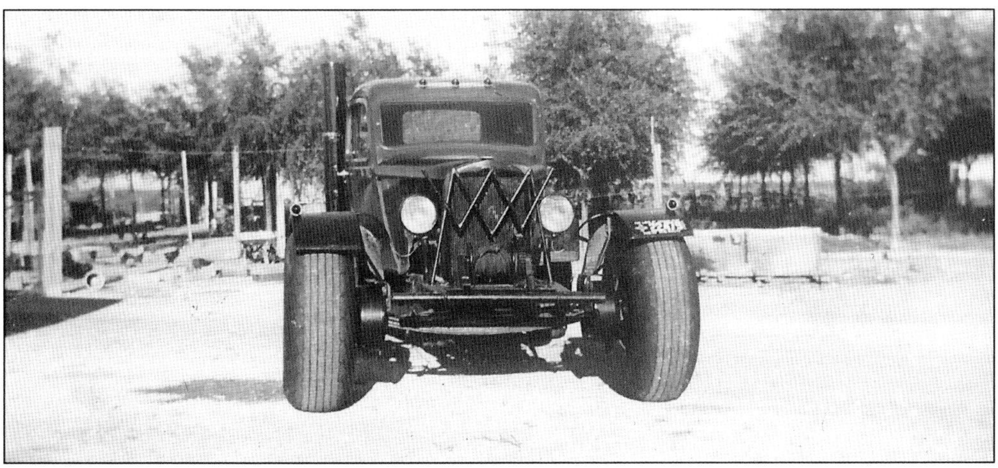

Pictured here is another of R.L. Jones Jr.'s pastimes. Because of his interest in cars, he built the county's first dune buggy some time in the 1930s. High clearance, a powerful engine, and plenty of bracing made it the perfect vehicle for crossing the rugged terrain of West Texas. According to R.L.'s son Robert, his father built this buggy "for the oil companies." (Jones family.)

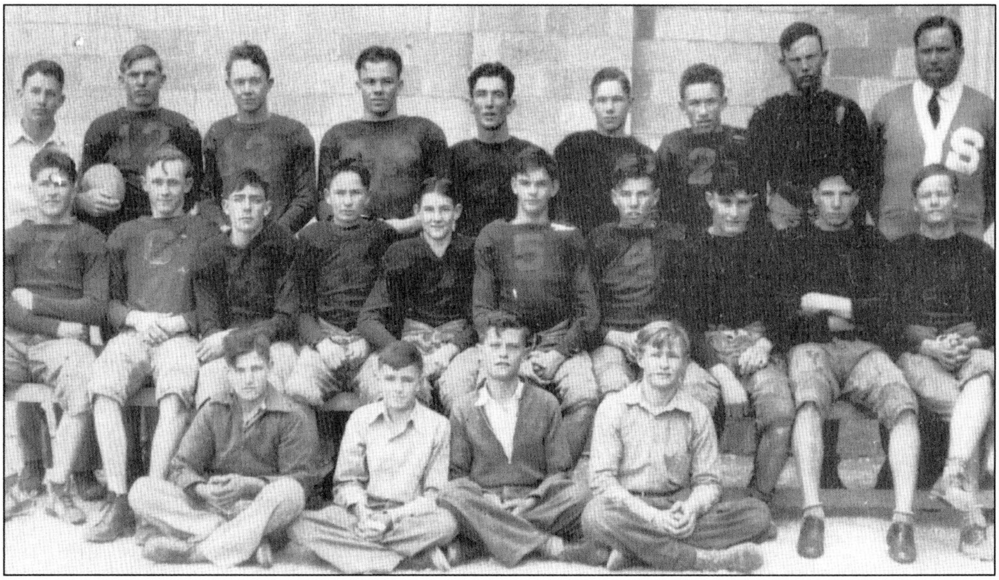

These three photographs show Seminole school athletic teams of the 1930s. Above is the first Indian football team (1933). From left to right are (first row, sitting Indian-style) Dale Goode, Johnny Kendrick, Glendale Stark, and Bill Wescott; (second row) Horace Jones, Raymond Patton, Judson Prindle, Alex Trimble, West Maben Jr., Dale Daniels, Jack Auten, Edd Thompson, Ben Birdwell, and "Gump" Stark; (third row) Rex Goode, Willie Sims, Johnny Patton, John D. Auten, Ramsey Longbotham, Scott Doss, Dale Zusoni, Garland Brock, and coach Dewey Davis. Below is the 1935 basketball team. From left to right are (first row) Raymond Patton, Johnny Patton, Dale Daniels, Horace Jones, Edd Thompson, John D. Auten, and Scott Doss; (second row) Ramsey Longbotham, Rex Goode, West Maben Jr., Judson Prindle, Gump Stark, Alex Trimble, and Bill Wescott. Coaching this team is again Dewey Davis, who was the school's superintendent by this time. (Both, Museum.)

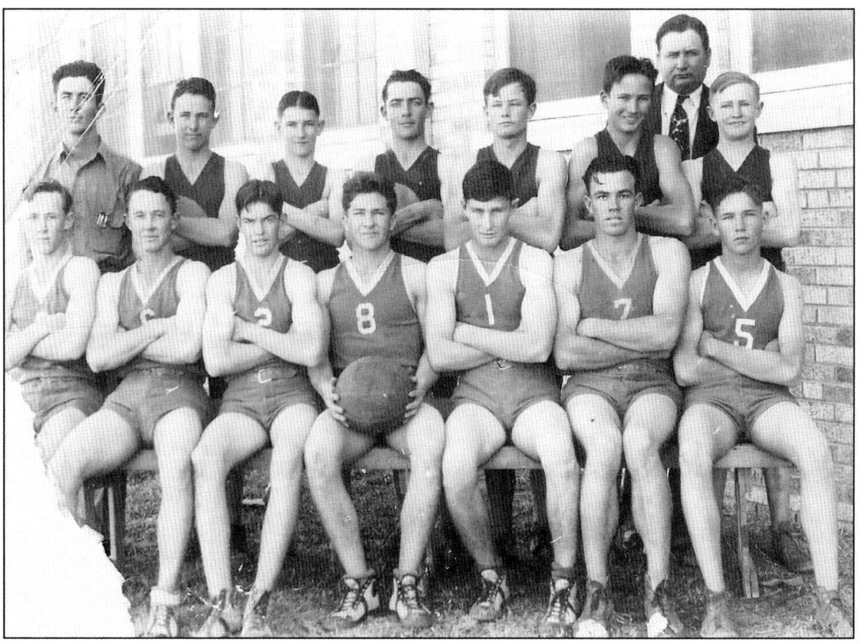

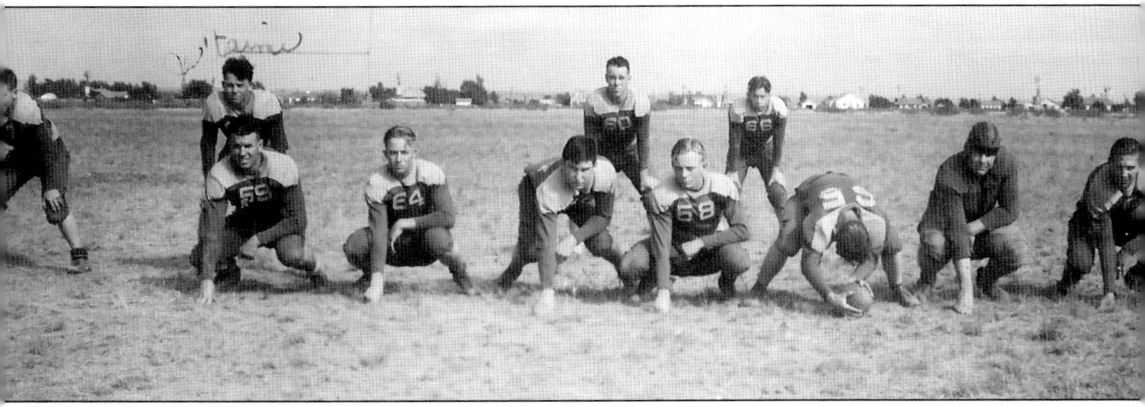

This is the 1937 football group. The roster included, in no particular order, J.E. Woodard, Coy Patton, Arvil Fincher, Billy Pittman, Jack Auten, A.C. Stanley, Bill Heath, Fred Mann, Dean Moore, and Billy Meeks. One other player has not been identified. (*Sentinel.*)

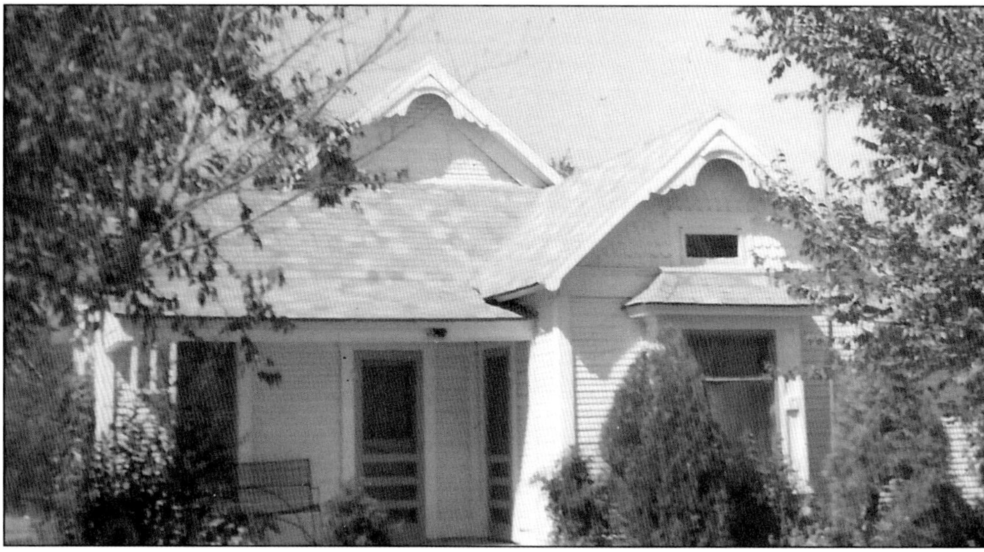

Built in 1907, this home stands at Southwest Avenue C and Second Street. Several families lived here, including Mr. and Mrs. Tom Ross and Mr. and Mrs. T.C. "Top" Heard. Bert M. and Olive Ancell bought the home in 1928 and lived in it when school was in session. In the summer, they moved to their ranch northwest of Seminole. The family kept the home until 1968, when it was sold to Olan Locker, who moved it to a location on the Lamesa Highway where it still stands. (Museum.)

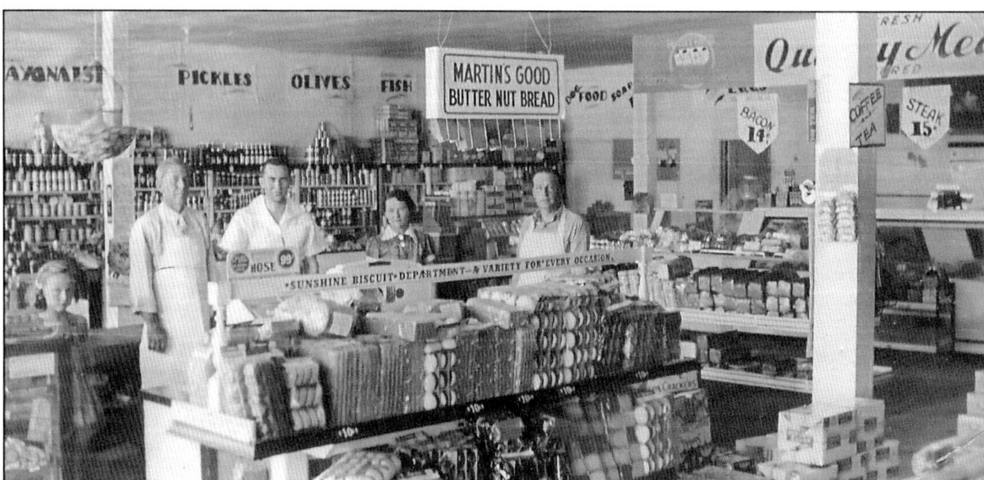

In the early to mid-1930s, Kidd's Grocery and Market sat about half a block south of the courthouse square on South Main Street, just north of the Masonic lodge. Inside the market, customers could find Martin's Butter-Nut Bread, Sunshine Biscuits (various baked goods—"A Variety for Every Occasion"), and a full meat market. (*Sentinel.*)

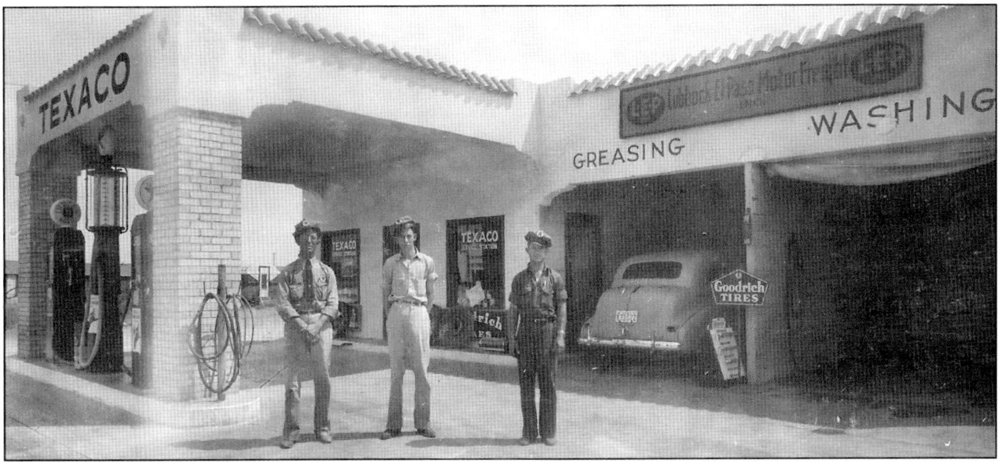

In the 1930s and 1940s, this Texaco station stood at the intersection of North Main Street and Northeast Avenue B—what is now the parking lot behind Bealls, Brown's Ace Hardware, and other stores that face the courthouse along Avenue A. Taken in 1938, the image shows the station's owner Ramsey Longbotham (left) with his employees Ray Anderson (center) and Charlie George (the coauthor's father). (George family.)

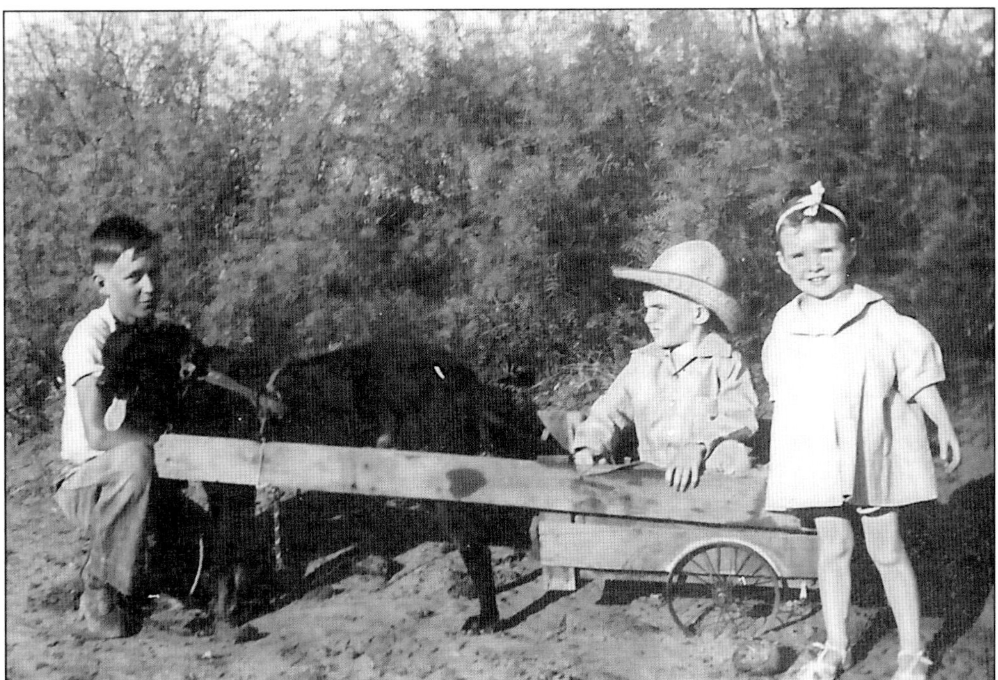

During the Great Depression, children sometimes had to improvise their fun. In this June 1936 photograph is Hardy Dalmont, who seems to have harnessed his dog Pup Boy to a wagon of some sort. Dayton Elam is in the wagon, and Debbie Jean Elam waits her turn for a ride. (Museum.)

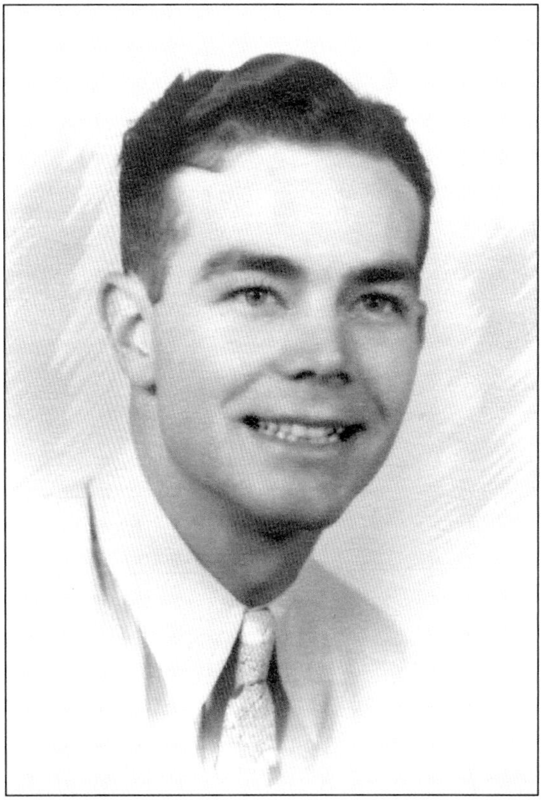

Reeves Cothes, son of C.C. and Gertrude Cothes, was named for Dr. W.J. Reeves, one of Seminole's first doctors. In 1932, after graduating from Texas Christian University (TCU) and the Danforth School of Pharmacy, Reeves returned to Seminole and worked at the pharmacy until his father's death in 1937. Active duty during World War II in Saipan, Tinian, and Iwo Jima kept him away from Seminole for a while, but he returned, married Modelle Moore, and continued operating Cothes Drug for several decades. (Museum.)

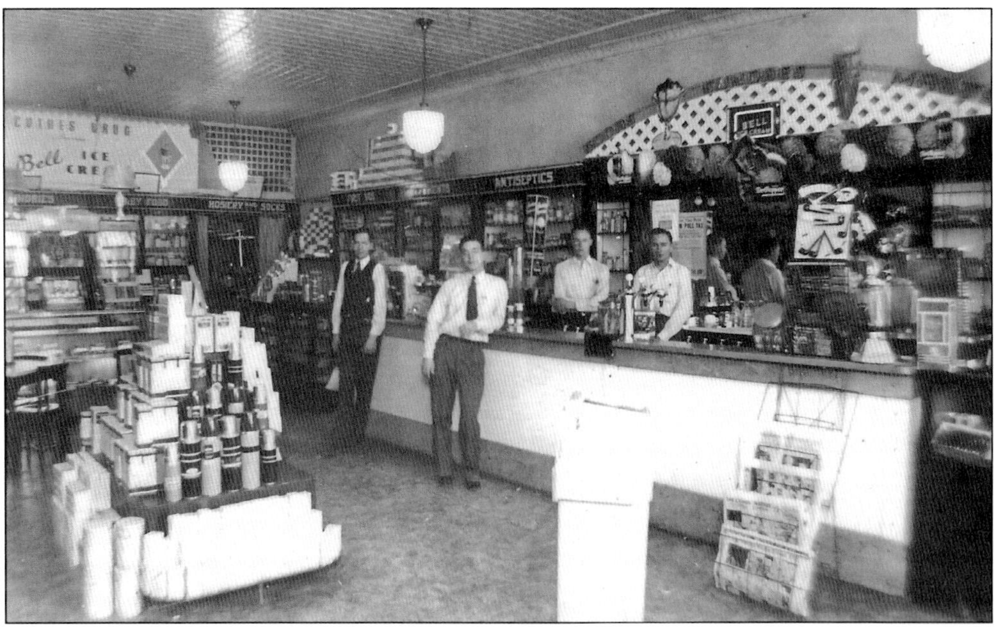

The interior of Cothes Drug in the late 1930s shows Reeves Cothes leaning against the soda fountain. Other employees are, from left to right, Harvey Jordan, Edward Todd, and Alex Trimble. Cothes Drug was always a top-notch pharmacy and a warm, friendly place to gather with friends at the soda fountain. (Museum.)

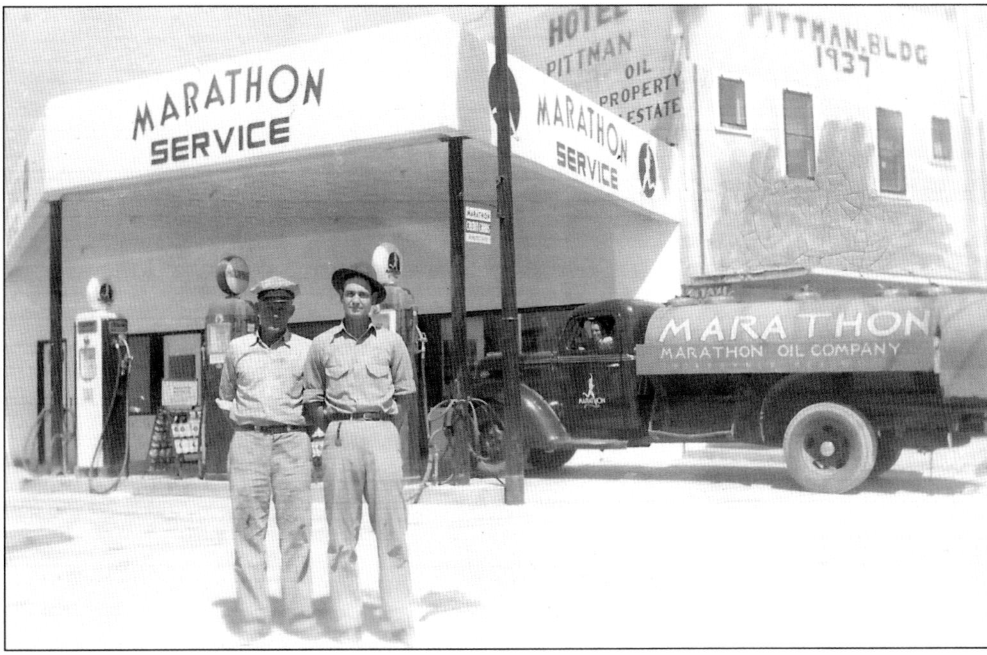

In the 1930s, during Seminole's oil boom, R.W. Pittman built the multistory hotel, café, and office building seen in the background. In the foreground is a Marathon service station. The hotel was torn down years ago, and other service stations have replaced Marathon at the northwest corner of the courthouse square; the newest is Swift Stop, which opened in 2011. (*Sentinel.*)

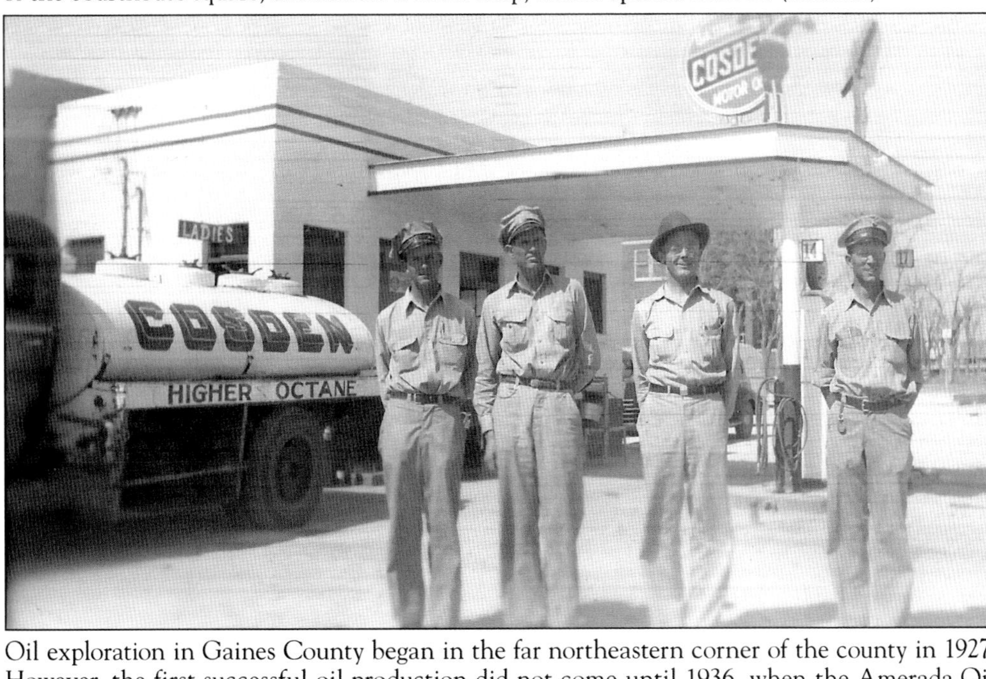

Oil exploration in Gaines County began in the far northeastern corner of the county in 1927. However, the first successful oil production did not come until 1936, when the Amerada Oil Company brought in a well west of town. After that, well after well came, ushering in Seminole's oil boom. As a result, numerous gasoline stations sprang up, including this Cosden Oil station located just west of the courthouse square on the Hobbs Highway. (*Sentinel.*)

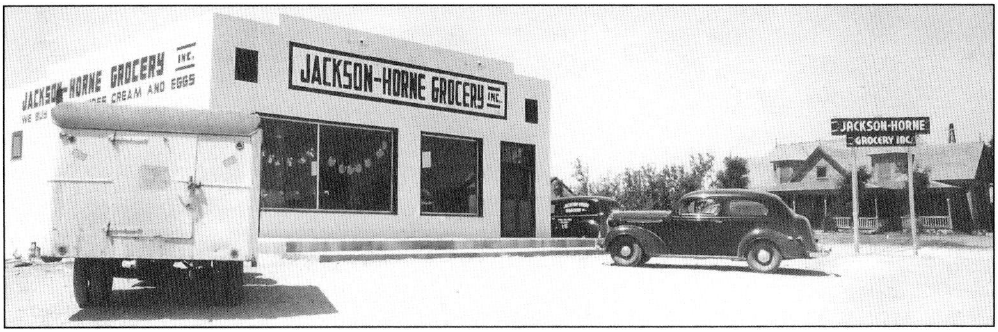

A booming oil industry brought many oilfield workers and their families to Seminole and the surrounding area. The rapid increase in population led to an increase in the number of stores in town. New grocery stores opened, like the Jackson-Horne Grocery, Inc., which was located at the corner of Southwest Second Street and Avenue C. The house in the distance on the right is the Ramsey home, one of the oldest in Seminole and still maintained in its original condition. (Jameson family.)

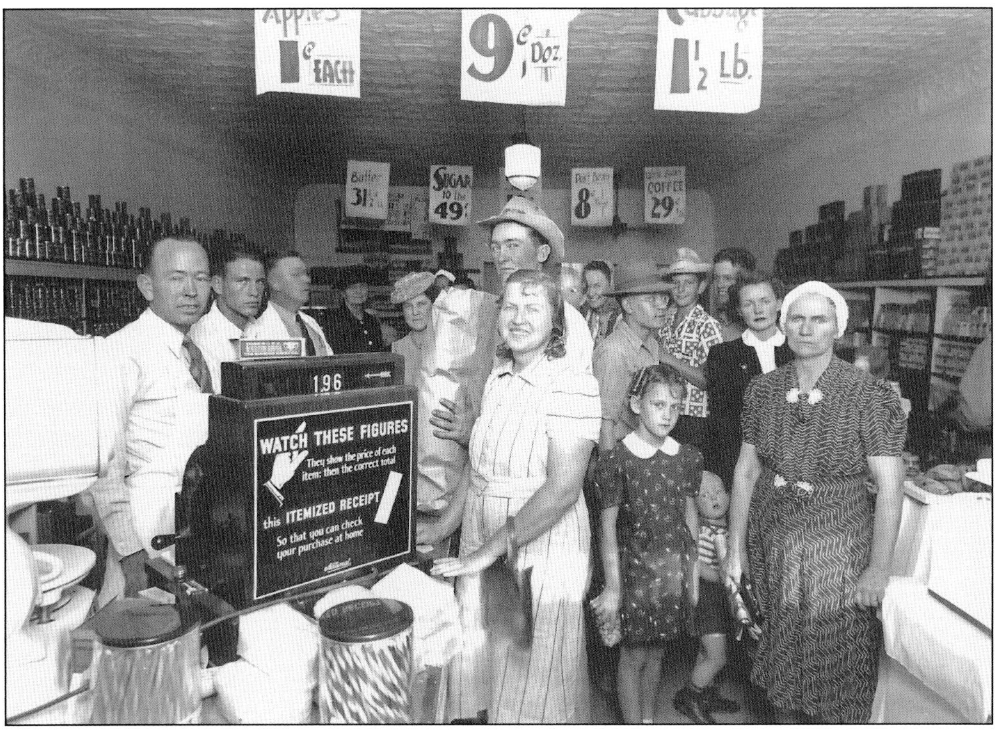

The interior of Jackson-Horne Grocery, Inc., which opened in 1938, shows Eddie Jameson at the cash register with Walker Dearing to his right and a store full of customers. The sign on the cash register explains to customers that they will receive a printed list of what they bought—a revolutionary idea at the time. (Jameson family.)

Randy and Belle Whitaker, pictured with their grandchildren in 1947, lived and worked on the Doss Ranch southeast of Seminole. A well-respected cowman, Randy also farmed thousands of acres of cotton and grew feed for his cattle. The grandchildren are, from oldest to youngest, Georgia, Geneva, Robert, Lavada, Eldon, Thelma, Susan, Lynn, and Kenneth. (Whitaker family.)

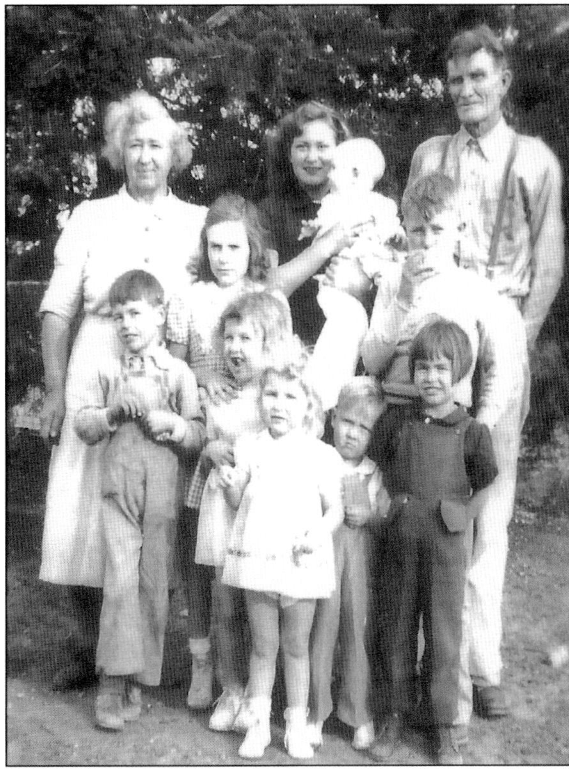

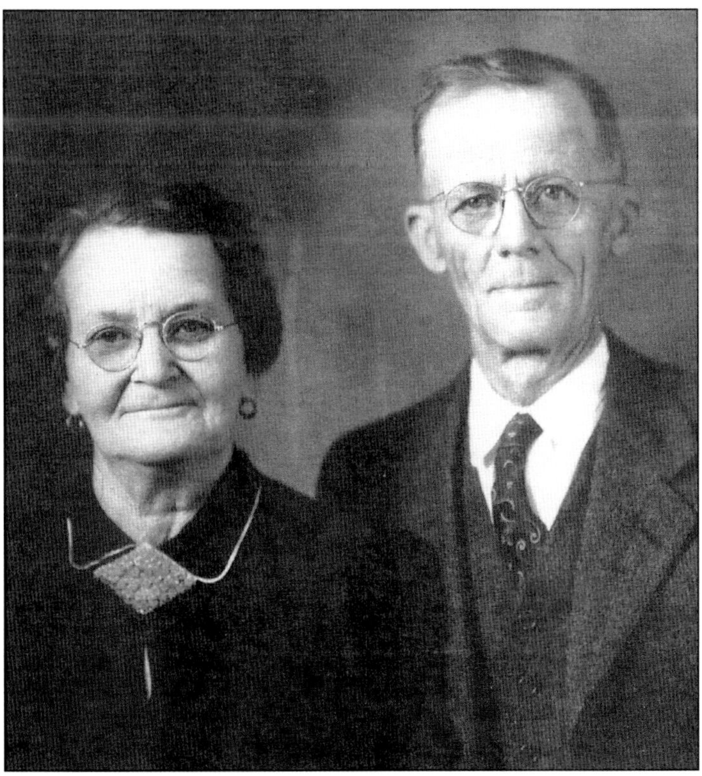

Taken on their 50th wedding anniversary in 1943, this photograph shows Guy and Bettie Page Stark, who had come to Seminole in 1904, helped organize the Methodist church at a gathering at Hackberry Grove, and built a business on South Main Street that helped develop Seminole into a thriving community. Guy died as a result of a freak accident in 1948, but Bettie lived on at their home until 1964. (Stark family.)

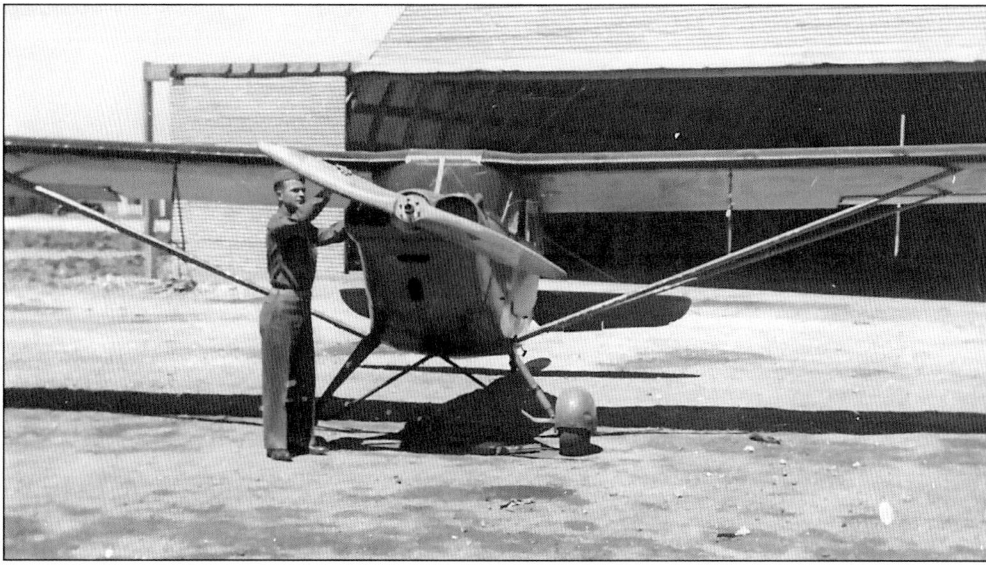

The first airplane bought in Gaines County belonged to Marbut and Charlie George. The plane, a 1941 Aeronca Chief two-seater with a 50-horsepower engine, had a range of 500 miles and a service ceiling of 15,000 feet. Charlie George (the coauthor's father) is doing a preflight inspection at a hangar built for them by Seminole pioneer Emma Austin at Southwest Eleventh Street and the Hobbs Highway, where Allsup's currently sits. (George family.)

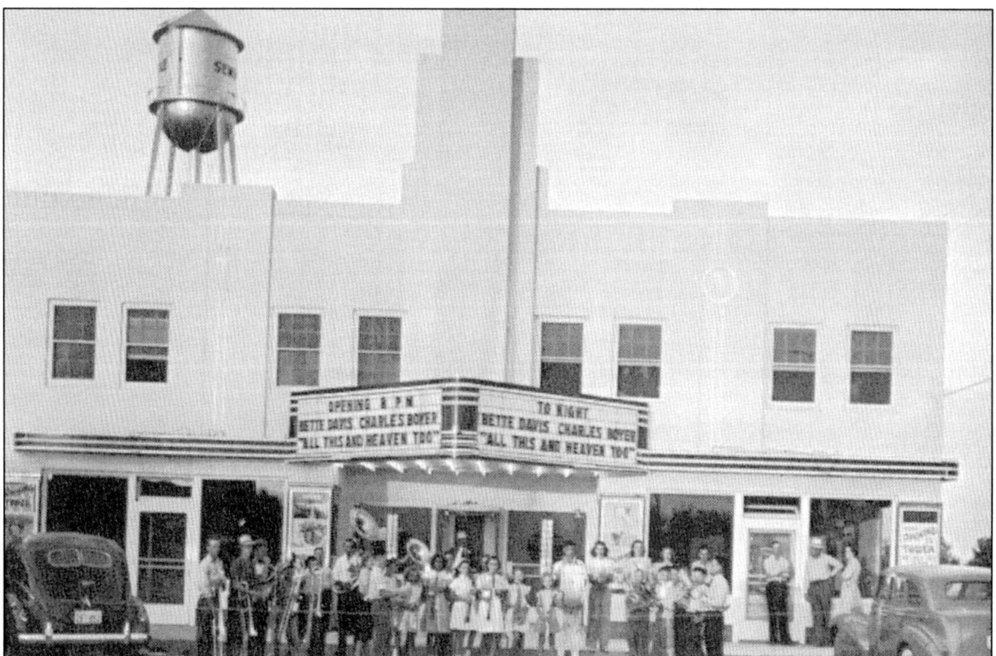

Owned by W.E. and Fronia Cox, the Tower Theater at 215 South Main Street was the site of this grand opening featuring the Seminole City Band on July 26, 1940. Although not the first theater in town, it was the nicest, with plush carpet, a balcony, and luxuriously padded seats. Today, the location is a small grassy park with trees and a gazebo. (*Gaines County, Texas Pictorial History.*)

December 7, 1941, brought war to the United States. During the war years, everyone had to pitch in to get things done, especially in the cotton fields. This photograph, taken in 1942, shows Seminole school staff members picking cotton. From left to right are Chris Hamilton Mills, Billie Poole, Alene McCrummen George (the coauthor's mother), Olene Shillingburg Bingham, Dale Cook, and Supt. Dewey Davis. (George family.)

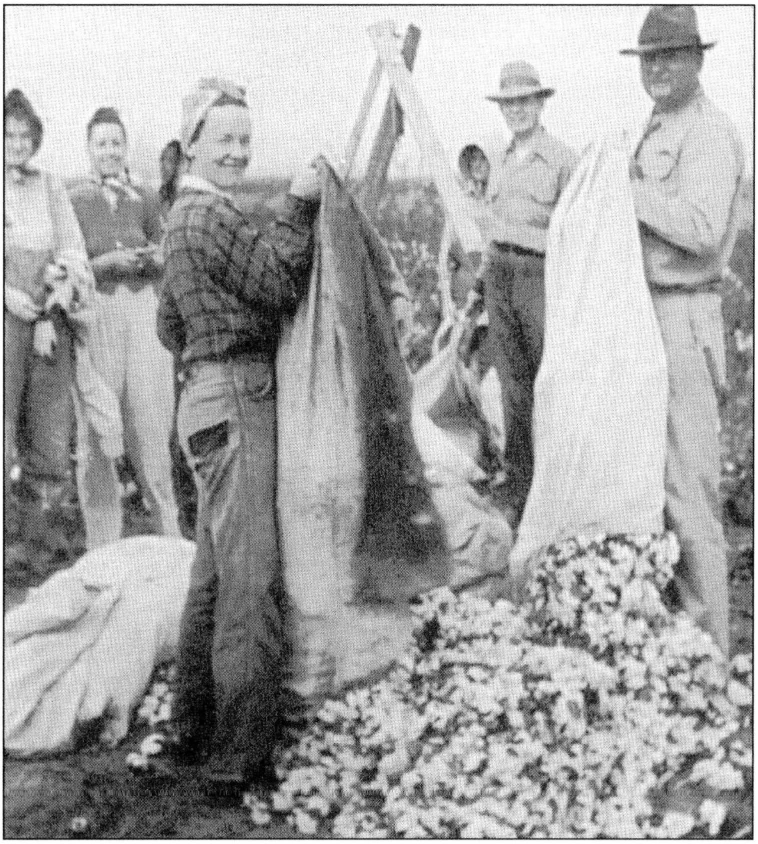

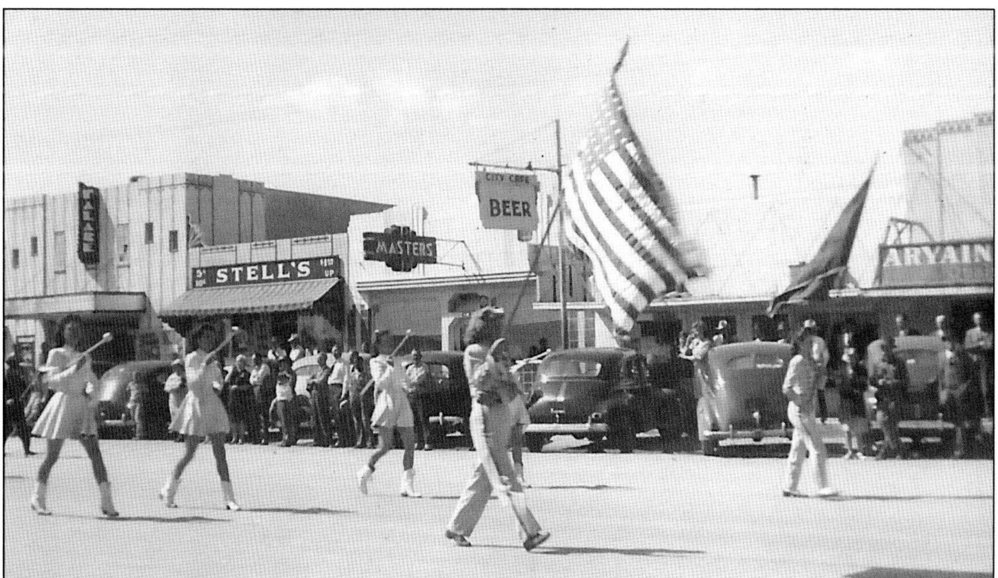

This parade some time in the early to mid-1940s shows Stell's Variety Store, Master's Café, City Café, and other businesses. What makes the photograph unique is that it was taken during one of only four years in the history of Gaines County when the sale of alcohol was legal. (*Sentinel.*)

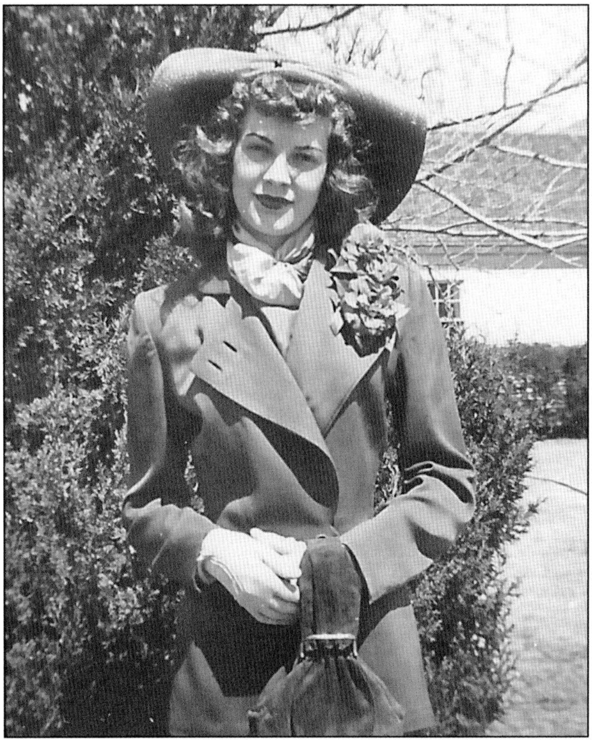

This ravishing beauty is Patricia Denton (now Pat Aryain) in a photograph taken in the fall of 1946, just before she was to be crowned Seminole's football queen. Patricia is the daughter of Rev. T.L. and Sadie Belle Denton. Up until that day, all her clothes had been handmade by her mother. For this special event, though, her mother insisted that she have her first store-bought outfit. (Aryain family.)

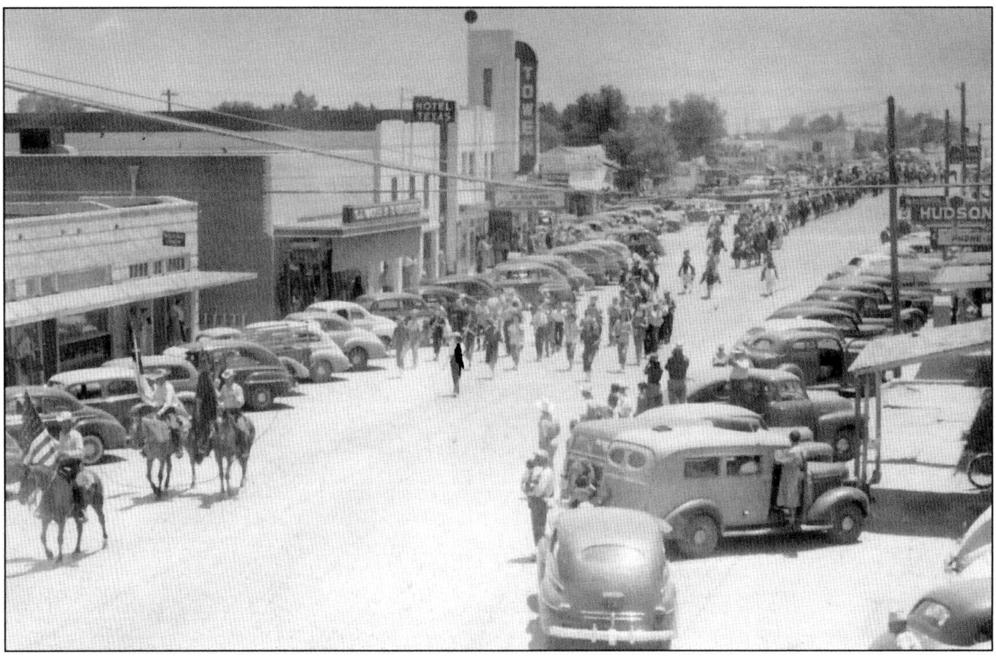

Another parade, this one possibly during 1946 homecoming or for the Gaines County Fair, shows South Main Street looking southward toward the Tower Theater. Looking closely, a barbershop, a Western Union office, a G.F. Wackers, and Hotel Texas are visible. Across the street from left to right stand Cox & Moore Insurance (where Moore-Haralson Insurance Agency is now), Kidd's Grocery & Market, and the Masonic lodge. (*Sentinel.*)

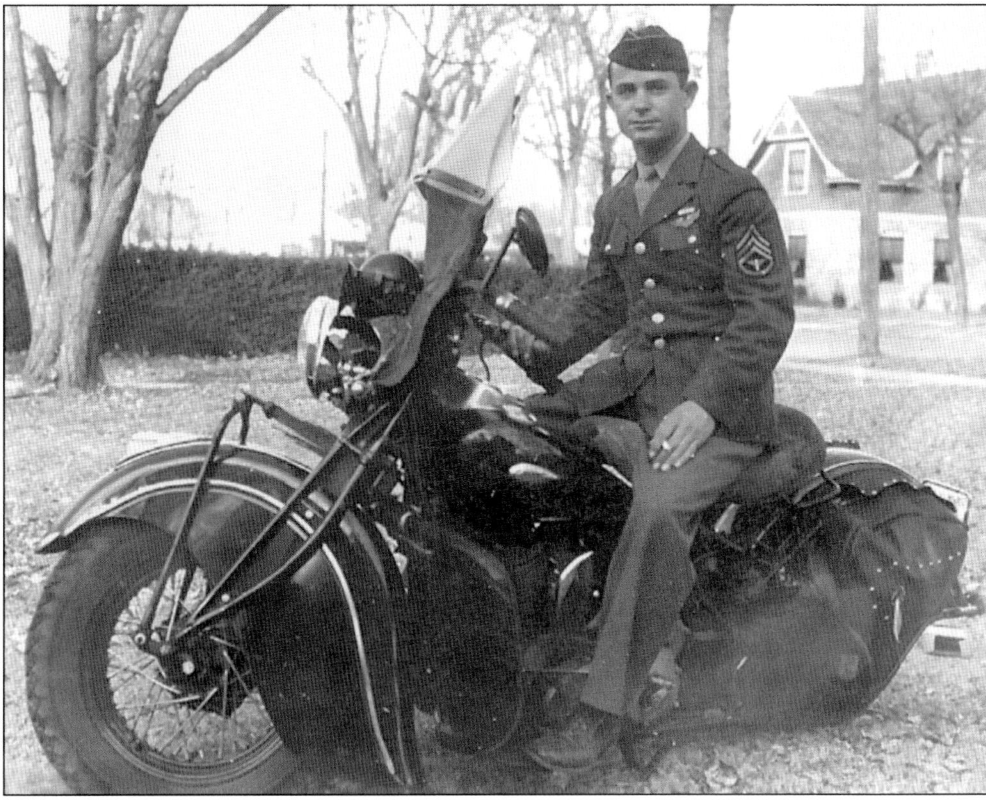

This photograph taken in the mid-1940s shows a dashing young airman—Charlie George—on his 1941 Indian Chief just before being shipped overseas to fly gliders in Operation Market Garden in World War II. George survived the war, returned to Seminole, began working in the oilfield, married a young teacher named Alene McCrummen, and raised two children. Charlie passed away at the age of 92 in 2007. (George family.)

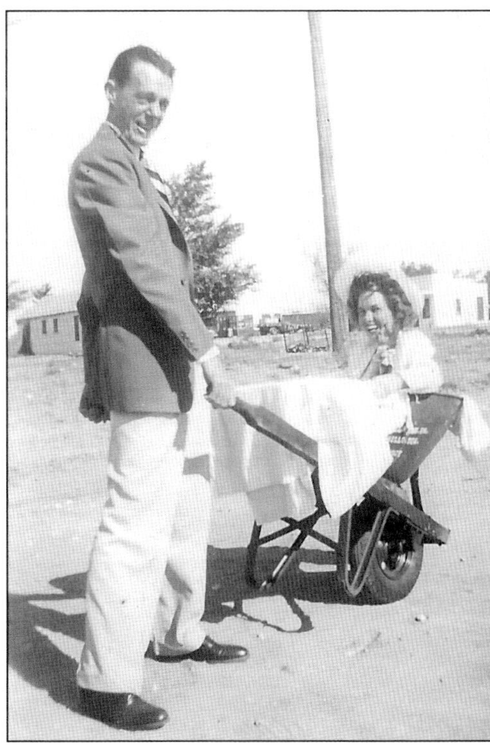

In this photograph, taken on June 6, 1946, Ulan Holbrooks pushes his bride, Dorothy Pittman Holbrooks, around Seminole's courthouse square in a wheelbarrow on their wedding day—one of those odd old wedding traditions. Dorothy was the daughter of Seminole pioneer R.W. Pittman. (Holbrooks family.)

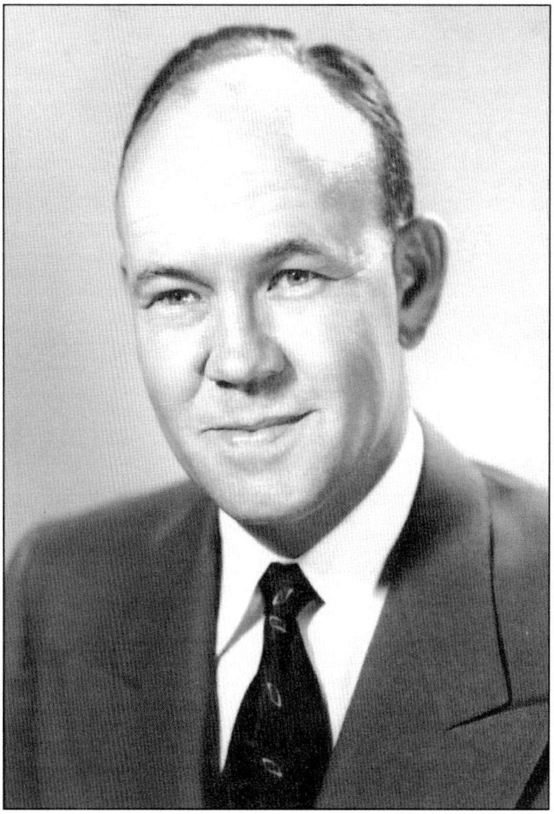

Attorney William T. (Bill) Curry and his wife, Bess, arrived in Seminole in 1947. Bill had been county attorney of Burnet County and assistant attorney general for Texas before coming to Seminole. Bill and Bess were active in the First Presbyterian Church, Rotary Club, and countless other causes. Bill was a kind, caring man, and he left a legacy that will last generations. Bess—now a realtor—still lives in Seminole. (*Sentinel.*)

During the oil boom from 1935 to 1960, oil companies built "camps," groups of houses for their employees' families. In Seminole, Phillips 66 built such a camp with 15 houses. Competition between the camps was intense but friendly. This 1947 picture shows the Phillips softball team. From left to right are (first row) Gene Brown, Eddie Dossier, batgirl Barbara Britton (Culver), Bill Burrows, and Jimmy Woods; (second row) Jess Greenfield, Lloyd Pyle, Lester Pyle, Tommie Roberts, and Joe Britton (player/manager). (Culver family.)

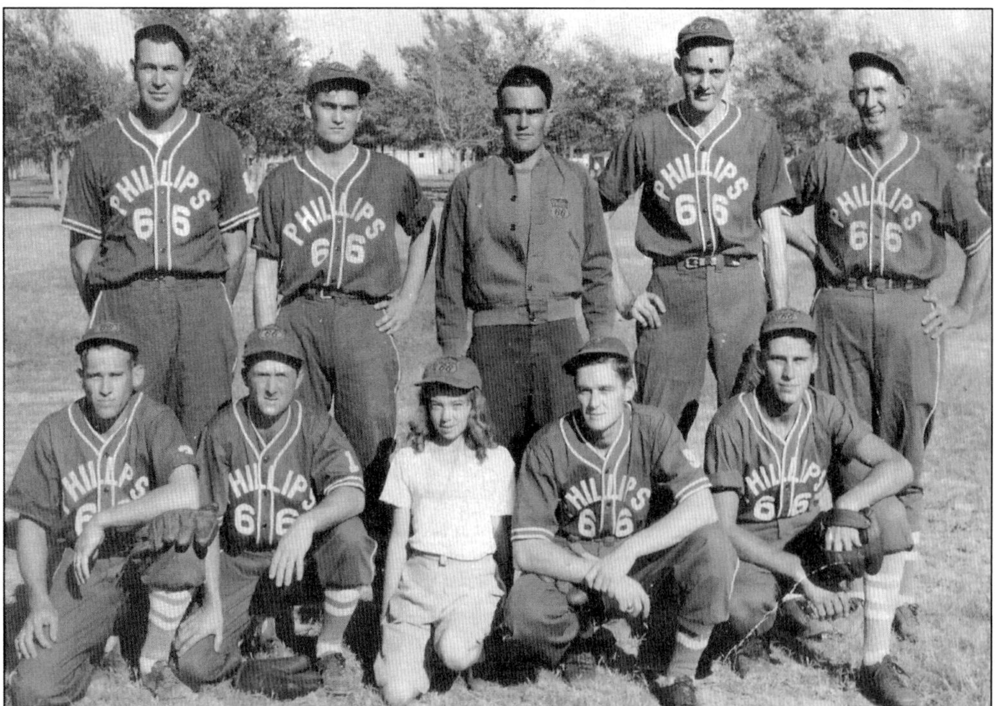

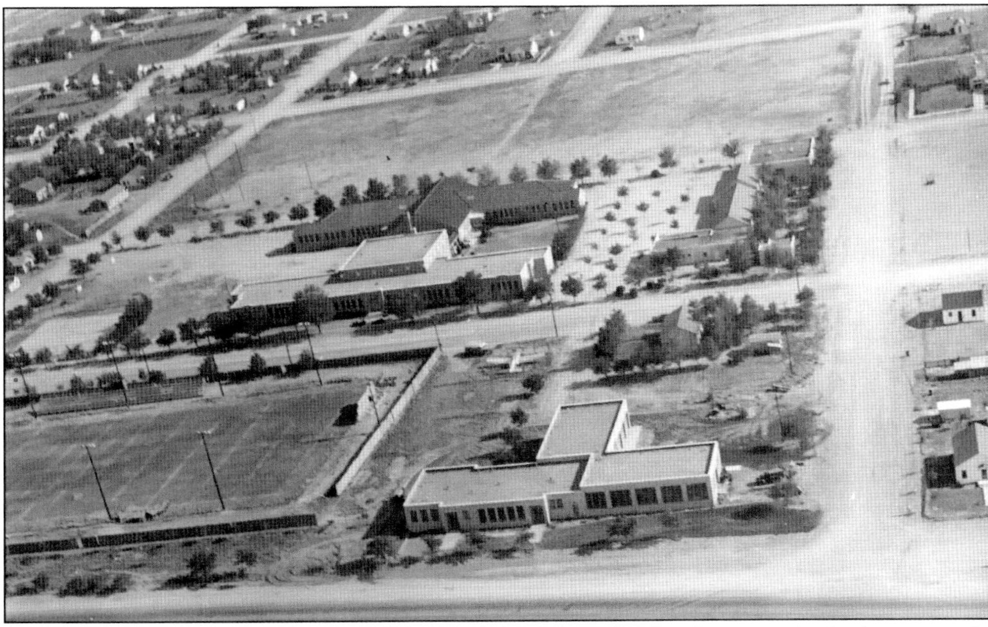

This 1947 aerial photograph looks south across the Seminole school system. At the bottom is the Hobbs Highway with the football stadium in the lower left, where the playground for Seminole Elementary now sits. The building in the lower right is a shop building that is still in use. In the center of the picture is what was then the high school, with the elementary building behind it, both of which have now been razed to make room for the current elementary campus. Behind those buildings is an open field that today holds Seminole Primary School. (Museum.)

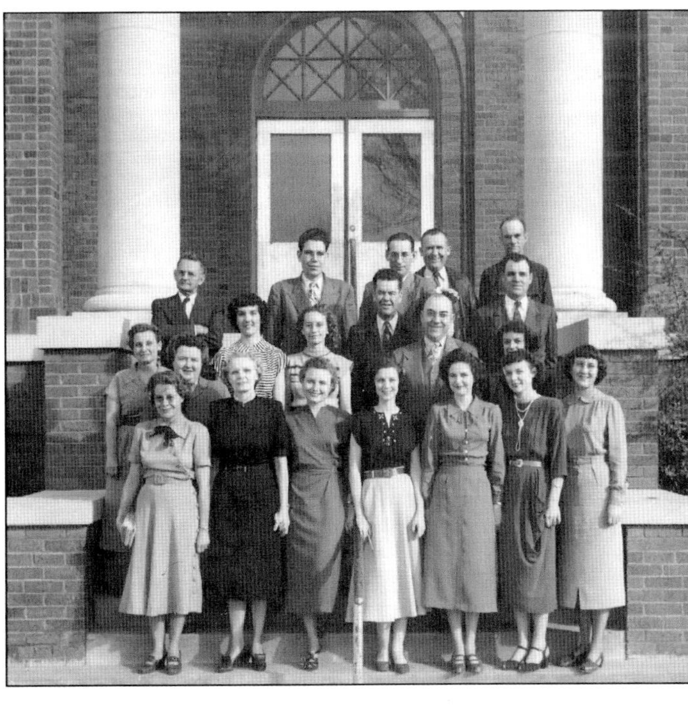

Gaines County Courthouse employees are standing on the courthouse steps in the late 1940s. From left to right are (first row) Sue Richardson, Ruby Smallin, Joyce Davis, Joyce Skinner, Mary Maloney, Mary Eunice Barrett, and Ruby Lewis; (second row) Edith Stanley, Nuel Mitchell, unidentified, Doris Earl, county judge C.C. Byar, and Mary Baldwin; (third row) J.R. Coker and Charley Ramsey; (fourth row) J.P. Kelly, Woodson Jones, Joe Anderson, Chester Browne, and Jim McClesky. (Museum.)

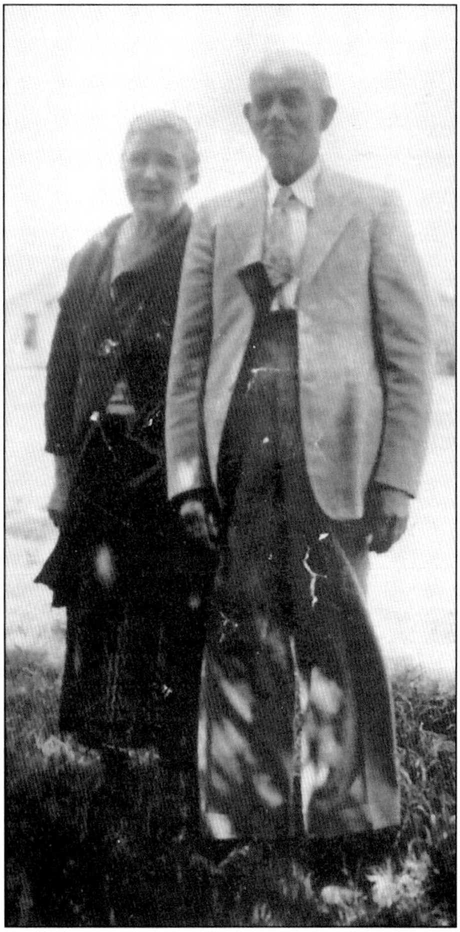

Seen here in the mid-1930s, Dan and Aurelia Cobb literally helped build Seminole from the ground up. Arriving in 1906, Dan built their home, two of the county's courthouses, part of the First Baptist Church (the Cobbs were charter members), the 1910 two-story Seminole school building, and many residences. He also hauled mail between Midland and Seminole and sold oil leases in his later years. Aurelia Cobb, an accomplished musician and former teacher, was active in her church and enjoyed doting on her grandchildren and great-grandchildren. (Museum.)

This group picture, taken in the 1940s, shows the congregation of First Presbyterian Church standing outside its stucco-covered church. Just to the right of center, wearing a dark dress and a light hat, is Emma J. Woody Austin, the sweet lady called by many the "Mother of Gaines County." She was also present in 1955 for the ground-breaking ceremony for the current First Presbyterian Church and donated the majestic oak tree that still graces its grounds. (First Presbyterian Church.)

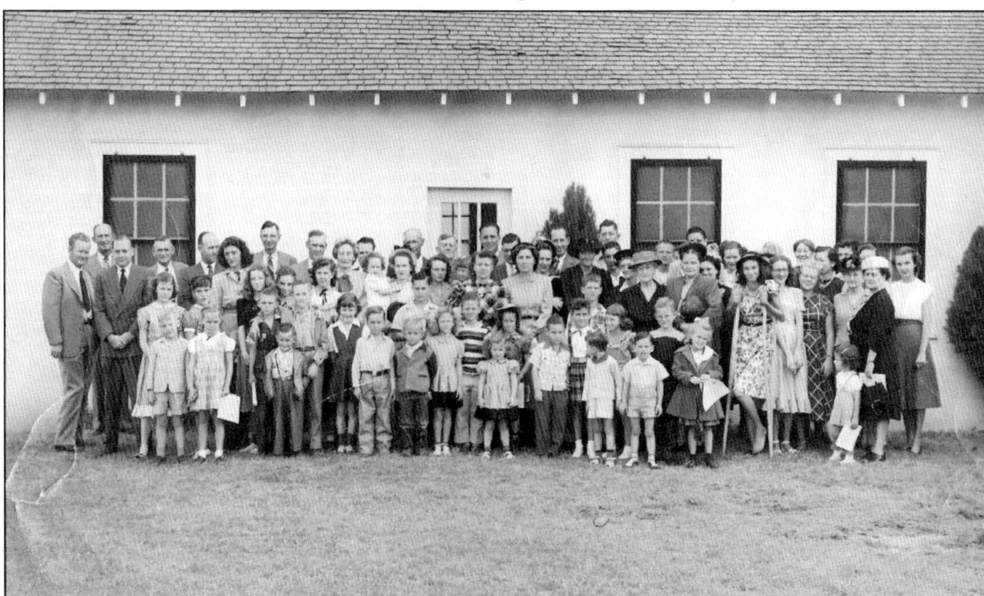

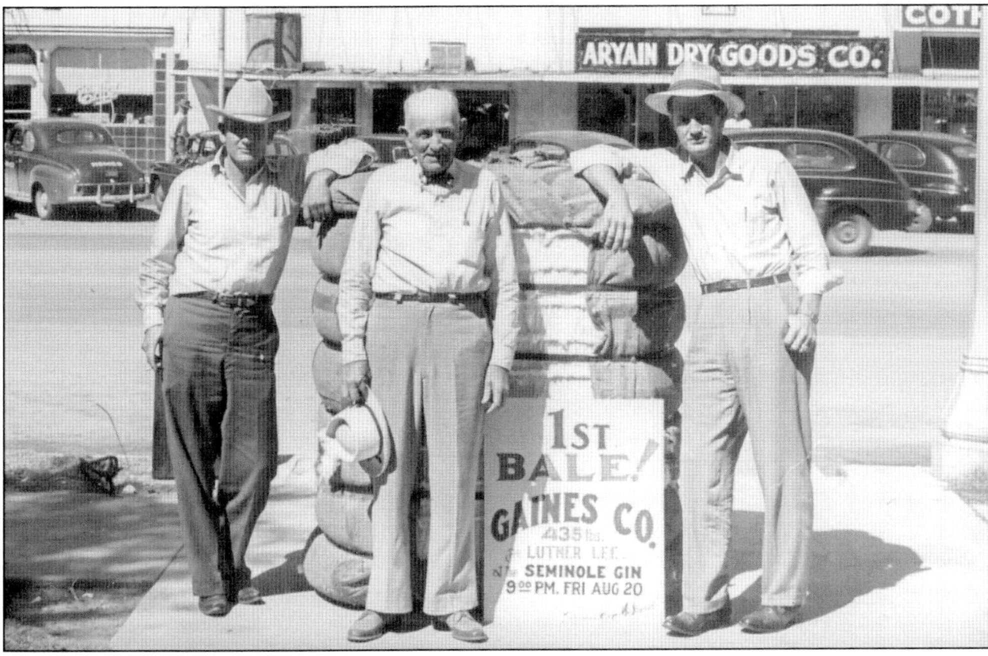

Since 1948, producing the first bale of cotton of the season in Gaines County has become an annual honor sought by many cotton farmers. In this photograph taken on South Main Street, the honor goes to Luther Lee (left), who lived in western Dawson County but farmed in eastern Gaines County. The man in the center is Homer Kyle. The man on the right is unidentified. (Seminole Chamber of Commerce.)

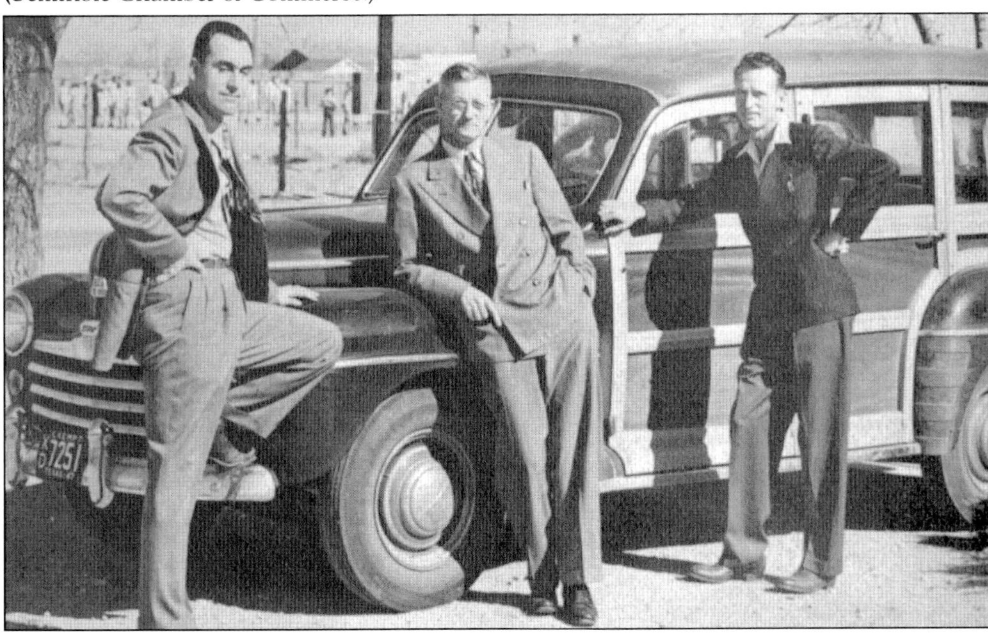

This photograph, taken in 1948, shows the administrators of Seminole schools. On the left is Ted Edwards, superintendent. In the center is W.H. Vanlandingham, high school principal (who students referred to as "Mr. Van"), and next to him is T.B. Livingston, elementary school principal. (Museum.)

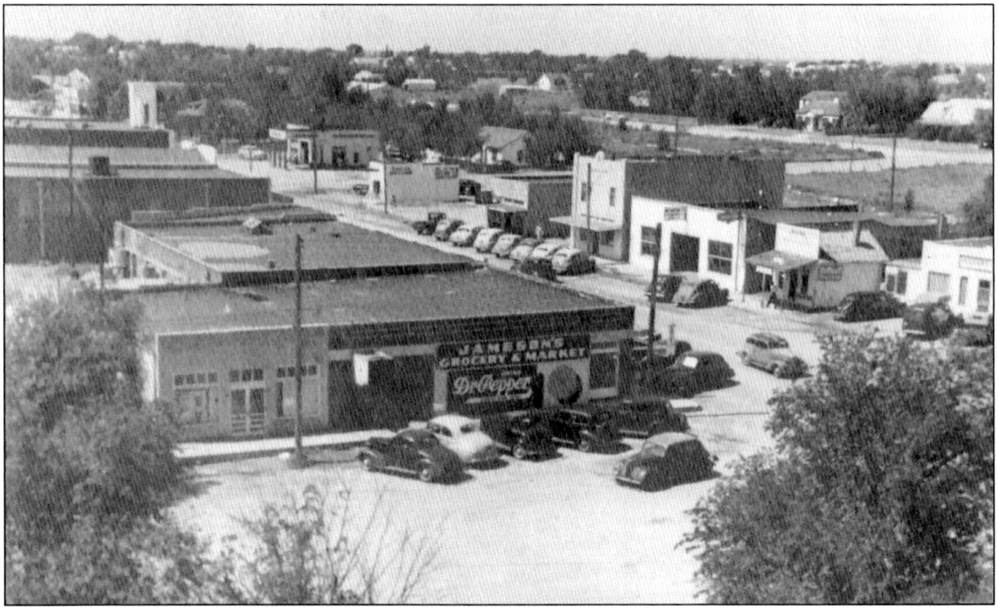

The five images on pages 62 through 65 comprise a panorama of downtown Seminole in 1948. The above image looks southwest, with Jameson's Grocery & Market on the corner of South Main Street and Avenue B, the Greyhound bus station directly across Main Street, then Cox & Moore Insurance, Hudson's Garage (where Kidd's Grocery had been), the Masonic lodge, Maloney Drug, and Seminole Newsstand. Below, about a half block west along Southwest Avenue B, are Ketner Furniture Store, the Gaines Hotel, Forrest Lumber Company, and finally, the Frozen Food Locker on the south side of the street. In the center of the photograph is Singleton's Department Store, with Smallin-Worthington Insurance Agency and Singelton's Funeral Home just to its west along the north side of Southwest Avenue B. North of Singleton's along Main Street are the Palace Theater and Malcolm's Variety Store. (Both, Museum.)

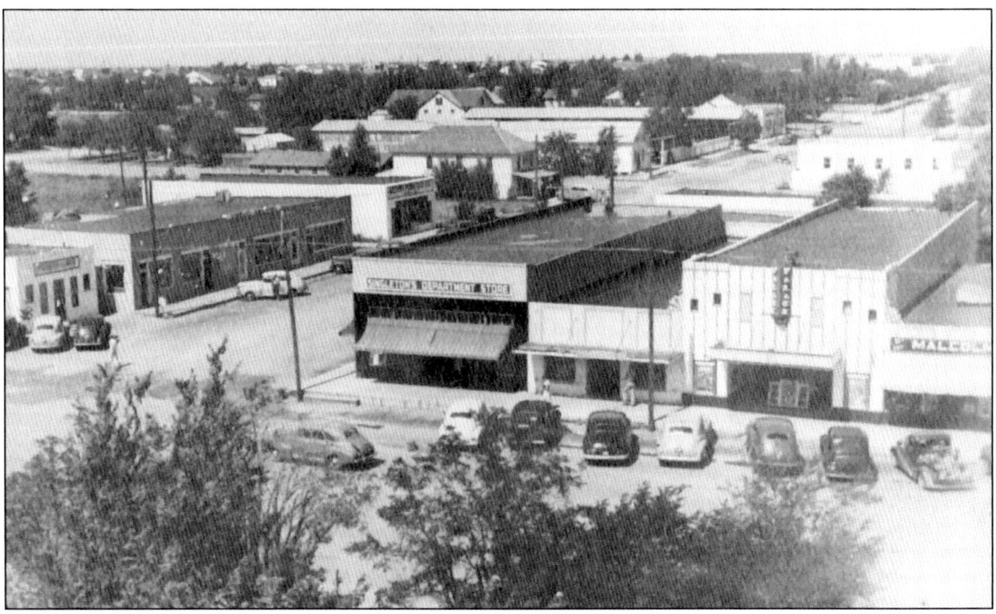

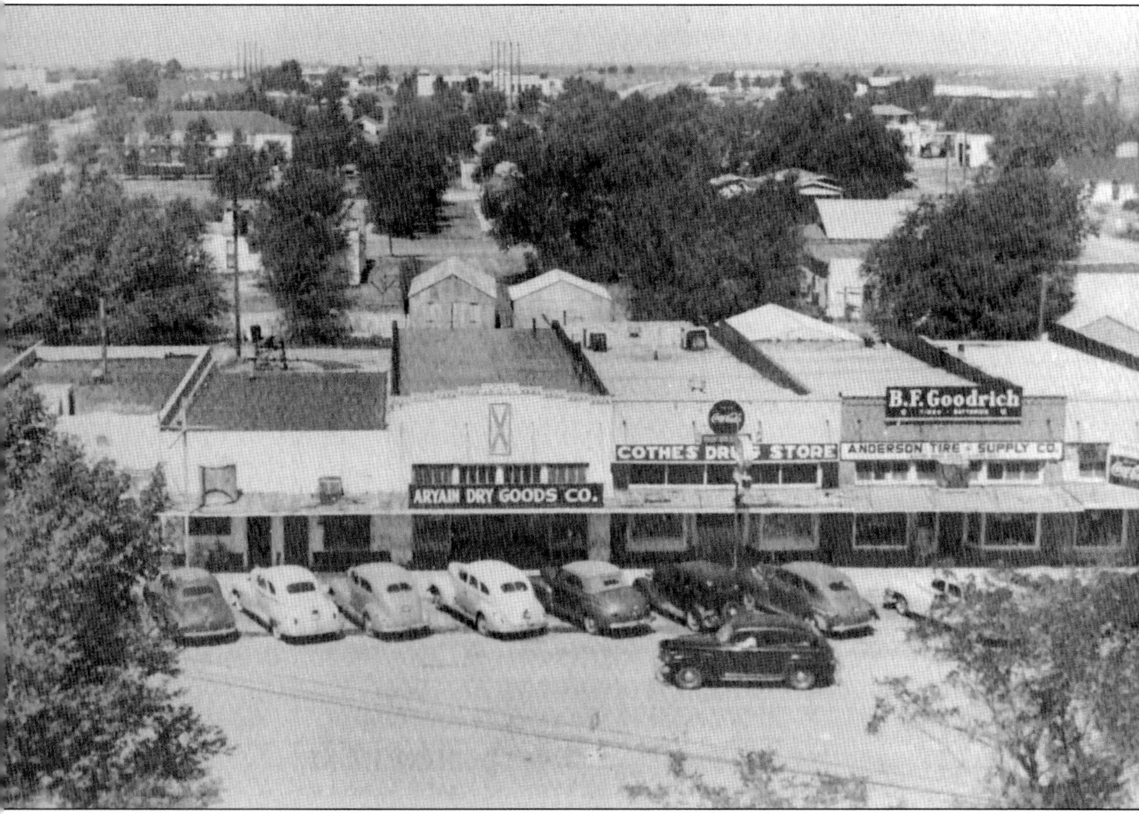

This view toward the west shows Master's Café, City Café, Aryain's Dry Goods, Cothes Drug, and Anderson Tire & Supply along Main Street. Just visible in the distance over the tops of those businesses are, on the left, the First Baptist Church, the First Methodist Church, and the lights of Wigwam Field. (Museum.)

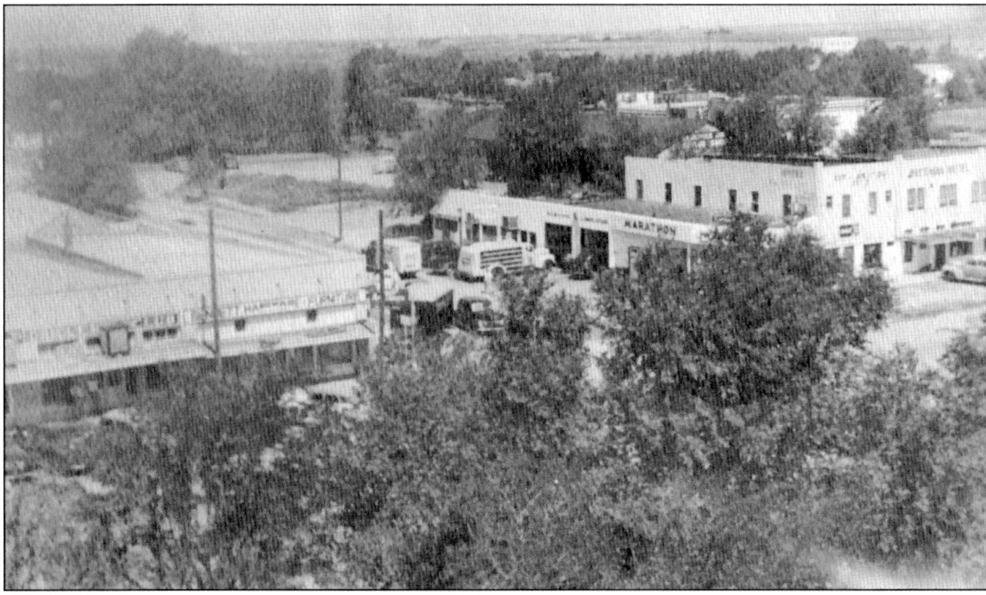

On the far left of this panorama segment are the Driller's Club and Bennett Hardware & Furniture. To the north across the Hobbs Highway is the Marathon station, the Pittman Building, and Pittman Hotel on North Main Street. The buildings just visible over the top of the Pittman Building are the R.L. Jones Jr. Repair Shop and Foremost Dairy Products, which most people in Seminole called the "icehouse." (Museum.)

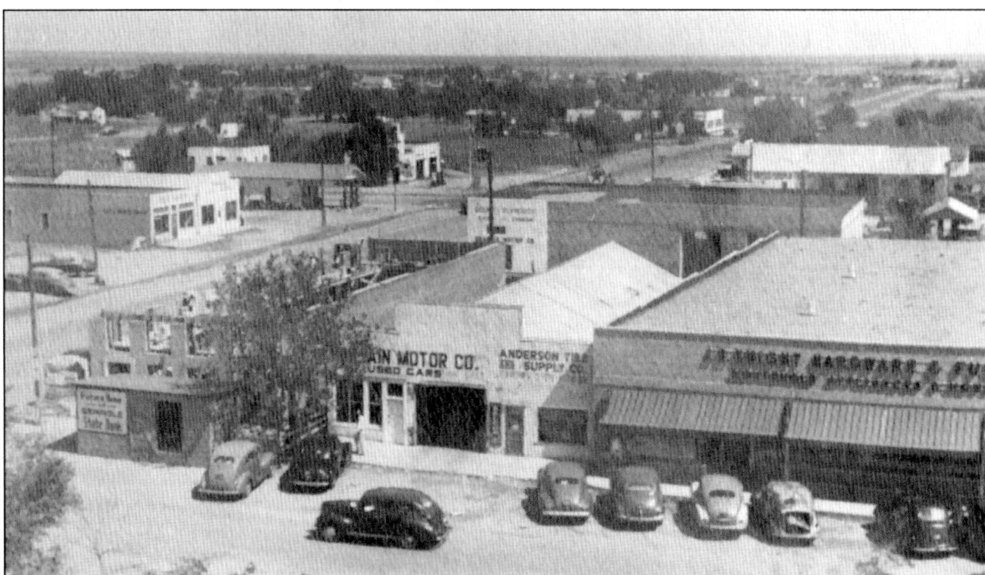

This view looks northwest from the courthouse. On the corner of North Main Street and the Hobbs Highway, the Seminole State Bank is under construction. When finished, this facility offered Seminole residents their first drive-through banking with one window on the northwest corner of the bank. Next to the bank are Partain Motor Company and J.B. Knight Hardware & Furniture. Just visible behind these stores along North Main Street are the Dodge/Plymouth dealer and Longbotham's Texaco. Across North Main Street in the mid-distance is the L.F. Hyatt Gulf service station. (Museum.)

On South Main Street across from the Tower Theater and north a bit is Maloney Drug. Max Maloney and his wife came to Seminole in 1940 and opened the pharmacy, which also sold candy, film, and cigarettes and had a soda fountain. Standing in the doorway is Max Maloney. (Mary Maloney Hughes.)

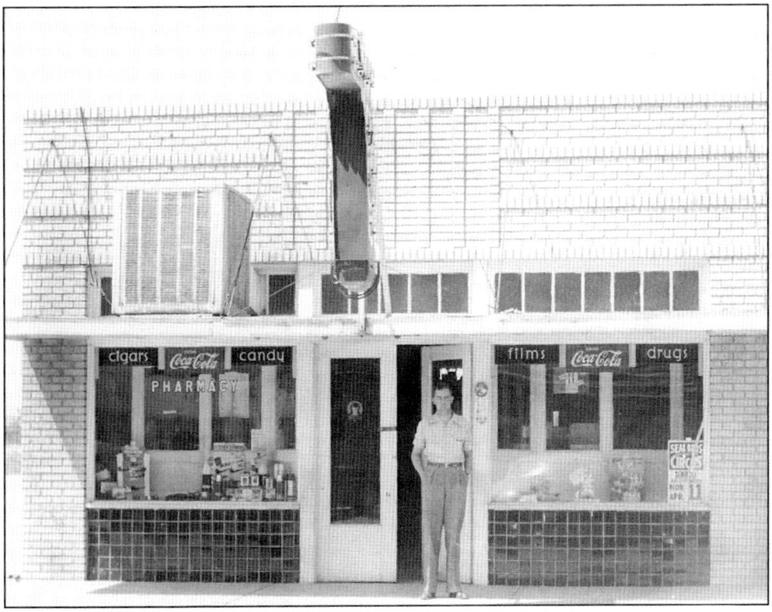

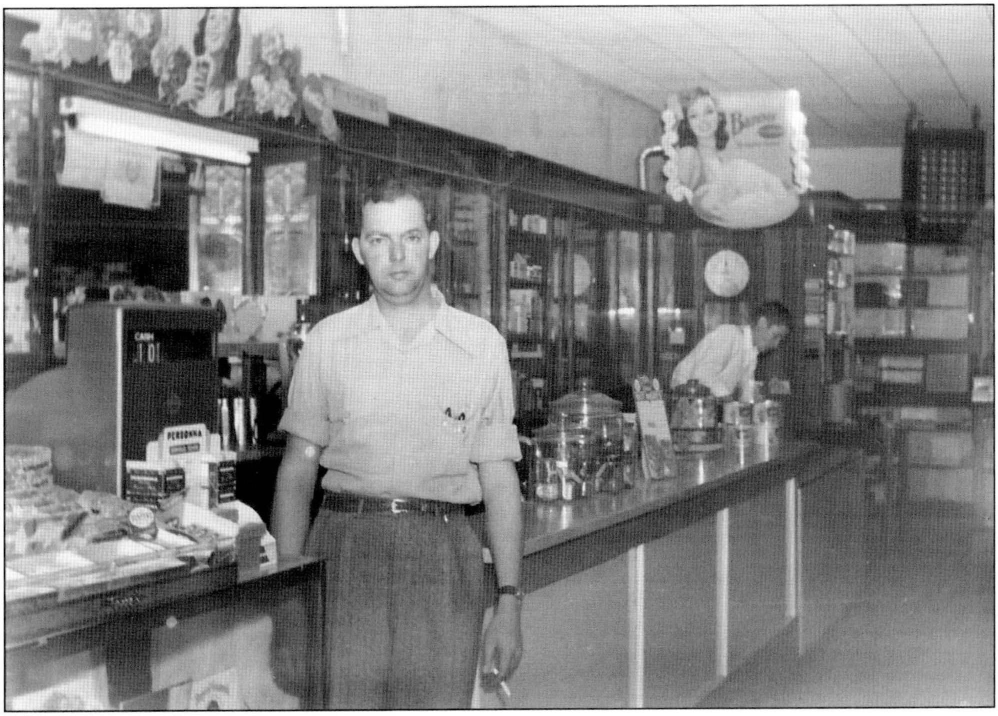

This image shows the interior of Maloney Drug with Max Maloney standing at the cash register and an unidentified employee in the back. During World War II, while both Max Maloney and Reeves Cothes were off fighting for their country, Seminole had only one licensed pharmacist—Max's father, C.C. Maloney. Until Max or Reeves returned, C.C. ran back and forth from Maloney's to Cothes to fill prescriptions. (Mary Maloney Hughes.)

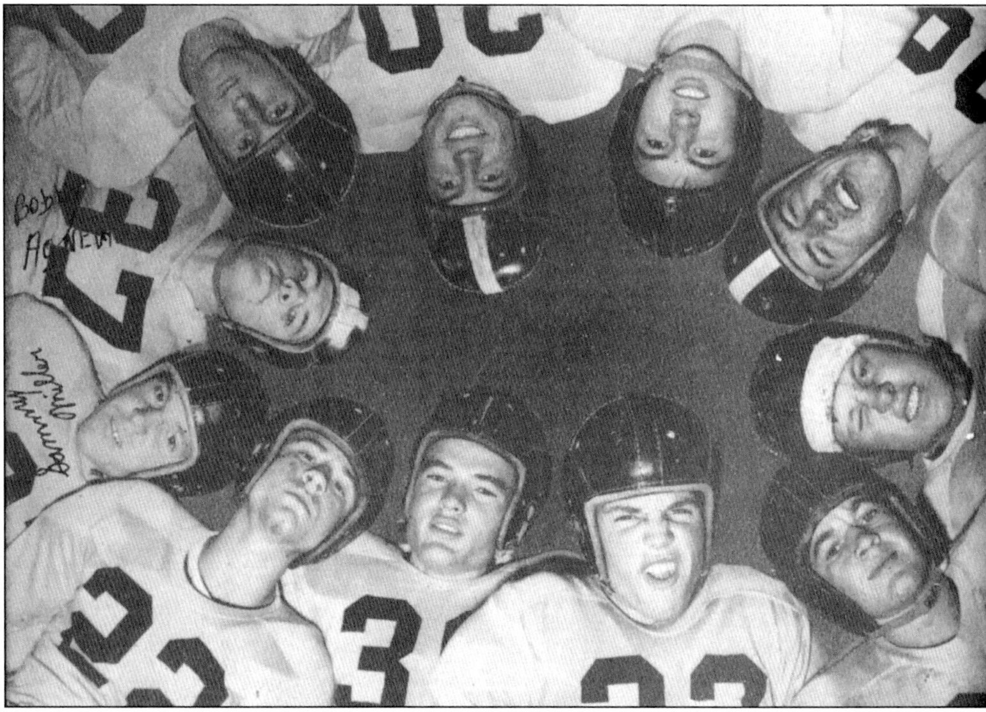

This football huddle—a rough-looking bunch—is made up of players from the 1948 Seminole Indian football team. These players from the 1947 Indian team are, clockwise from top left: Crowder Wharton, Bobby Hunter, Ralph Jones, Richard Stanfield, John Ancell, Ira Bobo, Val Joe Walker, Bill Neel, James Powell, Sammy Miller, and Bobby Agnew. The photo was taken by Tommie Roberts. (Museum.)

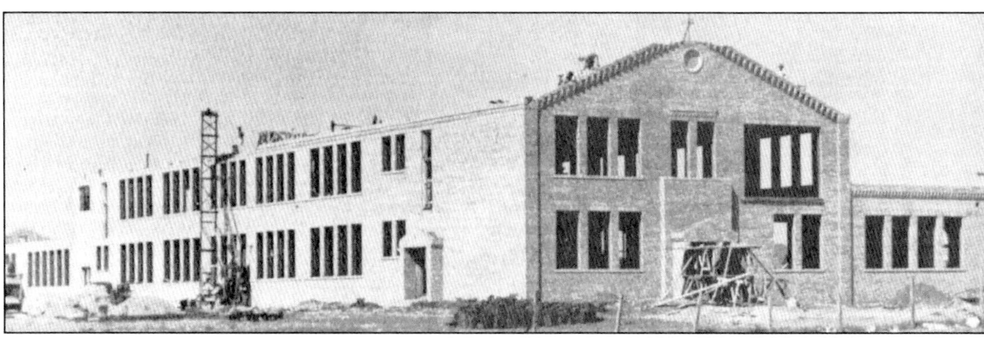

In the 1960s, people driving through Seminole often stopped and asked, "What college is that?" The proud reply was, "That's our high school!" Seen from the southeast in 1948 is the main building while under construction. The two-story building on Southwest Avenue B eventually had an auditorium and gymnasium. It served as Seminole High School until 1980, then Seminole Junior High School until 2011. Today, it houses primary students while their new campus is being constructed. (Museum.)

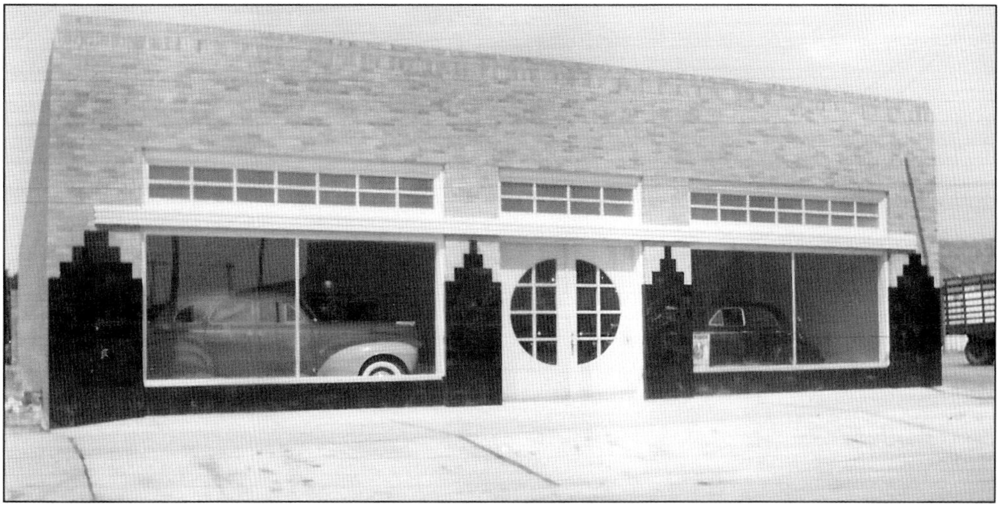

This building once stood across from the Tower Theater. It housed Seminole's Kaiser/Frazer automobile dealership in the late 1940s. The dealership was short-lived, however, because the parent automobile company was only in existence from 1945 to 1952. In that year, it was renamed Kaiser Motors, but the local dealership had closed by that time. (*Sentinel.*)

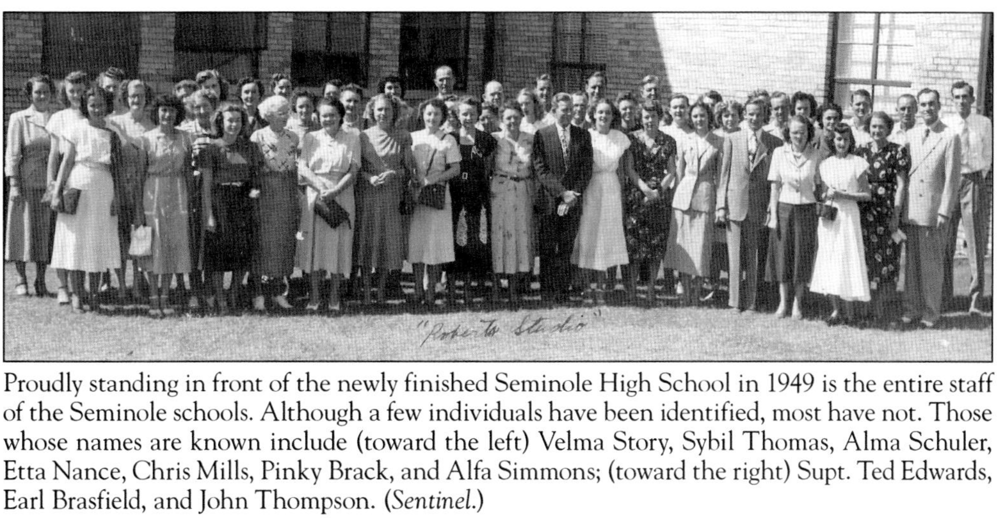

Proudly standing in front of the newly finished Seminole High School in 1949 is the entire staff of the Seminole schools. Although a few individuals have been identified, most have not. Those whose names are known include (toward the left) Velma Story, Sybil Thomas, Alma Schuler, Etta Nance, Chris Mills, Pinky Brack, and Alfa Simmons; (toward the right) Supt. Ted Edwards, Earl Brasfield, and John Thompson. (*Sentinel.*)

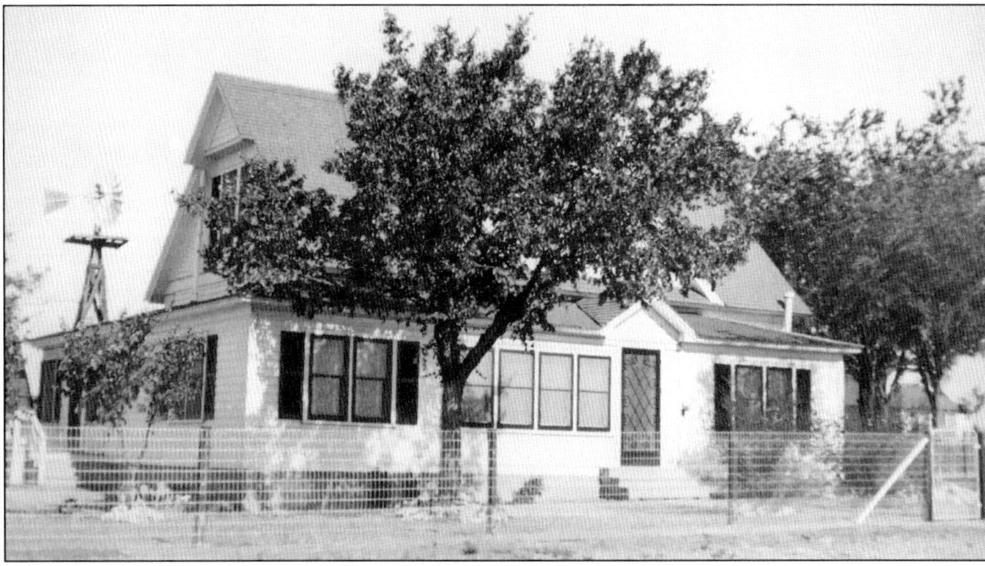

About 1910, M.S. and Meek Lane Doss purchased the former headquarters of the Hat Ranch, seen here. They remodeled it, modernized it, and made it into one of the most attractive ranch houses in the region. It was their home, a place friends and neighbors also loved, for almost 47 years until M.S. and Meek Lane decided to move into Seminole. (Museum.)

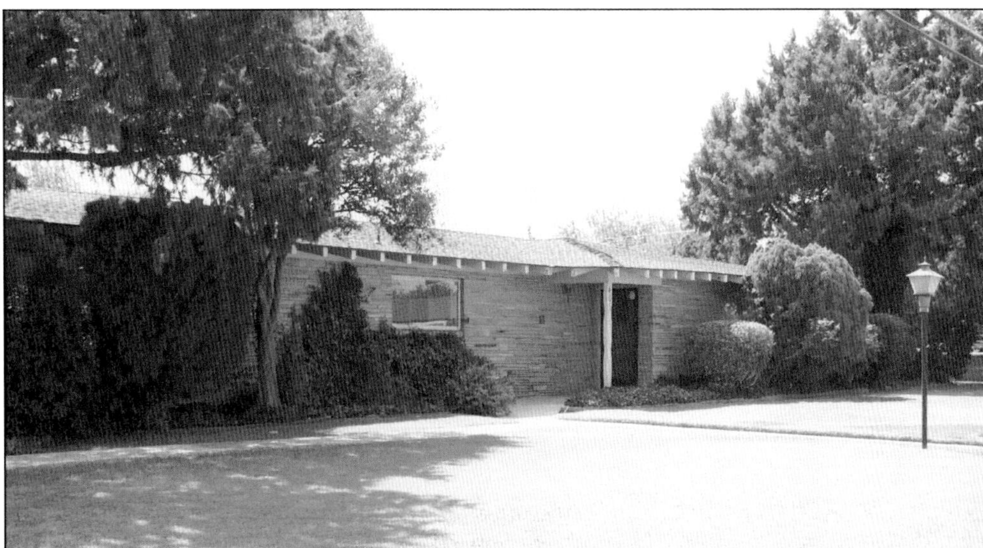

This beautiful stone home at 401 Southwest Avenue E became home to M.S. and Meek Lane Doss in 1957 when they moved into town. The Dosses contributed to many worthy causes: a dormitory and Olympic-sized swimming pool at the West Texas Boys Ranch near San Angelo, a youth center in Seminole, buildings for Boy and Girl Scouts in Seminole, and a beautiful chapel at First Methodist Church, where they were active members. This home now provides a meeting place for Seminole's Garden Club, the Music Club, and the Llano Estacado Porcelain Arts Club. (George family.)

Three

1950–1975

Room to Grow

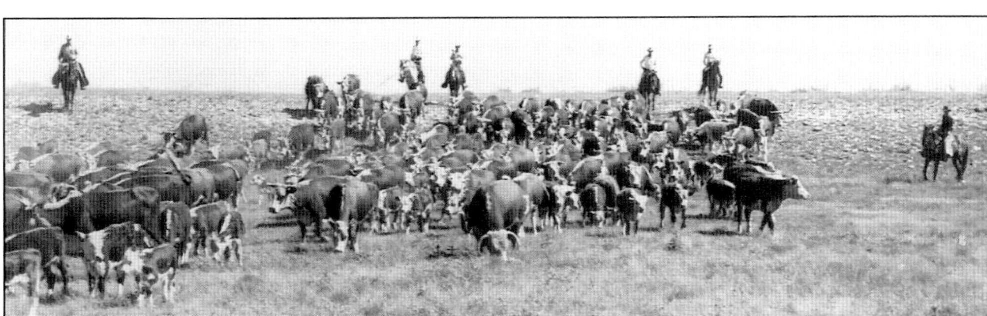

This 1953 image shows a roundup of Hereford cattle on the Rafter I Ranch in northwest Gaines County. Visible in the distance on the far left is A.C. Ward. Third from the left is Bert Sherman, and second from the right is Bill Ward. (Museum.)

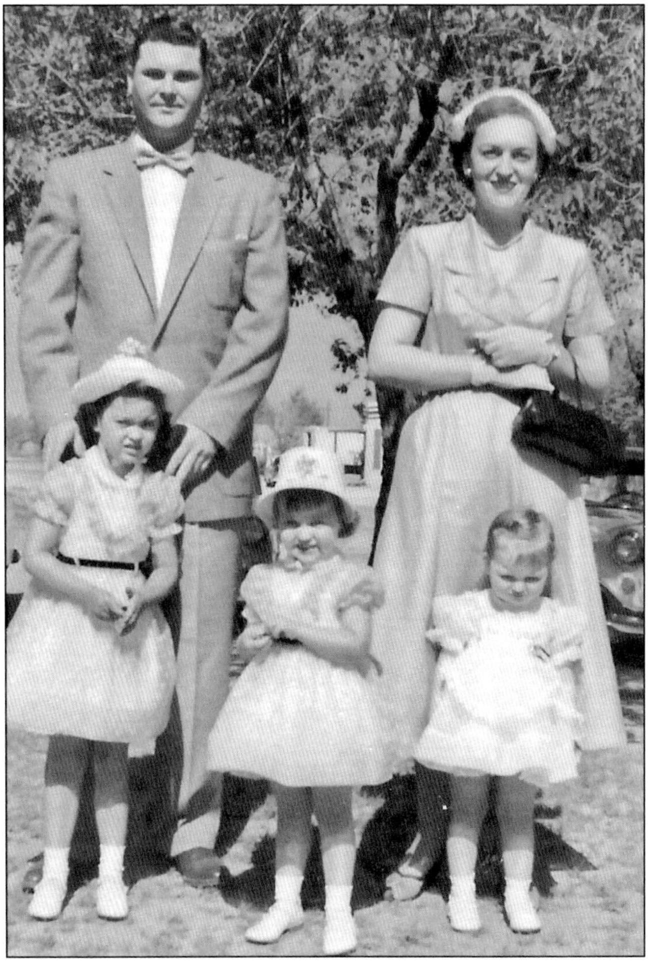

This photograph, taken in 1954, shows Gaines County judge Charlie Lawrence and his family. Charlie (left) has Charlotte in front of him. Charlie's wife, Dorothy (Dotsy), is on the right with Martha (center) and Linda in front of her. The only daughter missing is Becky, but she was not born for another two years. (Lawrence family.)

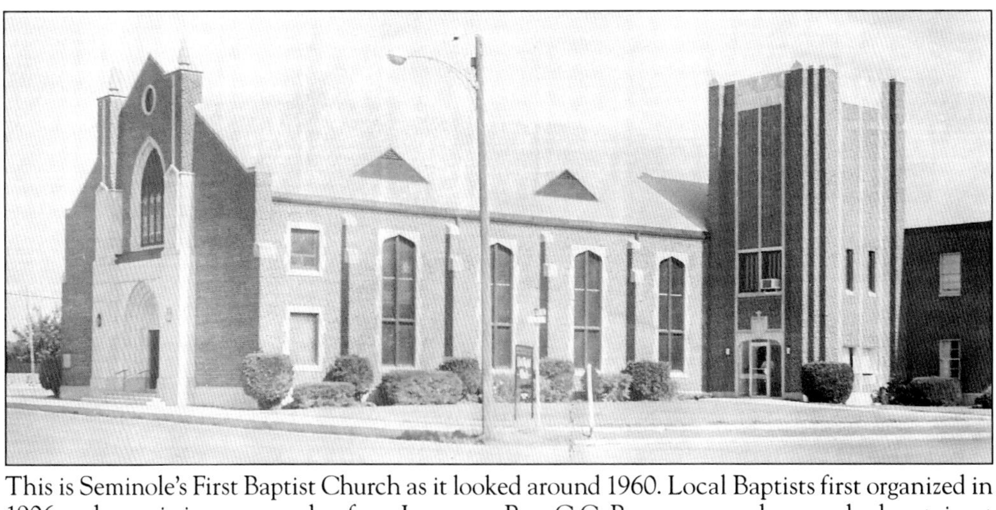

This is Seminole's First Baptist Church as it looked around 1960. Local Baptists first organized in 1906 under a missionary preacher from Lamesa—Rev. G.C. Berryman—who preached upstairs at W.B. Austin's home and later in the courthouse. In 1922, Baptists began construction of their own church building. That early wooden structure was replaced with this one in 1951. (*Sentinel.*)

Pictured here are Rev. T.L. and Sadie Belle Denton. They moved to Seminole in 1945, where Denton became pastor of the First Baptist Church. Under his leadership, plans for the new auditorium (seen on the previous page) were completed. The Dentons served the Seminole church until 1951, when they moved to Post. In 1957, they retired and moved back to Seminole. In all, Reverend Denton and his wife helped build over 100 churches. (Aryain family.)

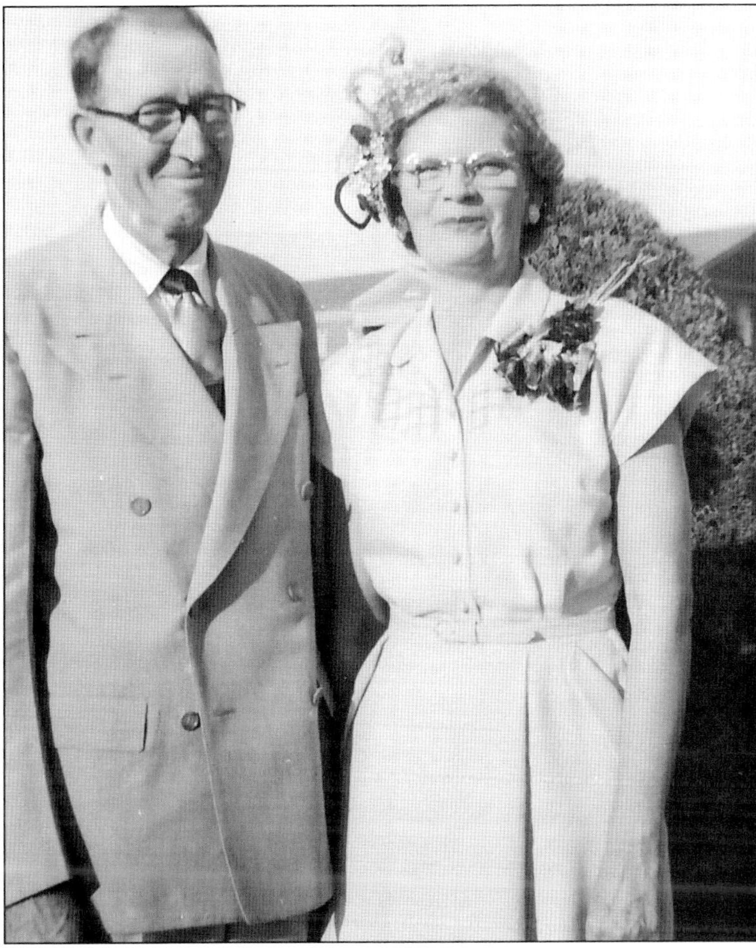

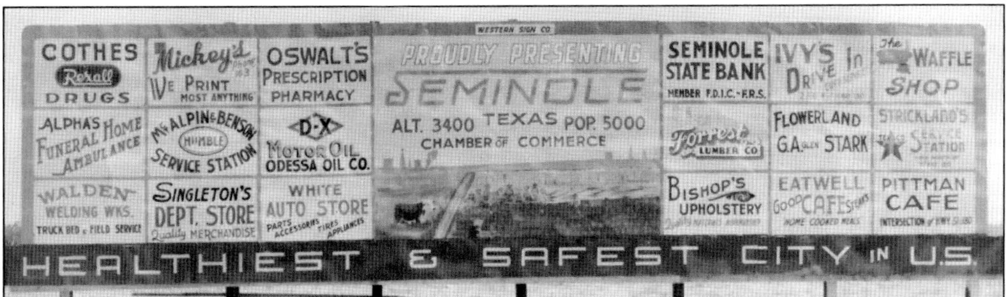

Proudly displayed at the edge of town in the late 1950s, this billboard features many local businesses as well as the town's population. In 1950, the town had only 3,480 residents. The 1950s were a busy decade for Seminole. A new hospital was built in 1953 and a county library in 1958. (*Sentinel.*)

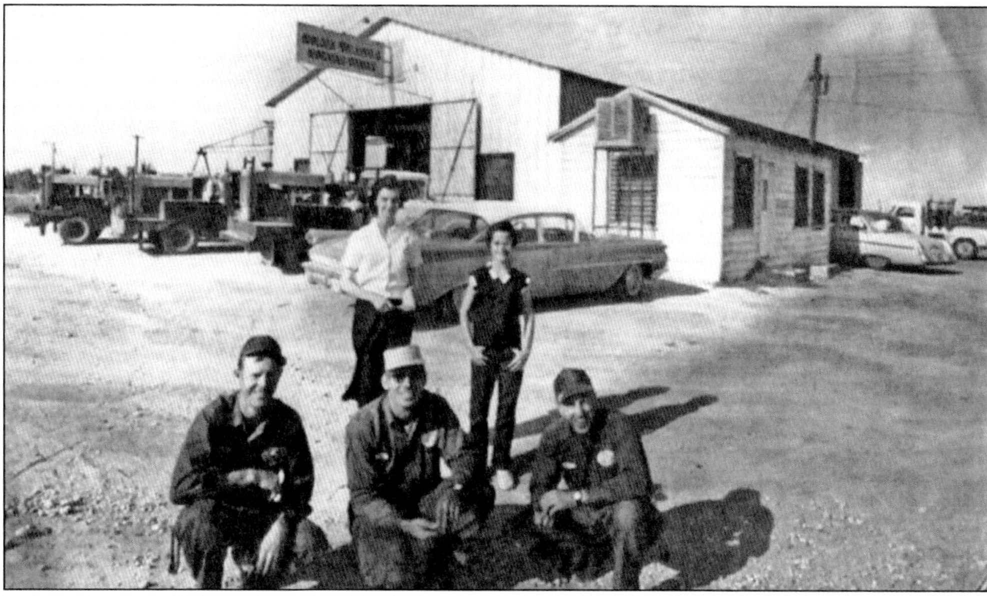

Pictured here is Walden Welding Works at 911 South Main Street, a busy place during the 1950s, especially with all the oilfield activity. In front of the business are, from left to right, (first row) Sonny Cox, O.B. Nelms, and Desmond L. Bruner; (second row) Margaret Walden and her sister Judy (Walden) Henry. (Walden family.)

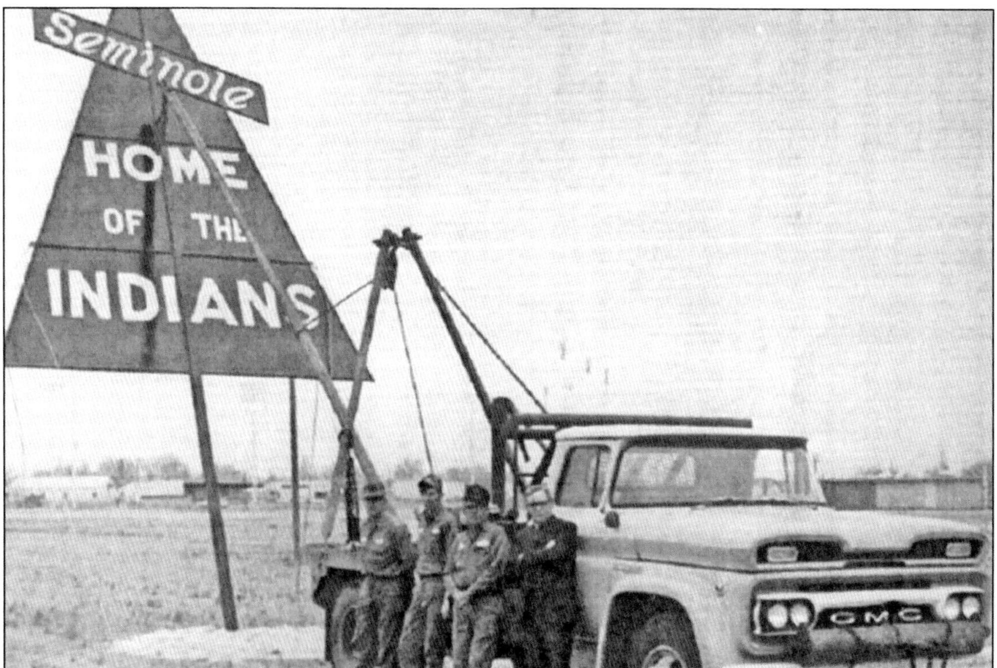

Walden Welding Works erected this Seminole Indian sign south of Wigwam Field along the Denver City Highway in 1970. In the photograph are, from left to right, O.B. Nelms, Deral Henderson, and business owner Bart Walden. The man on the right is believed to be Frank Nix, who was an English and drama teacher at the junior high and later principal at F.J. Young Elementary. (Walden family.)

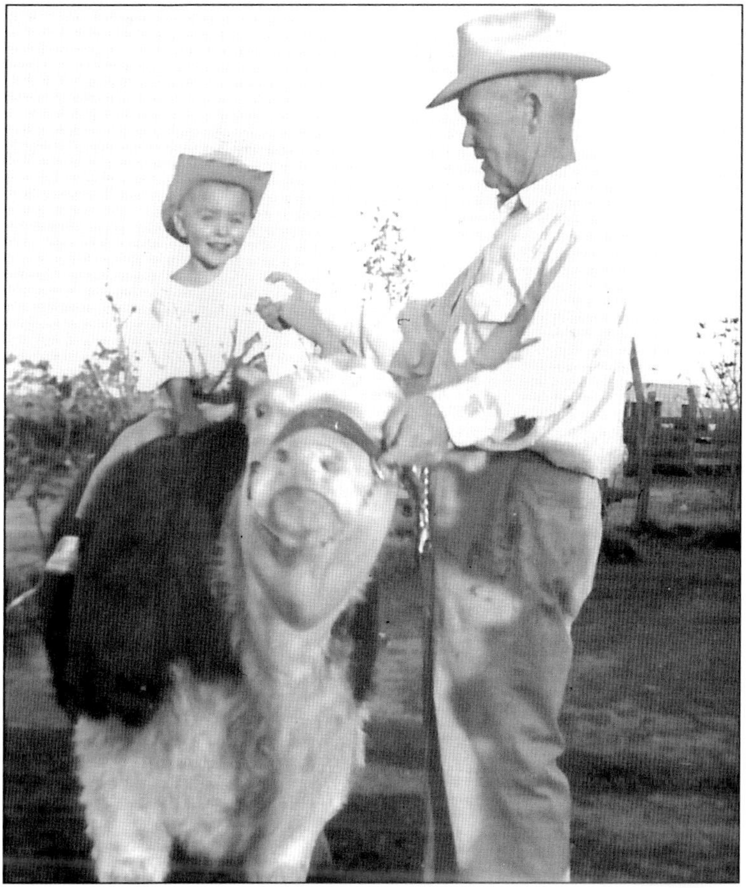

Pictured in about 1955 are R.H. "Rich" McCrummen (1889–1960) and one of his grandsons, Charles. Rich and Maude McCrummen lived just east of Seminole on a small farm, and he instilled in his children and grandchildren a love of livestock. Just a few years after this photograph, in 1959, Charles (the coauthor) won Grand Champion with a Hereford steer at Seminole's first stock show. (George family.)

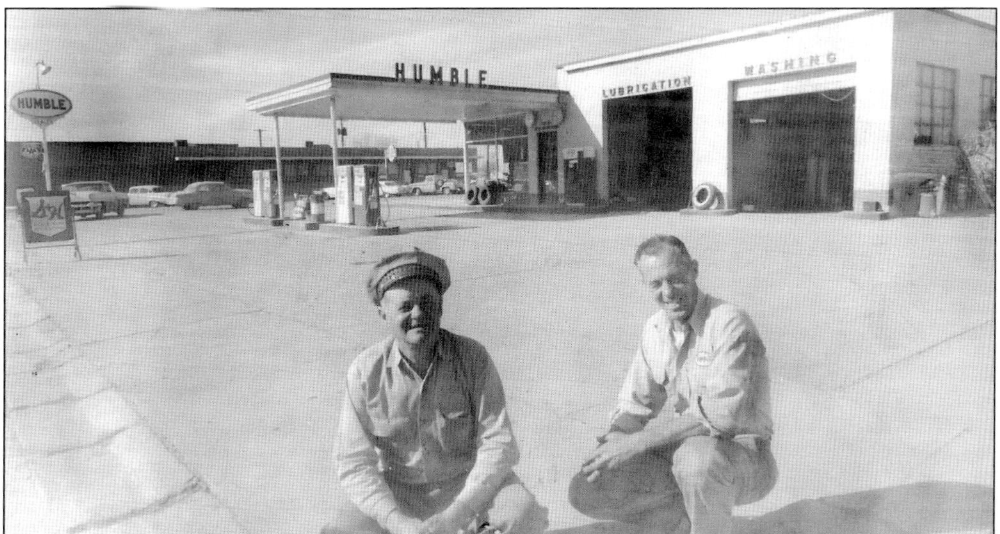

This photograph shows the Humble (later Exxon) service station that stood at the intersection of Northeast Second Street and Avenue A in the mid-1950s. The men kneeling in front are Cecil Warren Holbrooks (left) and Ulan Holbrooks. (Holbrooks family.)

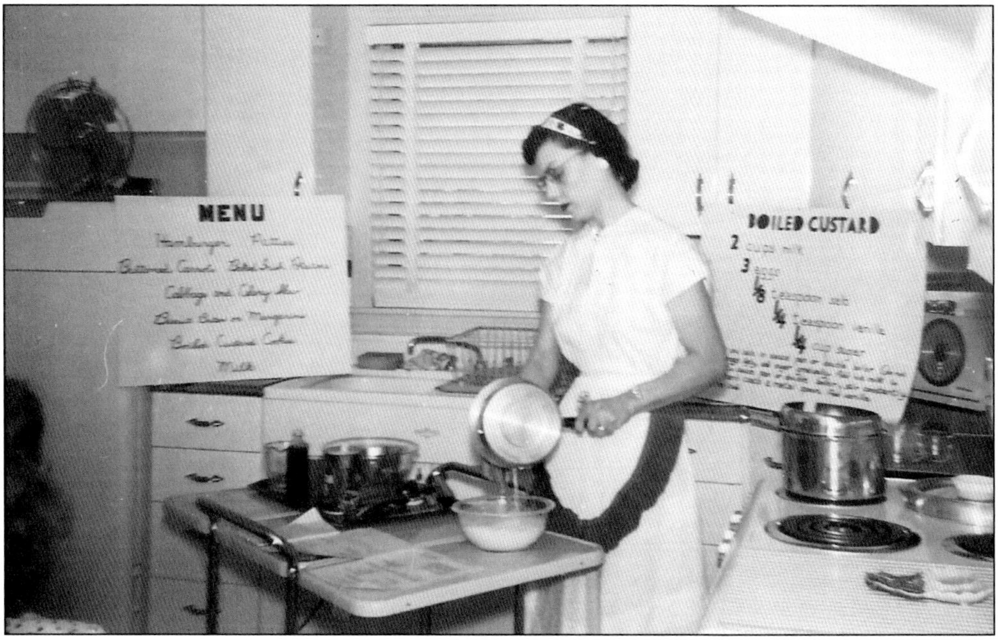

Pictured in May 1955, this home demonstration agent shows a group of homemakers how to make boiled custard. Anyone who has ever had homemade banana pudding made this way will remember just what a treat it was! (*Sentinel.*)

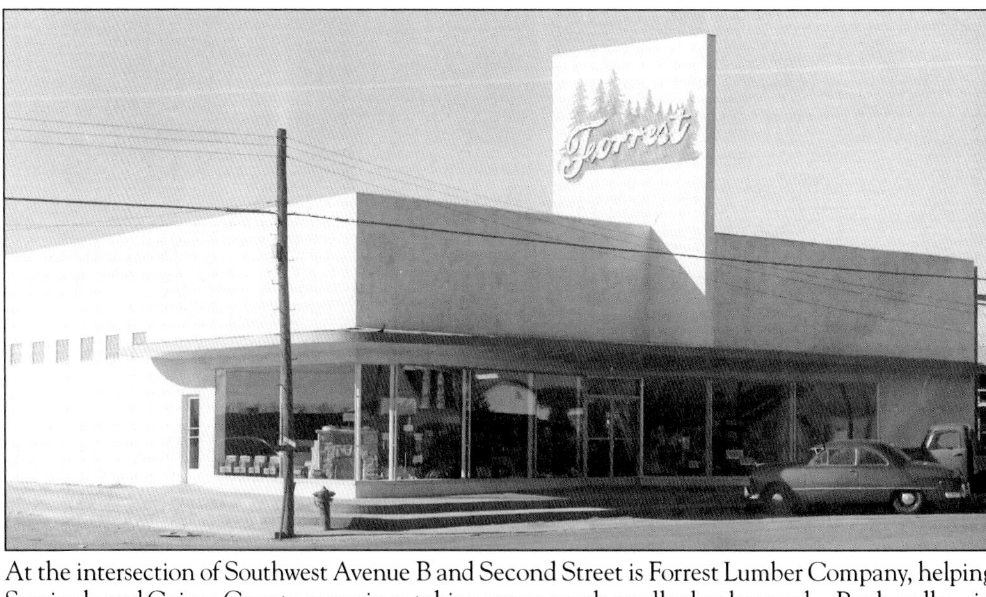

At the intersection of Southwest Avenue B and Second Street is Forrest Lumber Company, helping Seminole and Gaines County grow since taking over a much smaller lumber yard—Panhandle—in 1935. Forrest more than doubled its storage and display area by 1940, and by 1955, when this photograph was taken, it occupied almost half the block—nearly 35,000 square feet. (*Sentinel.*)

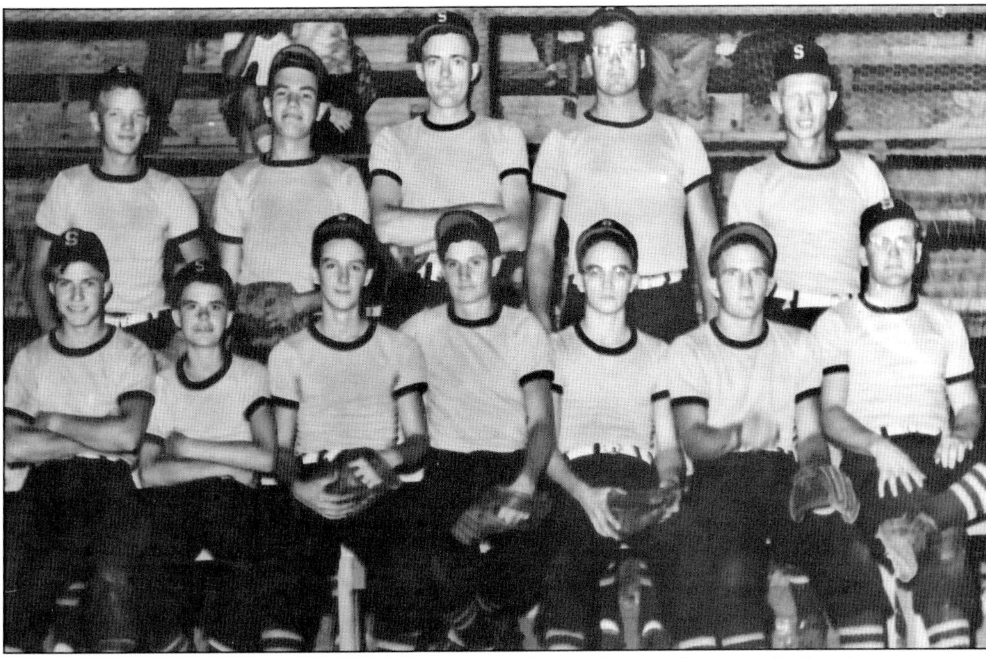

In the early 1950s, companies and organizations formed baseball teams for local competition. Seen here, one such team included the following players and coaches, from left to right: (first row) Harold Karr, Leland Caffey, unidentified, Karl Don Hughes, James Daugherty, James Jackson, and Howard Hassell; (second row) Marcus Crow, Crandall Young, Tommie Roberts, Metz Lafollette, and Jake Harrell. (*Sentinel.*)

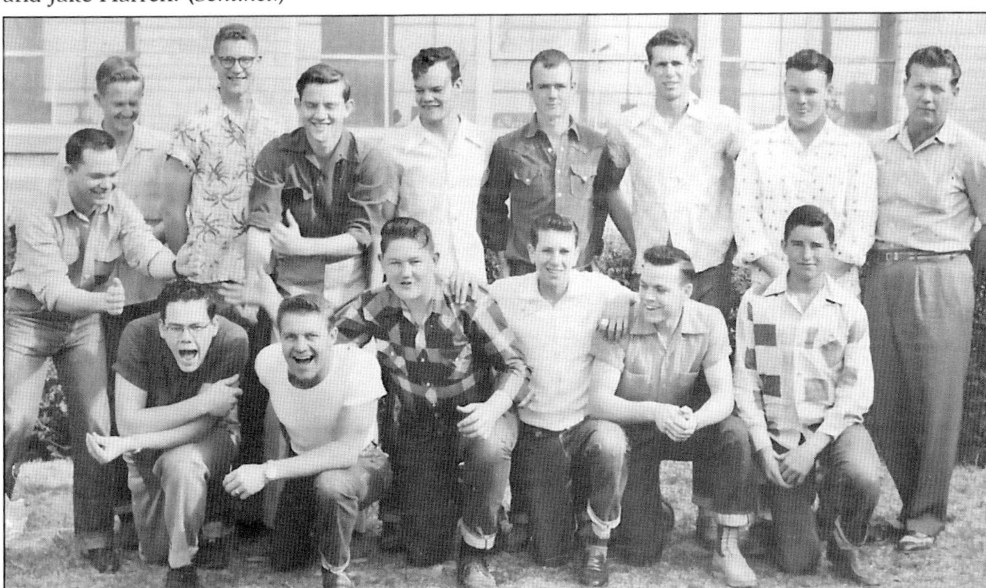

Mugging for the camera in 1954, this group of Seminole High School industrial arts students includes, from left to right, (first row) Bill Box, Ronnie Phillips, Winfred Baggett, John Dozier, Carol Cox, and Donald Scantling; (second row) Sisco Ruth, Gene Parrish, Tommy Oliver, Bill Lindley, Lynn McCrummen, Martin Dulin, Jackie Gothard, Bill Trammell, and shop teacher Woodrow Bowman. (*Sentinel.*)

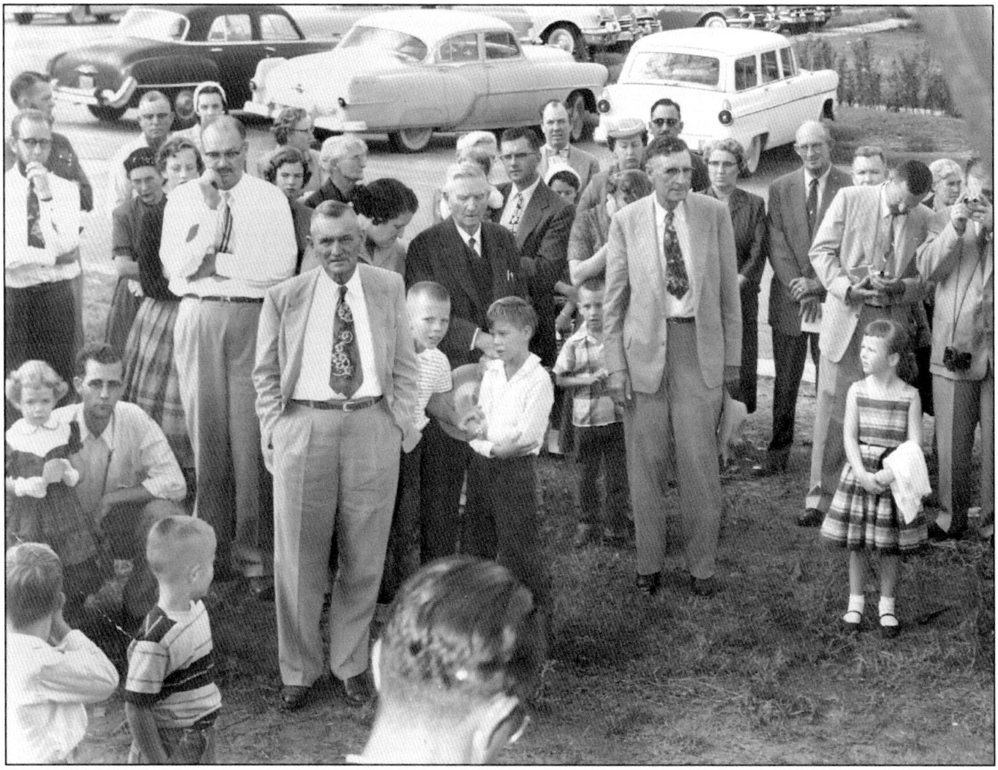

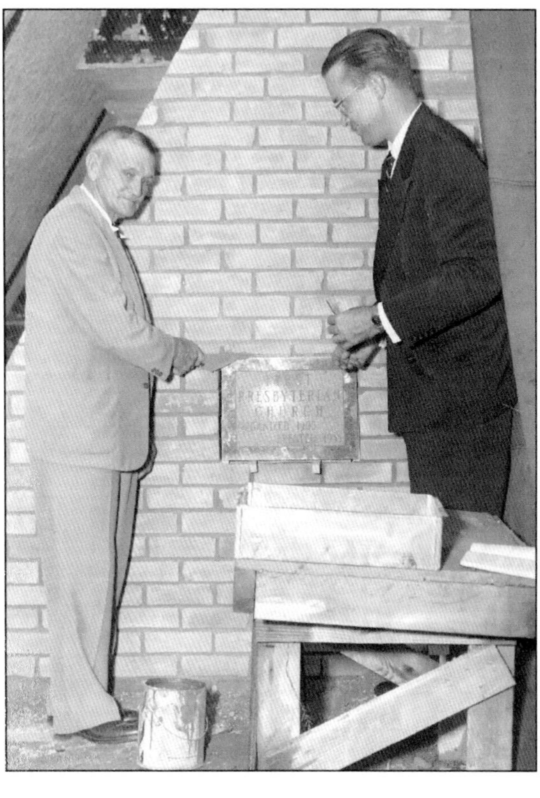

This photograph shows the 1955 dedication ceremony of the new A-frame First Presbyterian Church at Southwest Third Street and Avenue C. Those in attendance at the ceremony included, in no particular order, Dewey Chestnut, Con Hood, Bart Walden, Mary Walden, Margaret Walden, Jim Vining, Scott Doss, Louise McCombs, Pat Reagan, Edith Vining, Roe Doss, Hyle Doss, Chester Robertson, Pauline Ogg, Roy Sherman, Ruby and Joe Britton, Carlos Alexander, and Jim Graves, among others. (First Presbyterian Church.)

Scott C. Doss (left) helps Rev. Burke Kerr install the cornerstone on the front of the new First Presbyterian Church in 1955. It was largely the drive and enthusiasm of Reverend Kerr and his family that helped make this sanctuary a reality; it replaced the stucco structure across the street. (First Presbyterian Church.)

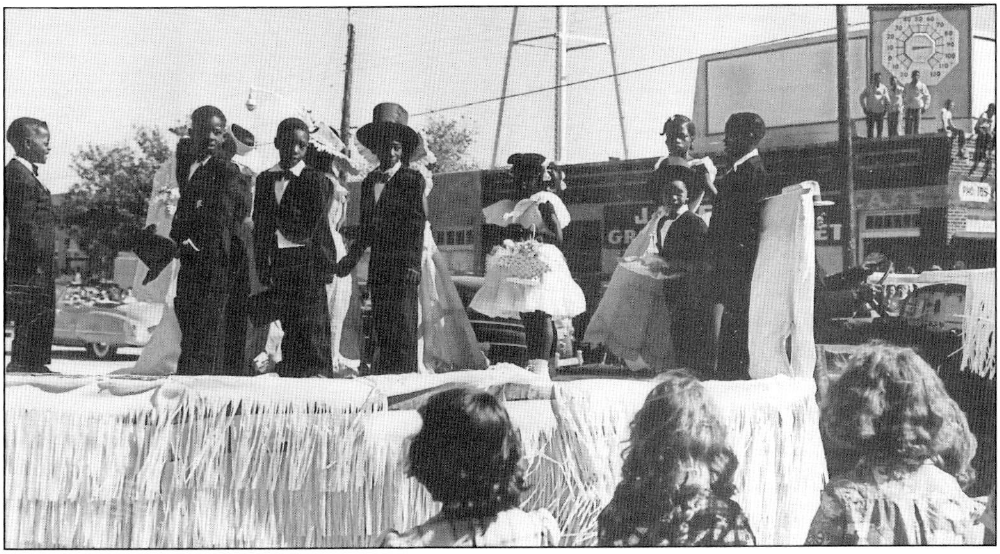

At Gaines County's 50th birthday celebration in 1955—its sesquicentennial, or Golden Jubilee—the city held a grand parade. This entrant was called "Tom Thumb Wedding." In the background across from the southeast corner of the square is one of Seminole's water towers, which was later removed. The roof of Jameson's Grocery can be seen on the right with its large thermometer and several spectators. (*Sentinel.*)

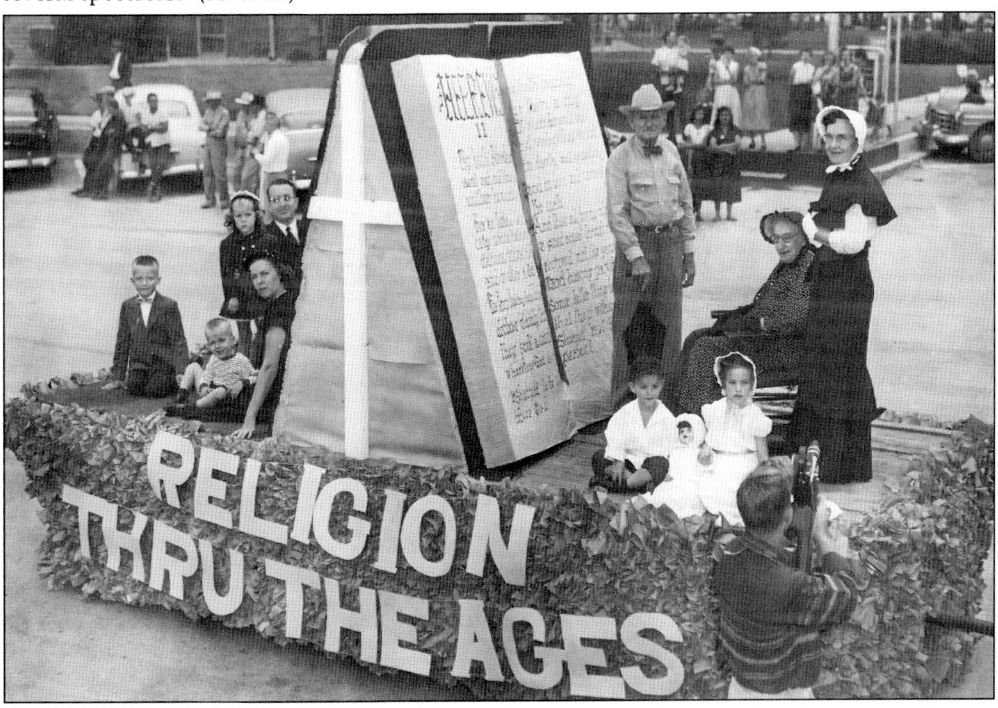

This float in Seminole's sesquicentennial parade displays the historic church on one side with Scott Doss standing and Emma Austin seated at right. Behind Austin is Alene McCrummen George, and sitting in the foreground are her children Charles and Charlotte George. On the left end of the float, representing the modern church, are First Presbyterian's Rev. Burke Kerr and his family. (George family.)

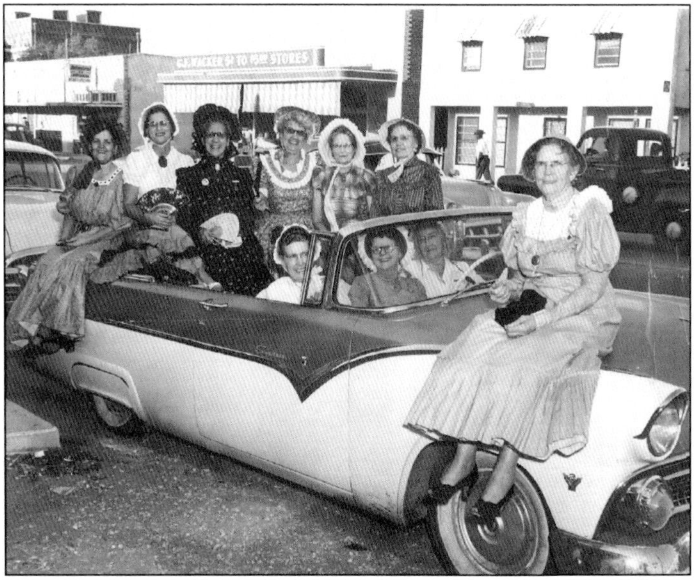

Another entrant in the parade is this carload of ladies in turn-of-the-century clothing. From left to right are (seated in car) Mabel Curry, Julia Duff, and Bess Maloney; (seated along the back) Mrs. T.F. Lindley (Alice), Dinah Munnerlyn, Meek Lane Doss, Eunice Stark, Mattie Stone, and Ruby Smallin. On the hood of this 1955 Ford Fairlane Sunliner convertible coupe is Janie McAlpin. (Mary Maloney Hughes.)

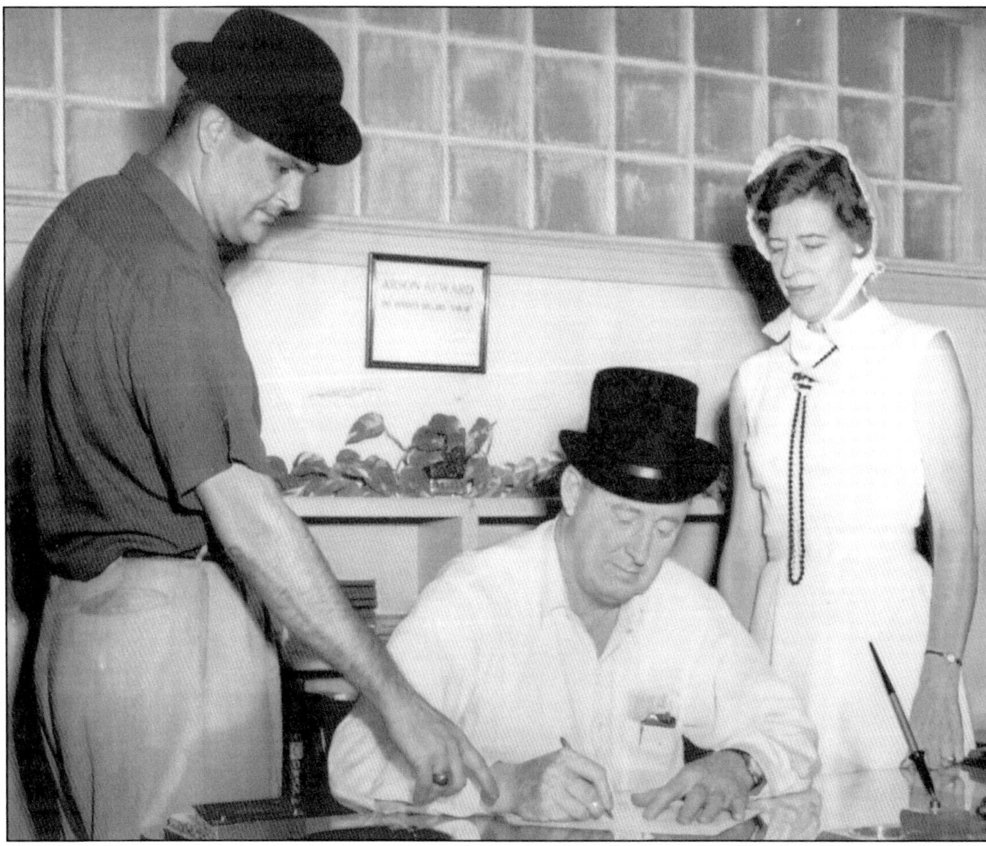

During the Golden Jubilee, men grew beards or paid fines. Women wore period costumes, and many men wore these black hats. In this photograph, taken in 1955, Judge Charlie Lawrence and Ruby Frost watch as Seminole mayor Earl Denton signs the proclamation honoring the 50th anniversary of the organization of the county. (Museum.)

In this sesquicentennial photograph, these men had somehow violated one of the "laws" of the Golden Jubilee festivities and were locked in this cage on the square (all in good fun, of course). Judge Lawrence stands smiling in the back center, behind a man thought to be Dr. Harold "Rowdy" Dow (with a pipe in his mouth). At the right of the cage is Tommie Roberts, holding onto the top of the cage. The other "criminals" have not been identified. (Tommie Roberts.)

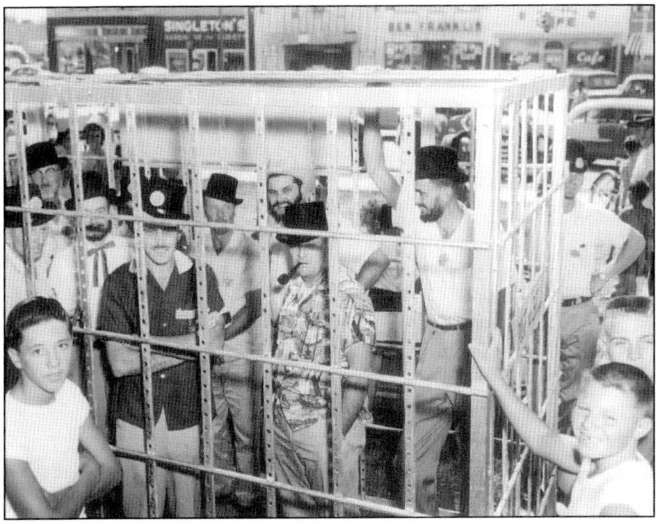

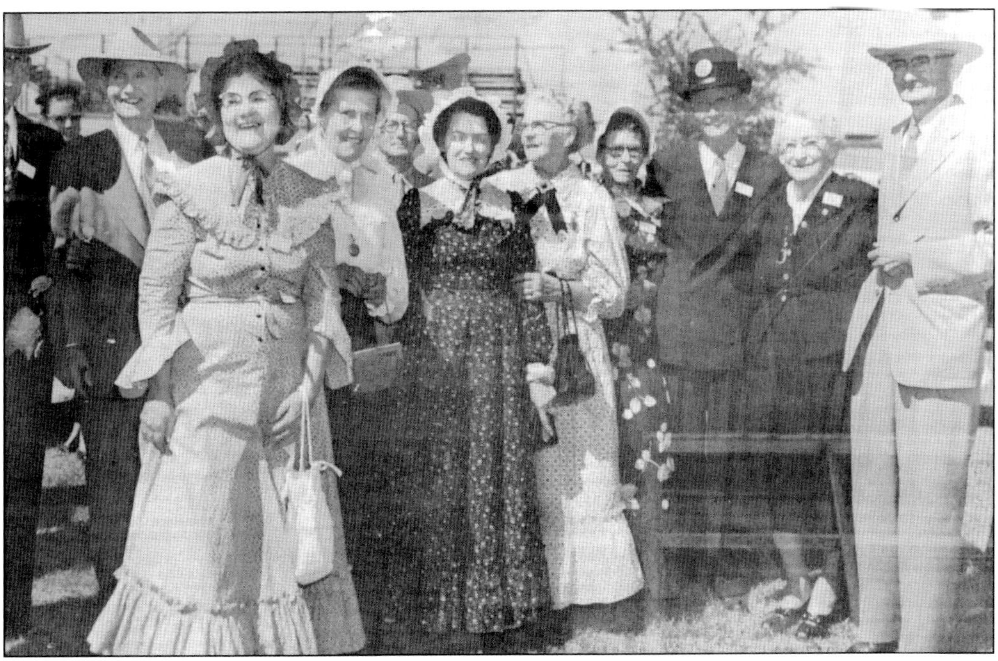

This picture taken in 1955 and later featured in the *Seminole Sentinel* shows a group of Gaines County pioneers. From left to right are Milliard Eidson, M.S. Doss, Pauline Rollins, Mabel Curry, R.W. Pittman, Jewel Cobb, Kate Elam, Georgia Malone, Sam Malone, Emma Austin, and John Elam. (First Presbyterian Church.)

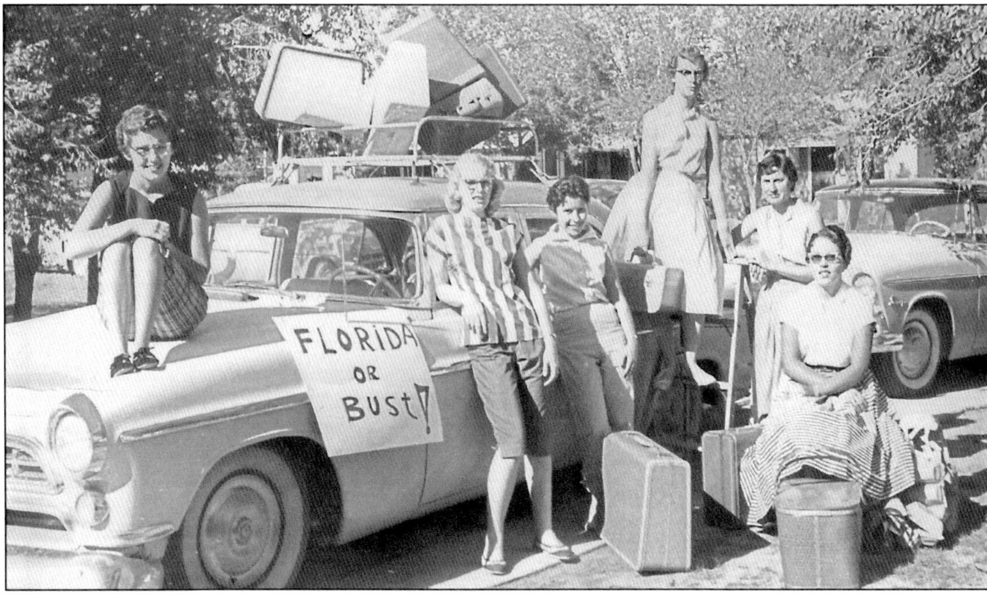

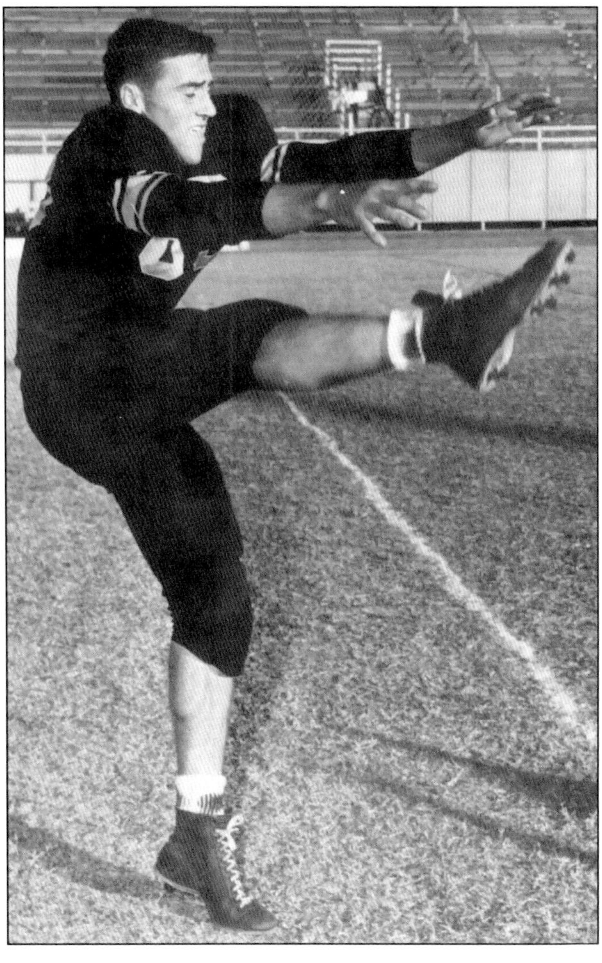

Here is a group of Seminole beauties packed and loaded for a trip to Florida. The occasion is not known, but the photograph was taken some time in the mid- to late 1950s, and the girls include, from left to right, Betty Oswalt, Barbara Green, Mickey Story, Sherry Carson, coach Floyce Vermillion, and Melba Smith. (*Sentinel.*)

This photograph appeared in the 1955 Seminole High School annual. The subject, obviously a gifted athlete, served as kicker for the Indians football team. He fell in love in Seminole, married his high school sweetheart—Barbara Britton—but then left town to pursue a career in education before returning home. For those who have not figured it out yet, this is Jim Culver. (Tommie Roberts.)

These three smiling individuals are in Aryain's Dry Goods on South Main Street. The date is probably the late 1950s or early 1960s, and Jameil "Dink" Aryain, the store's owner, is in the center helping Charlie Lawrence try on a new straw hat. Watching is Flo Satterwhite, another customer of Aryain's. (Lawrence family.)

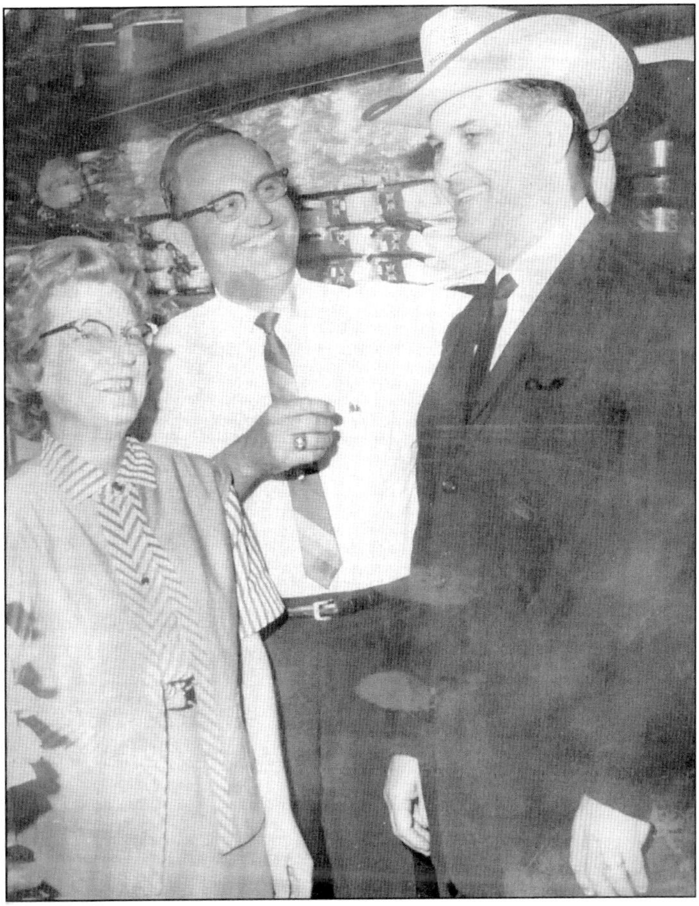

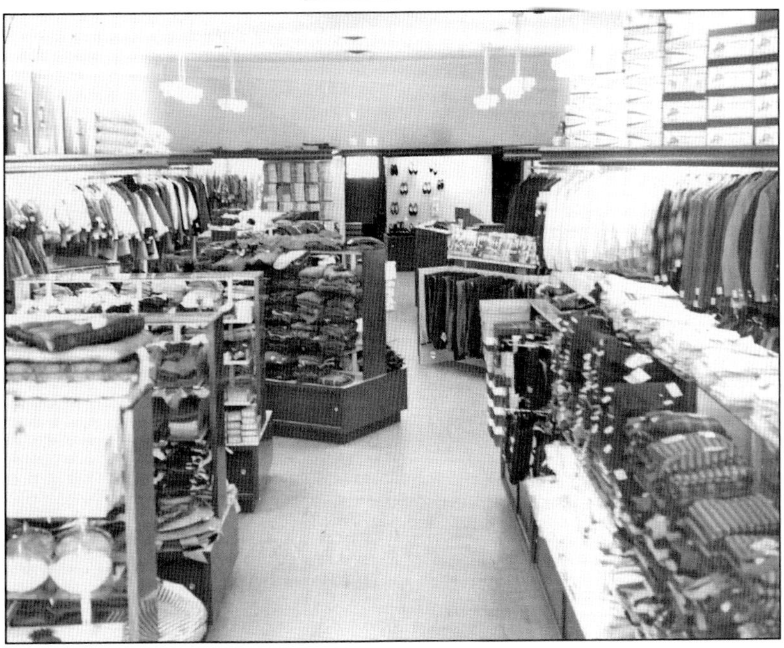

This is the interior of Aryain's Dry Goods after one of its many remodelings. Just like his father before him, Dink made sure that his store was up-to-date and that he had whatever clothing his customers were looking for. (Aryain family.)

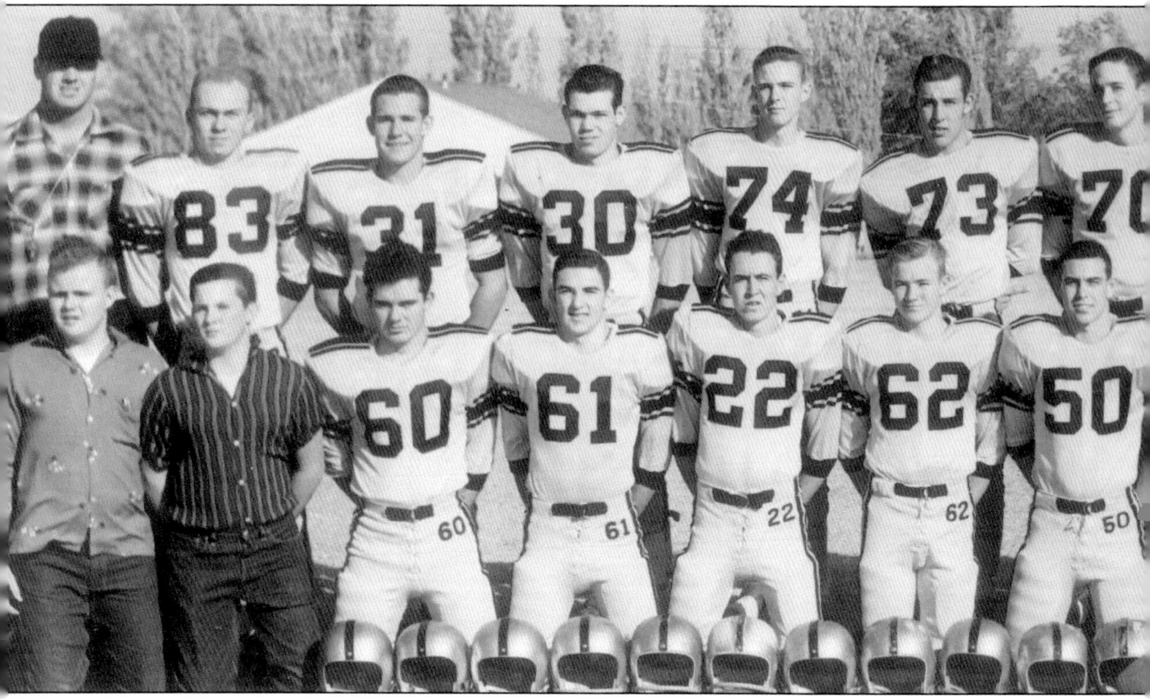

This two-page spread shows the members of the 1957 Seminole Indian football team. Shown from left to right are (first row) managers Jerry Sullivan and Donald Teston, James Lutrell, Charles Tomlinson, Addrin Gene Jones, Larry Williams, Mickey Warlick, Kenneth Saylor, Dennis Richardson, Jerald Steward, Bill Wallace, Don Sanders, and Leland Caffey; (second row) coach

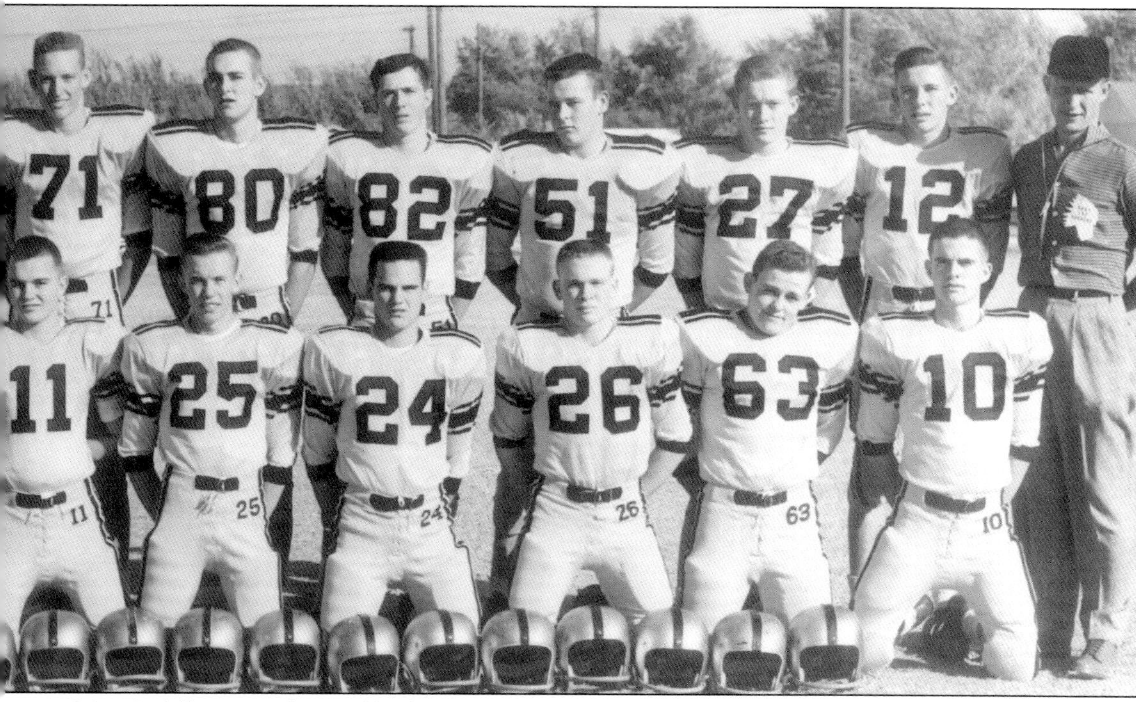

Metz Lafollette, Neely Woolfarth, Carol Norton, Donald Hort, Lawrence Kirk, Tommy Moore, Joey Hughes, David Anderson, Archie English, Billy Bob McLaughlin, Jerry Patton, Kenneth Cook, Wayne Anderson, and coach Jake Harrell. (Tommie Roberts.)

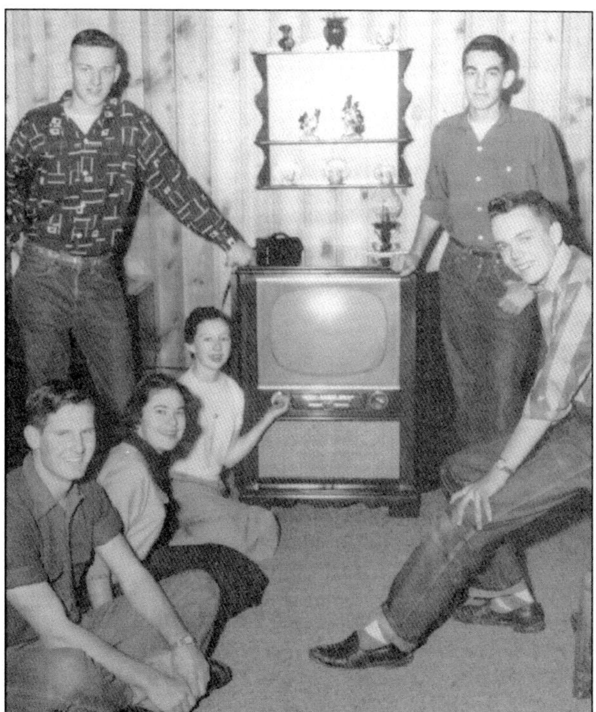

In this typical 1956 American living room, the senior class officers of Seminole High School are sitting around a television. They are, from left to right, Bill Burnett, Harry Walker, Albernita Braden, Jeannie McMurry, Ross Johnson, and Lewis Redell. Television sets were not common in the mid-1950s. Not everyone had one, they were black and white, and those who were lucky might have been able to pick up three channels. (Museum.)

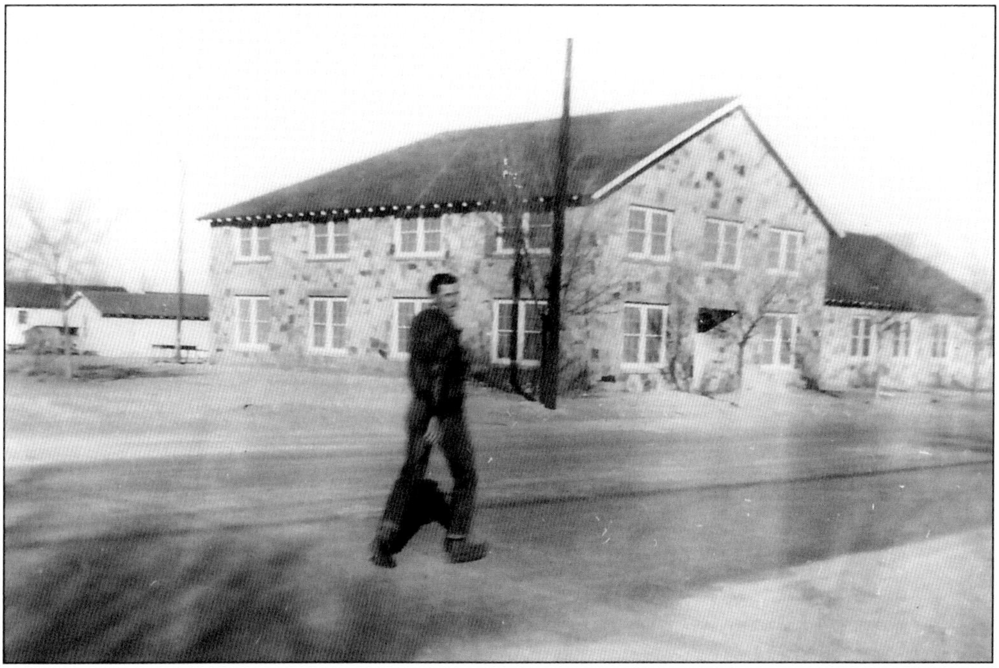

Pictured here is the First Methodist Church as it appeared between 1938 and the late 1950s. The original wooden church building, constructed in 1908, was replaced with this rock structure in 1938. As it was built during the Great Depression, funds for the church were scarce, but as was written in the church's records, the congregation "had little to give, but gave gladly what they had." The man in the foreground has not been identified. (Jameson family.)

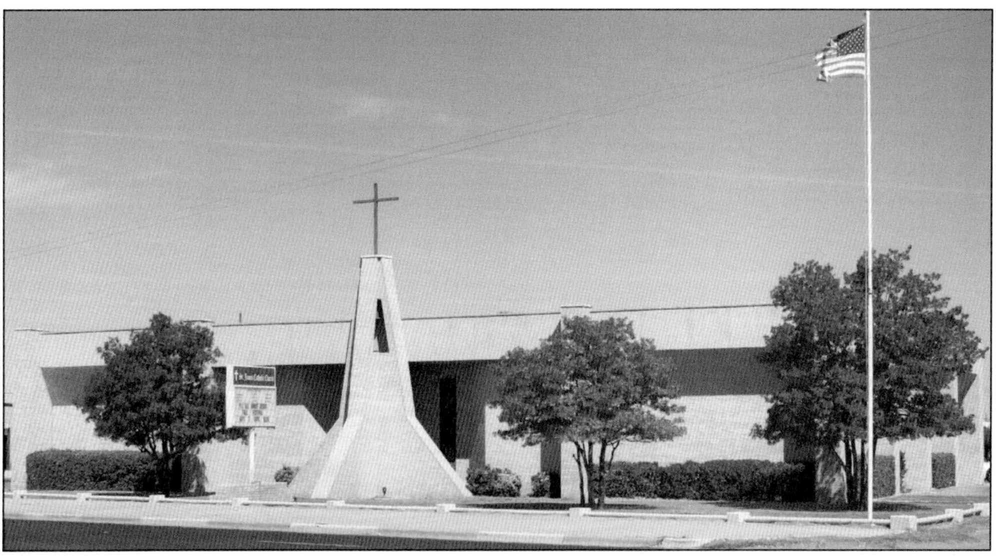

During the first 50 years of Seminole's existence, only a handful of Catholics lived here, and they had to drive 30 miles to Hobbs, New Mexico, to go to mass. Beginning in the 1940s, Catholics began meeting for mass in Seminole once a month—at the Tower Theater, the old Palace Theater, Aguilar's Boot Shop, the courthouse, and other locations. In 1966, St. James was formally made a parish. The building seen here was constructed in 1982. (George family.)

Nuel Mitchell, pictured here, was five years old when her parents moved to Seminole. She attended school in the building on page 20, graduating in 1928. After college, she returned and began a decades-long career at the courthouse. By the time she retired, she had been secretary to six county judges. Someone once asked how long she had been working there. A coworker joked, "They found her sitting at a desk and built the courthouse around her!" (Lawrence family.)

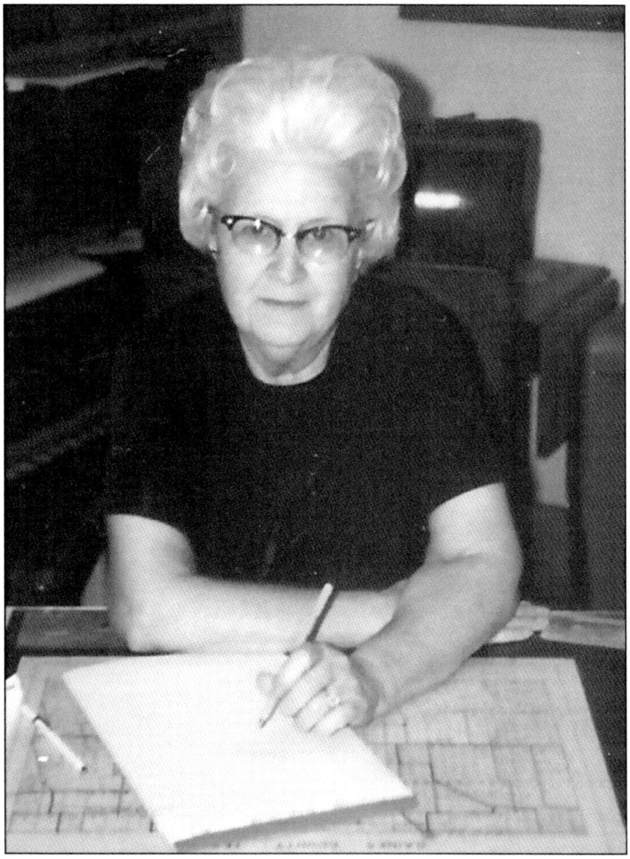

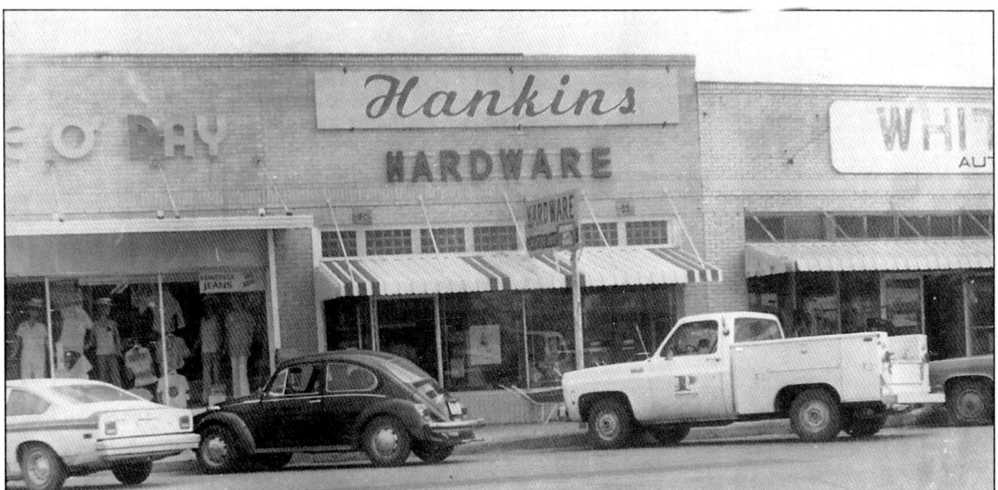

In the mid-1960s, one of the best places to go in Seminole for hardware was Hankins Hardware on the north side of the courthouse square. On either side can be seen Mode-O-Day (a dress shop) and White's Auto. (*Sentinel.*)

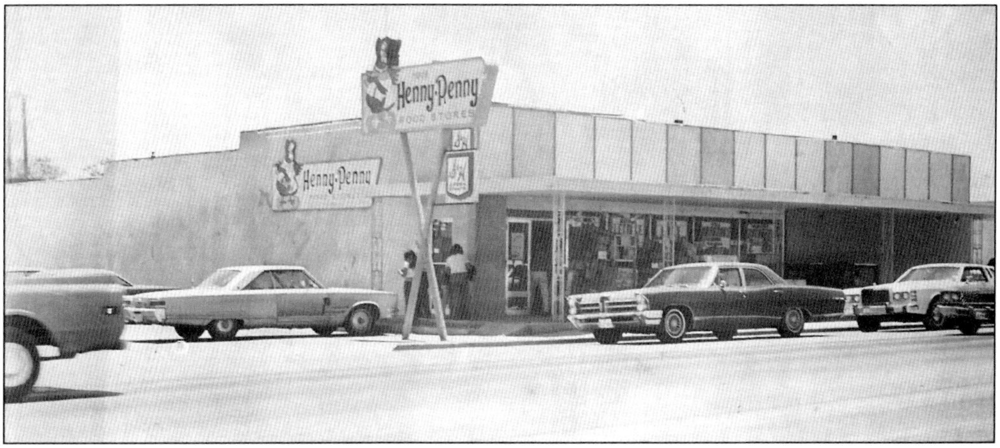

Another store where shoppers could find pretty much anything they needed in the mid-1960s was the Henny Penny Food Store on South Main Street. And they gave out S&H Green Stamps. Remember those? Shoppers collected them each time they shopped, and once they had glued them all into booklets, they could trade them in for cookware, serving dishes, sporting goods, and all sorts of things. (*Sentinel.*)

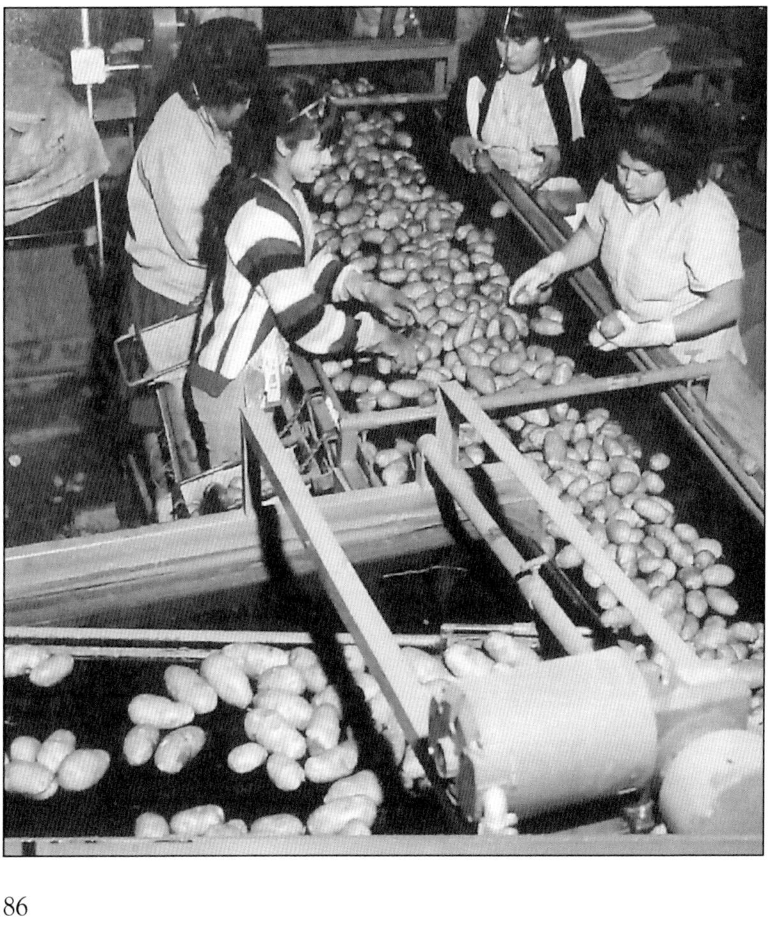

This photograph, taken in the 1960s or early 1970s, shows employees of the Howard Gault Potato Company sorting potatoes, preparing them for sale. At that time, hundreds of acres of Gaines County were planted in potatoes, and Gault ran a large processing plant on the Hobbs Highway. Potatoes are still grown in the Seminole area, but not on as large a scale. (Museum.)

In 1967, this young Seminole beauty—Katy Lafollette (now Katy Scroggins)—was elected Peach Queen for Gaines County and the very first Texas Peach Queen. In the 1960s, hundreds of acres of peach trees had been planted in the Seminole area. Katy, daughter of longtime resident, teacher, coach, and administrator Metz Lafollette, later taught physical education and coached volleyball. (Katy Scroggins.)

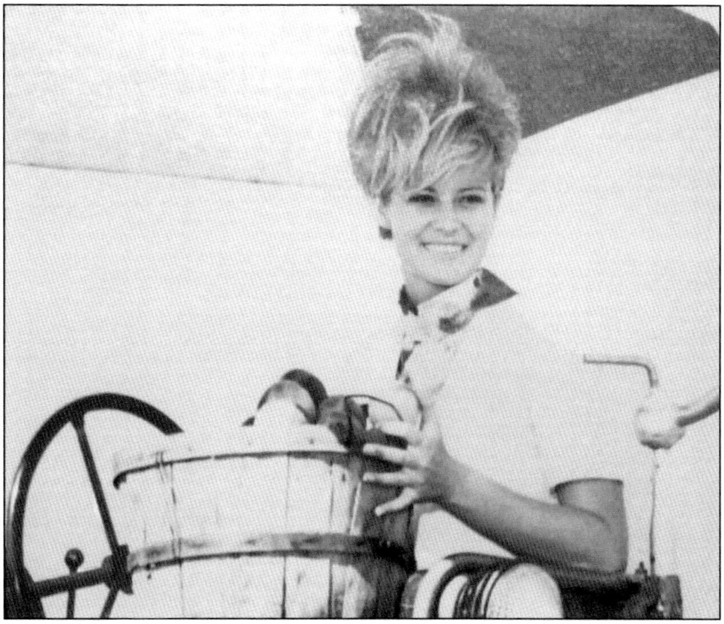

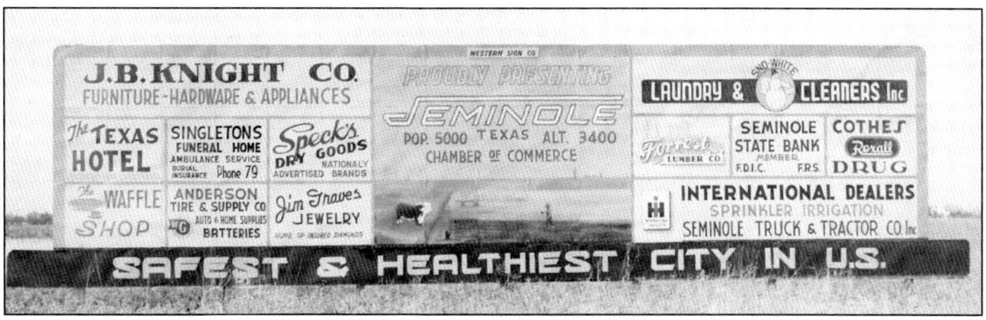

This billboard, erected a few years after the one on page 71, also featured local businesses. Many of the businesses advertised on that first sign were still in existence when this second billboard was erected. (*Sentinel*.)

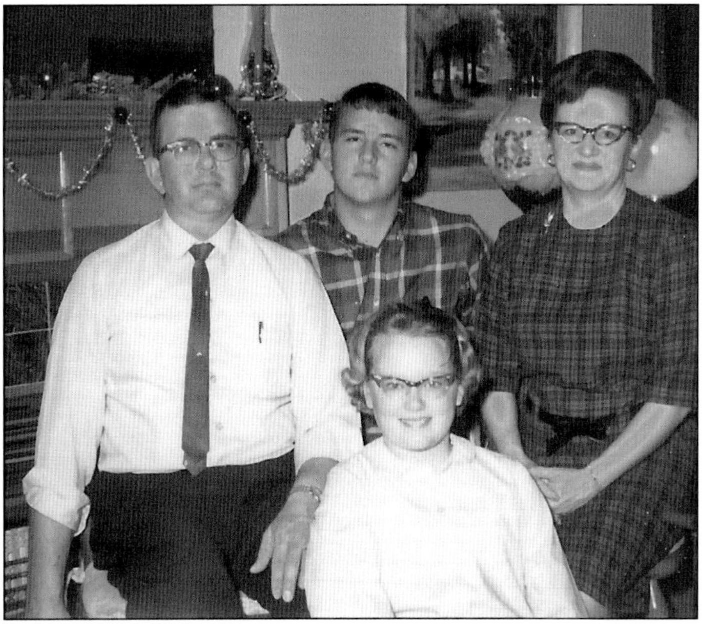

It is Christmastime around 1965 at the home of Hyle and Florence Doss on Southwest Second Street and Avenue F. Also seen here are their children: Skeet in the back and Polli in the front. Hyle, now of Midland, is the son of the late S.C. and Maggie Doss and, like his parents, was a loyal and active member of First Presbyterian Church while a Seminole resident. (Doss family.)

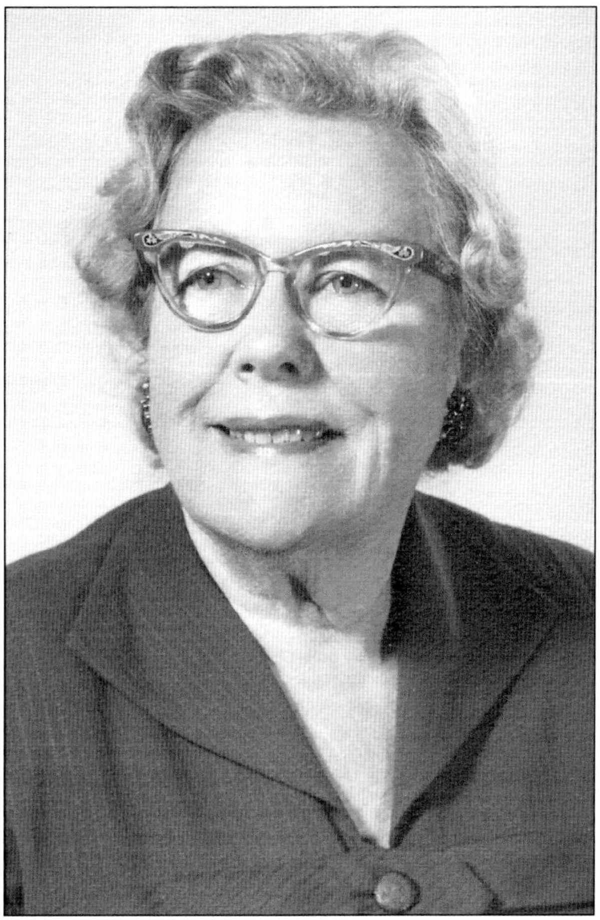

Seen in a photograph from the 1950s, this sweet lady is Emma Maude Burns McCrummen, wife of R.H. McCrummen (and the coauthor's grandmother). She was born in 1891, daughter of Rollie Burns, one of Lubbock's pioneers, but lived the last decades of her life in Seminole. She also was the first resident at Seminole's first nursing home, located just east of the Seminole City Park. (George family.)

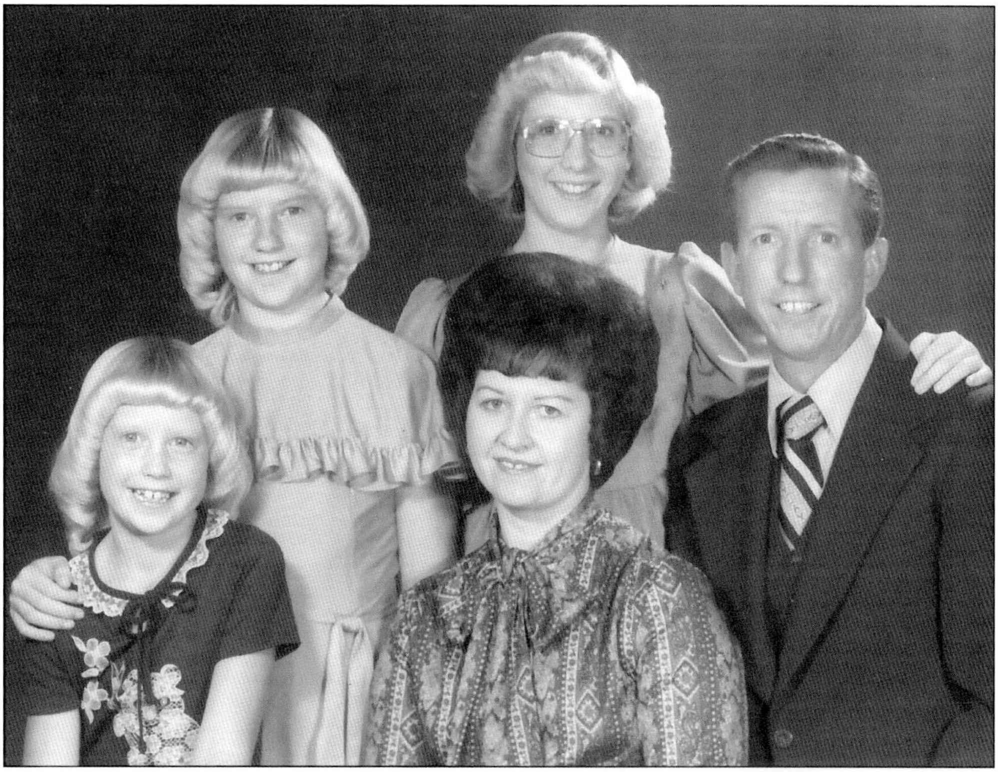

Pictured in the 1970s are Leo and June Copeland with their daughters (from left to right) Rhonda, Pam, and Denise. The family moved to Seminole in 1975 after living many years in Arizona. Leo drove a Seminole school bus for 20 years, preached at Seventh Street Church of Christ for 27 years, and served as associate pastor at Westside for 4 more years before retiring from the ministry. Leo has been writing for the *Seminole Sentinel* since 2007, interviewing families and getting acquainted with Seminole residents. (Copeland family.)

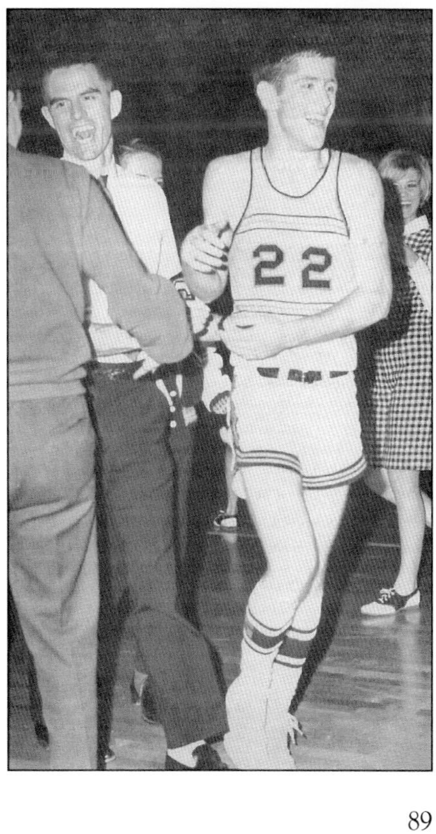

We won! In this photograph from 1966–1967, an unidentified spectator congratulates an ecstatic coach Leland Caffey with equally happy basketball player Darrell Price and smiling cheerleader Katy Lafollette in the background. Perhaps the Indians had just won another district or regional title. During that time, Seminole High School had something of a streak in basketball championships. (*Sentinel*.)

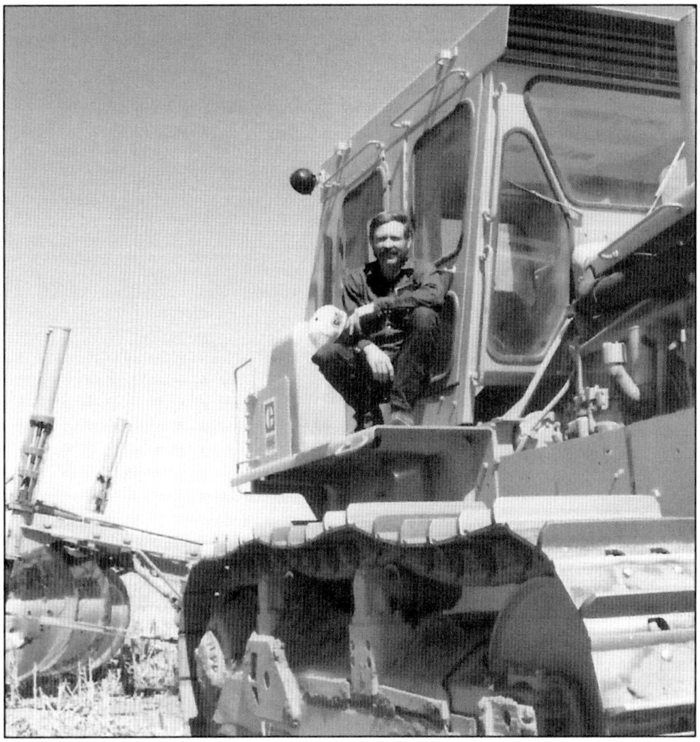

An agricultural practice that has made cotton and peanut farming successful has been "deep-breaking"—using a large disc plow to cut through the topsoil and to blend it with the clay beneath to prevent loss of soil during windstorms. This requires a powerful tractor, as seen in this 1976 shot of farmer Lynn Whitaker on his rig. (Whitaker family.)

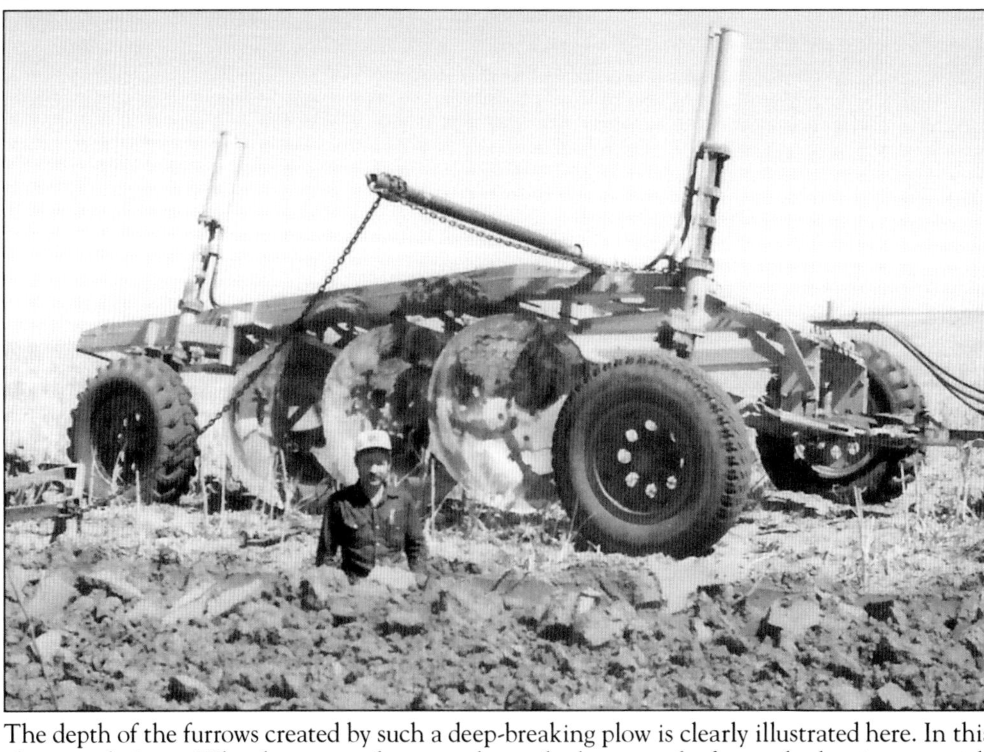

The depth of the furrows created by such a deep-breaking plow is clearly illustrated here. In this photograph, Lynn Whitaker is standing upright in the bottom of a furrow he has just cut with the 50-inch disc plow behind him. (Whitaker family.)

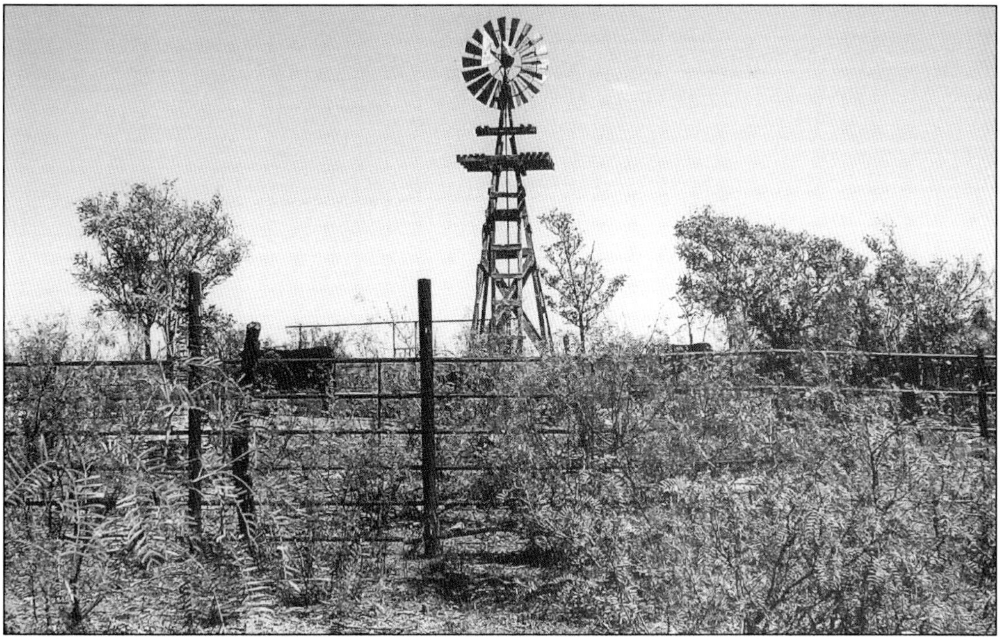

Today, the windmill and a cattle pen are all that remain of the original J.B. Thompson residence on the ranch southeast of Seminole along Farm to Market Road (FM) 1429 near the Fairview community. (There is more about the Thompsons and the historic significance of their ranch in the next chapter.) (Museum.)

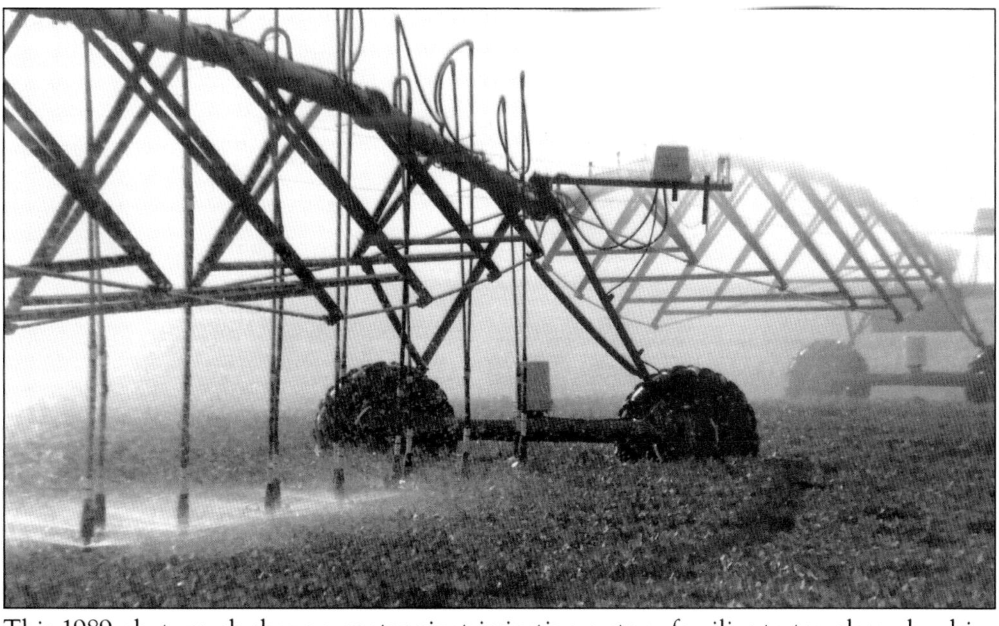

This 1989 photograph shows a center-pivot irrigation system, familiar to travelers who drive across (or fly over) Gaines County these days. These circular farms have not always been the norm, though. In the 1960s, Jack Setser (father of coauthor Linda Setser George) worked for Ross Irrigation, whose office was located on the western edge of Seminole. Jack sold the first center-pivot irrigation system in Gaines County. (*Sentinel.*)

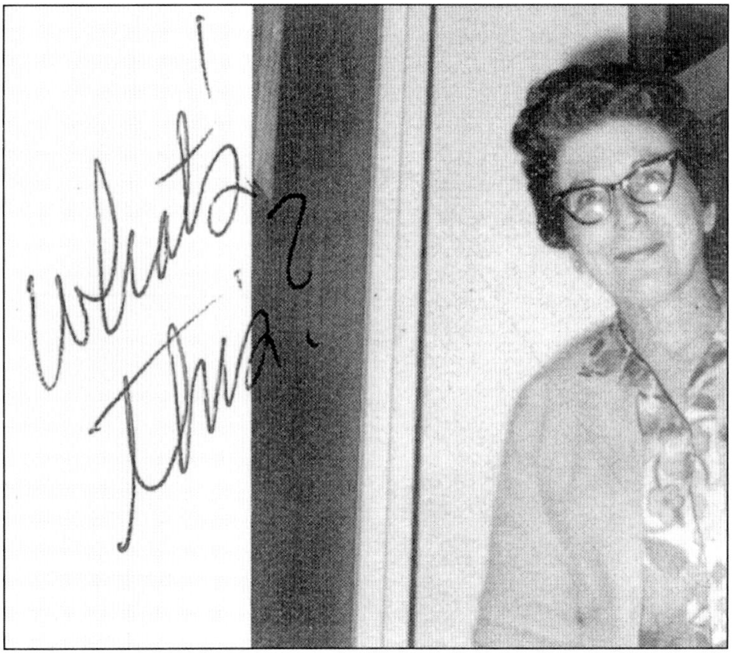

This is one of the most beloved teachers who ever graced the halls of Seminole High School—Dora Price—peeking around the corner in a candid photograph taken from the 1967 *Tepee*. Her handwritten comment—"What's this?"—was typical of her quirky sense of humor. Mrs. Price recently passed away, and she will be sorely missed by all who knew and loved her. (George family.)

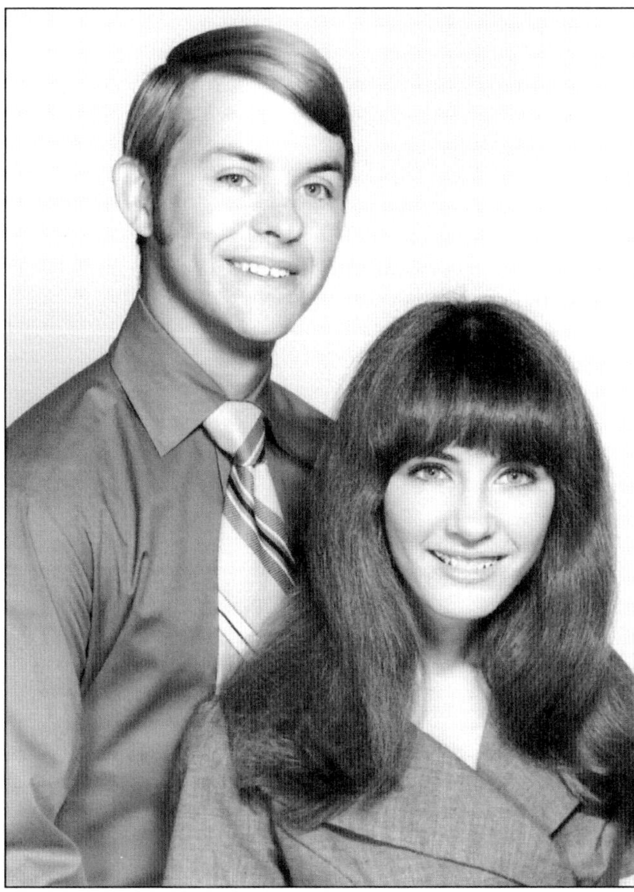

What's this, indeed! This photograph of the authors, Charles and Linda George, was taken in 1971, the year they were married—when they were both young and skinny! Now, more than 40 years, two children, one grandchild, and 70-plus books later, they may not be young, and they may not be skinny (Linda says, "Speak for yourself!"), but they are still going strong! (George family.)

Four

1975–2011

Then and Now

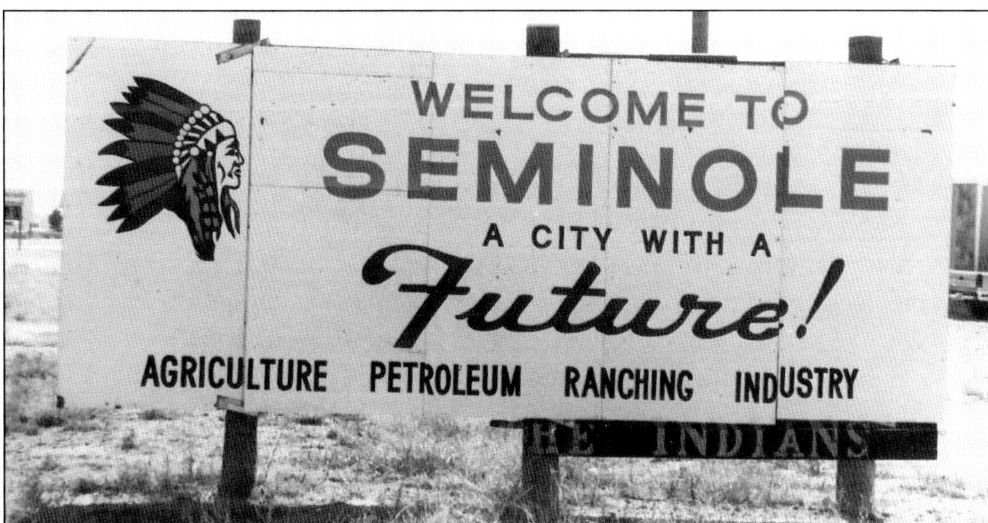

In 1990, visitors to Seminole were greeted by one of these signs at each entrance to town. The optimism reflected in this chamber of commerce creation has always been a feature of Seminole and probably always will be. (*Sentinel*.)

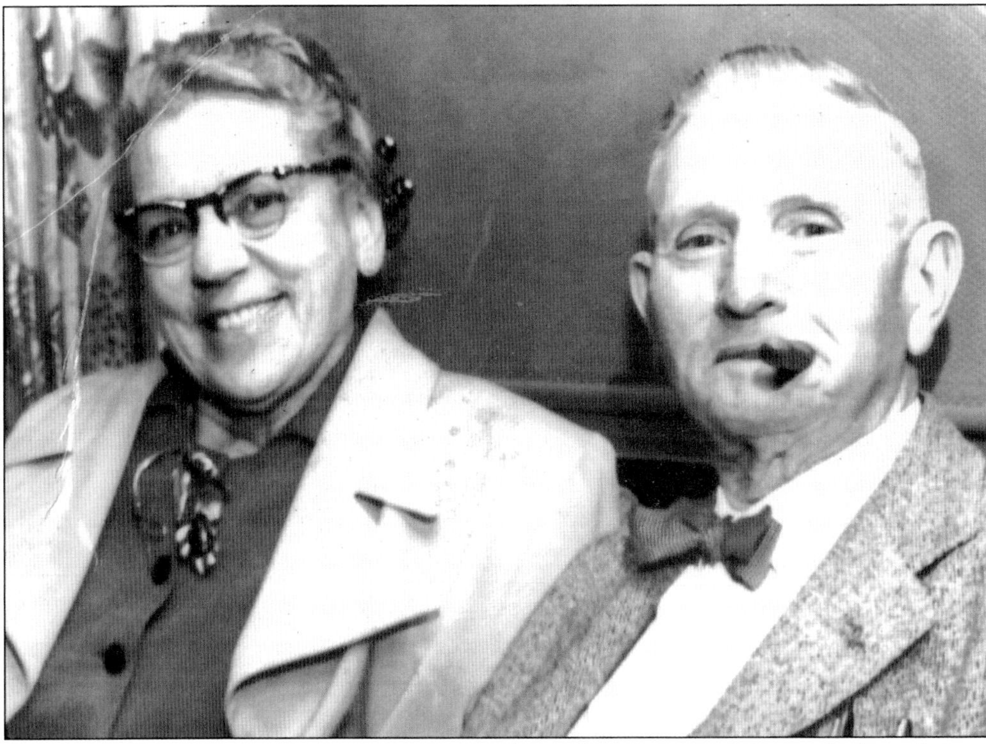

Perhaps no Gaines County pioneers' names are better known around Seminole than those of these two individuals—Meek Lane and M.S. Doss. Through diligence and hard work, they made a success of their ranch and helped other residents along the way establish Gaines County and Seminole, its county seat. Cattle ranching and later the discovery of oil on their land gave them the means to help even more. (Museum.)

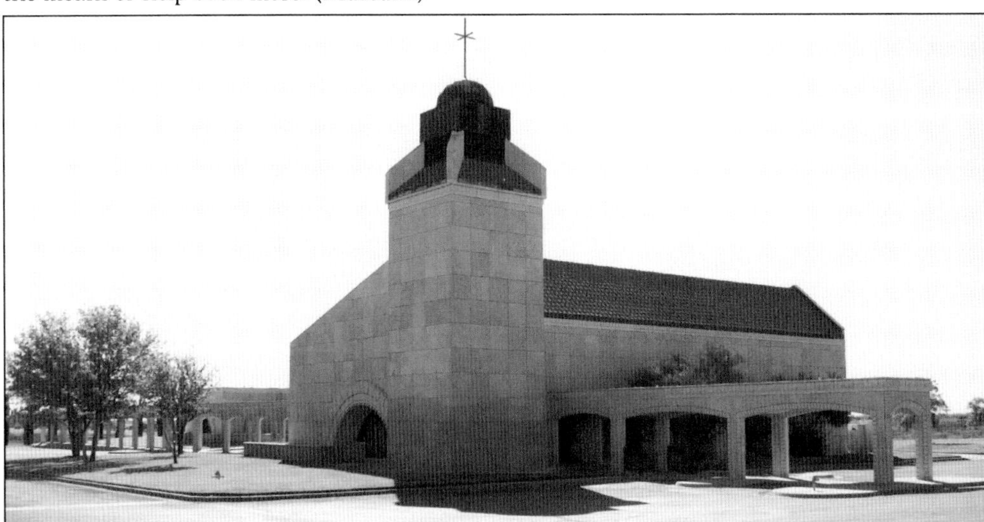

An enduring legacy of the M.S. Doss family was the construction of this magnificent chapel and mausoleum, which is open to the public at the cemetery south of Seminole. The building also serves as headquarters for the Doss Foundation, a philanthropic entity set up to continue the Doss family's commitment to worthy causes. (George family.)

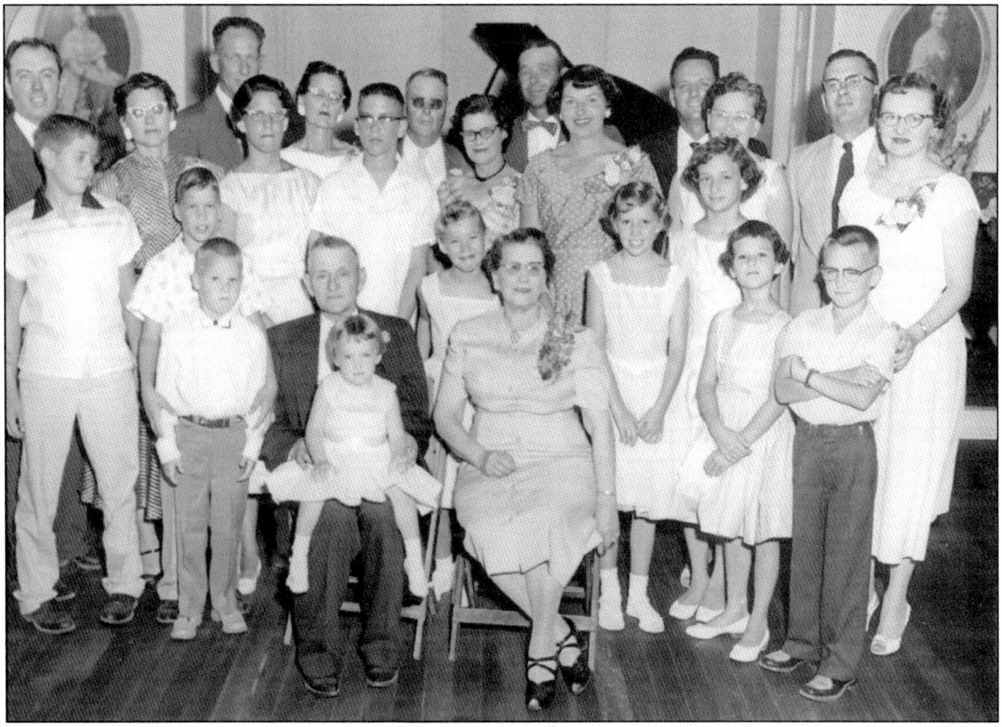

This photograph was taken at the 50th wedding anniversary of S.C. and Maggie Cox Doss on July 14, 1957. Members of the Doss family present for the occasion include, from left to right, (first row) David Doss, Scott C. Doss (seated), Polli Doss Satterwhite (in Scott's lap), Maggie Doss, Beverly Peters Sawyer, and R.C. "Skeet" Doss; (second row) Scotty Roberson, Steve Roberson, Marsha Doss Monahan, Claudia Doss Carlson, and Suzanne Peters Carlton; (third row) Beth Doss Roberson, Carole Mabe Williams, Doss Mabe, Cleo Doss Wilson Crosby, Marge Sharp Doss, Bobbie Doss Peters, and Florence Gwaltney Doss; (fourth row) Chester Roberson, J.R. Mabe, Bernice Doss Mabe, Gene Wilson, Scott Monroe Doss, Gene Peters, and Hyle Doss. Scott died five years later, in 1962, and Maggie died in 1990 at the age of 100. (Doss family.)

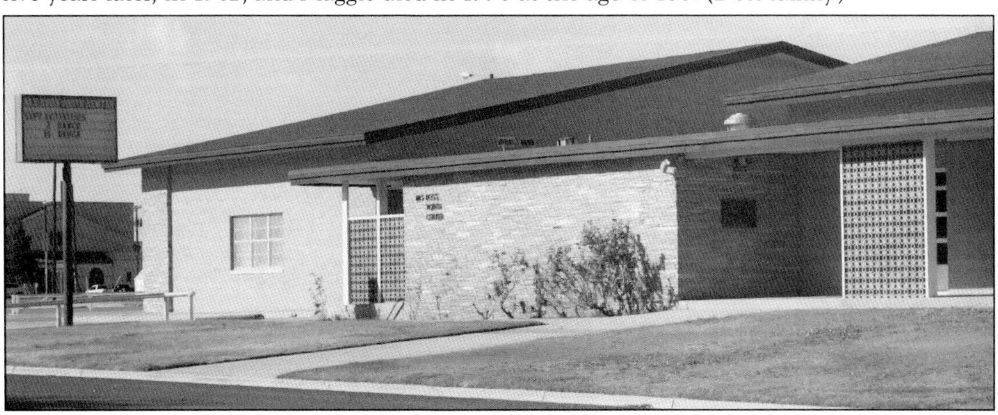

This shows only a portion of the M.S. and Meek Lane Doss Youth Center, located just west of the Seminole City Park. Originally built in the mid-1960s, it has expanded over the years but has never stopped serving the youth of Seminole and Gaines County. Longtime director Bob Black was the center's first and was loved by all. The center's current director (also loved by all) is 1966 Seminole High School graduate Mike Shain. (George family.)

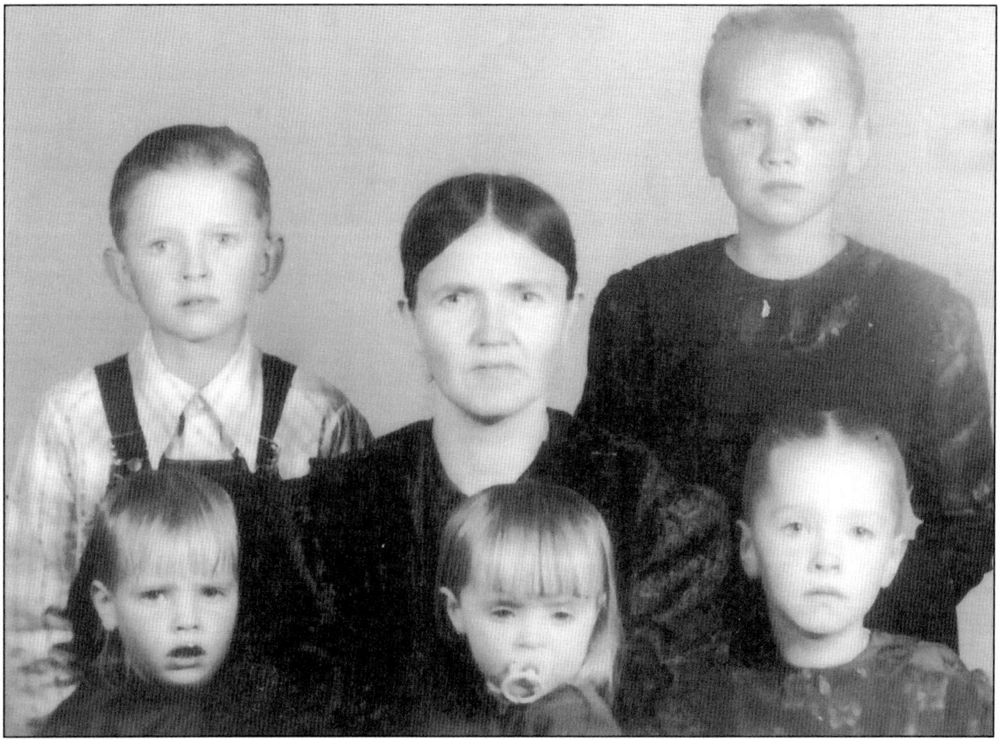

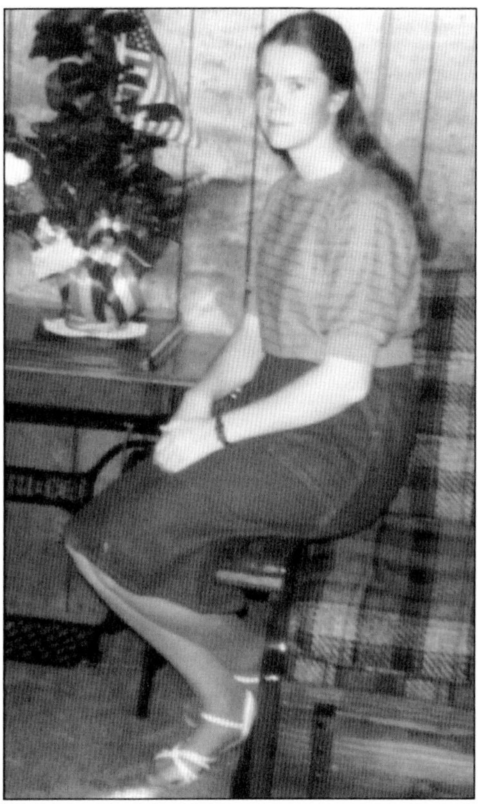

Seeking a place to live and prosper, 300 German families—many of them Mennonites—immigrated to Seminole from Cuauhtemoc, Chihuahua, Mexico, in 1977. Among them were David and Anna Rempel and their five children. This is the passport photograph for Anna and her children. (Tina Rempel Siemens.)

As one of the older Rempel children, Tina attended Seminole public schools her first year and is grateful to her teachers for helping her, as she spoke no English. The next year, she attended a German school on Southeast Fifth Street with English as one of its subjects. One of Tina's proudest moments was on October 31, 1985, when she attained her US citizenship. The flowers were a gift from "Pappy" and Laura Hoffman. (Tina Rempel Siemens.)

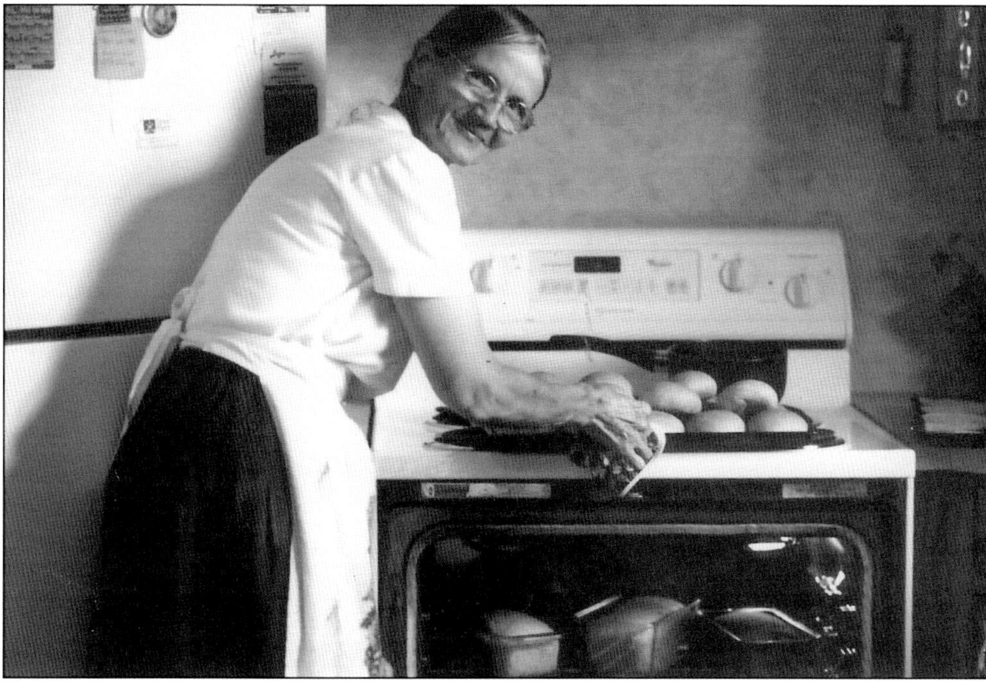

Seen here in 2007, Anna Rempel has long been known for her delicious home-baked bread. She is also a very courageous woman. She and her five children made the long journey to Seminole riding in the back of someone else's pickup, arriving at night. They were among the first 10 of the German families to come to Seminole. (Chamber.)

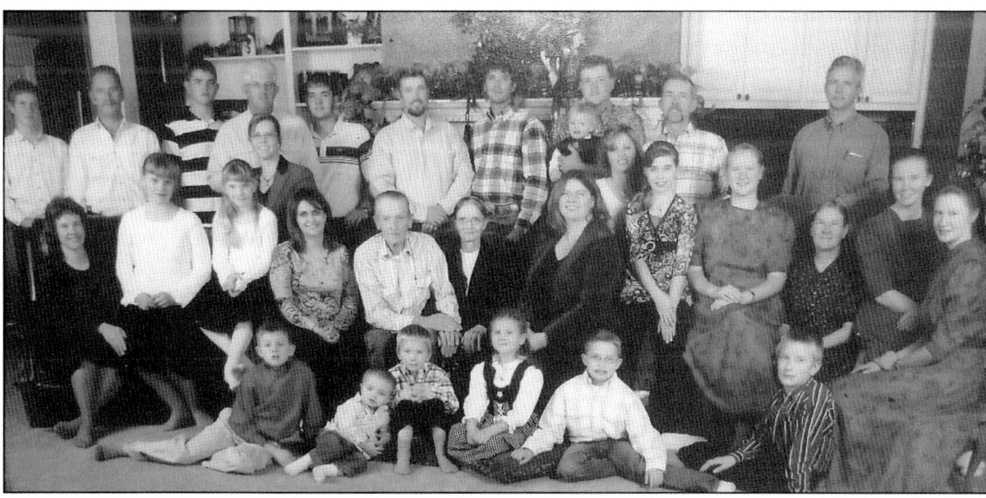

Pictured are David and Anna Rempel (center), their children, and their children's families at the home of Tina and John Siemens in 2007. Just 30 years earlier, the Rempels had arrived in Seminole in the back of a pickup truck they did not own, bringing very little with them. Hard work, determination, and a strong faith helped them achieve their dream. After all, Tina says, their family's mottoes have always been "Let's pray about it" and "Never give up." (Tina Rempel Siemens.)

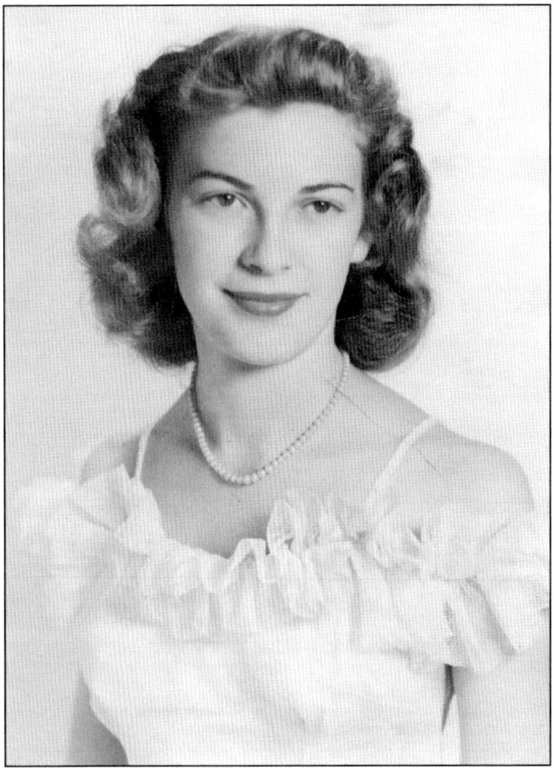

This beauty, the 1946 Seminole High School Football Queen, is Pat Denton (now Pat Aryain). After high school, she enrolled in Oklahoma Baptist University and went on to Texas State College for Women (later called Texas Women's University) in Denton. Once married to Jameil (Dink) and back in Seminole, Pat opened a private kindergarten. When Seminole schools opened theirs, she went to work for the Seminole Independent School District. (Aryain family.)

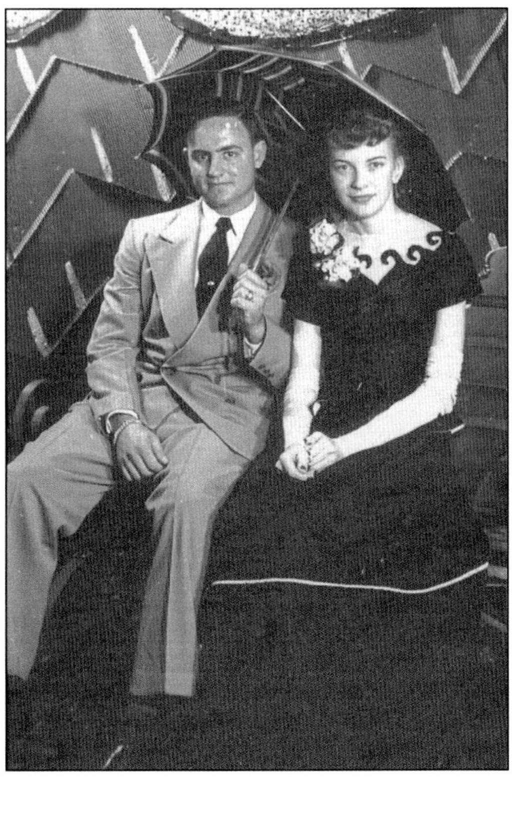

When Pat Denton was a freshman at Texas State College for Women in 1948, there was no doubt in her mind who she would ask to escort her to the prom. She and Dink were engaged to be married, and they made a beautiful couple. Come to think of it, they still do! (Aryain family.)

When Queen Victoria had been on the throne for 60 years, England celebrated what it called her Diamond Jubilee. The word "diamond," after all, comes from the Greek *adamas*, meaning "unconquerable and enduring." On October 22, 2010, Dink and Pat Aryain celebrated their diamond wedding anniversary. The term could not be more fitting. (Aryain family.)

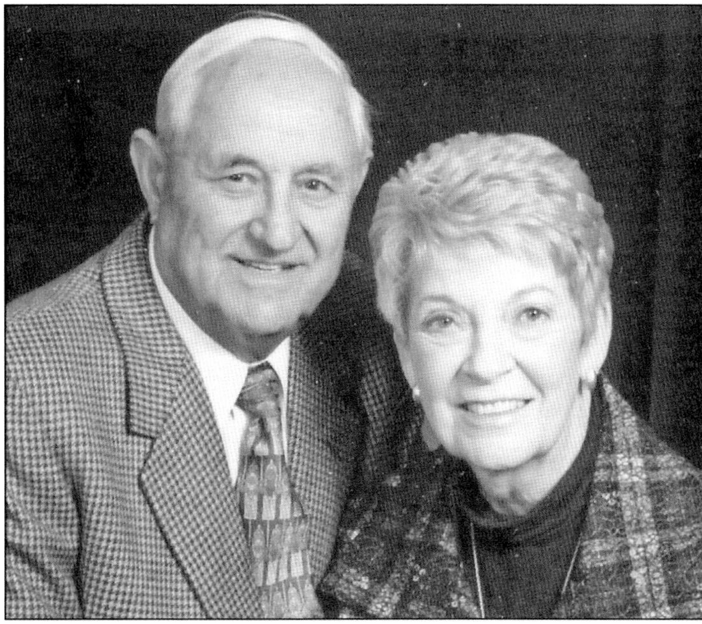

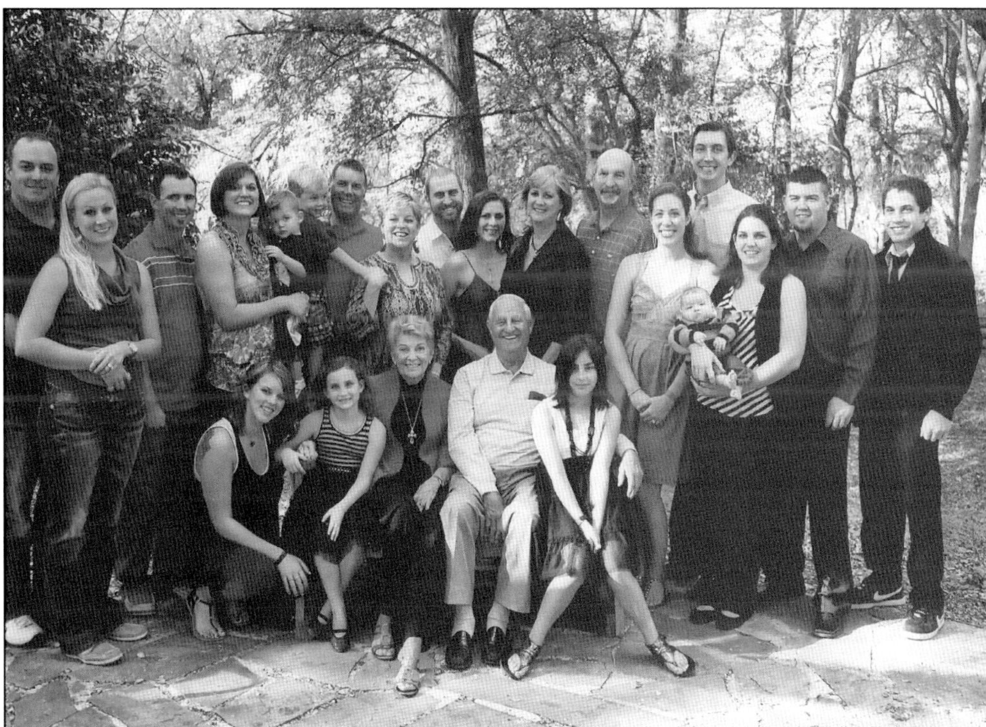

This group consisting of most of the Aryain family came together on Dink's and Pat's 60th wedding anniversary. Pat is active at First Baptist Church and still teaches (as a substitute) at F.J. Young Elementary School. Dink is active at the First Presbyterian Church and volunteers at its food pantry. He also plays golf almost every day. Conceding to his family's wishes that he carry a cell phone, Dink now has one, safely stored in his pickup truck's glove compartment. (Aryain family.)

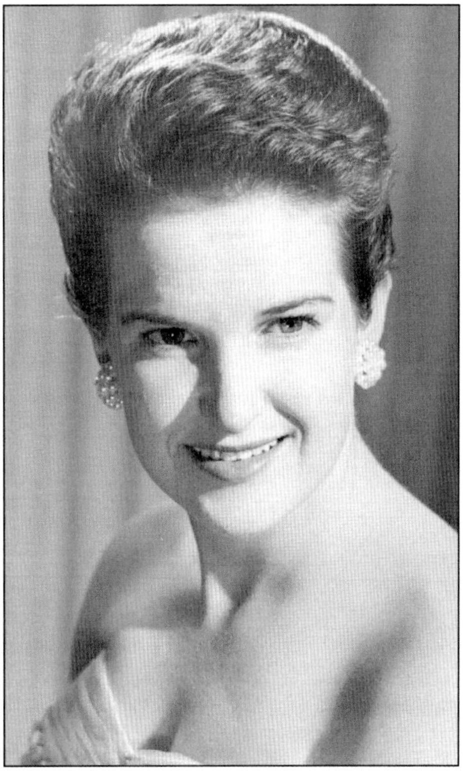

This young beauty is 1958's *Tepee* Queen Sandra Ward, daughter of longtime Gaines County rancher A.C. Ward and his wife, Irene. After attending college at Texas Women's University in Denton, she returned to Seminole to teach, beginning a 42-year career molding the lives of her students. (Museum.)

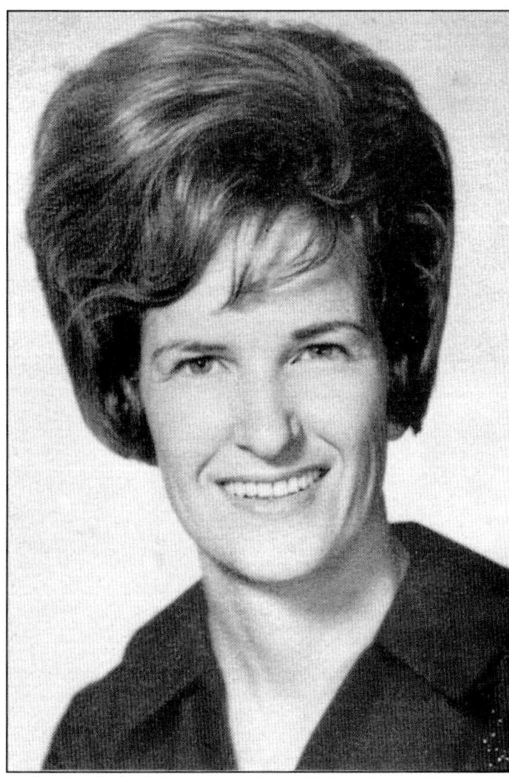

This picture from the 1967 Seminole *Tepee* shows teacher Sandra Ward. During her tenure at Seminole High School, she taught science and social studies. Her favorite teaching experience was general science when she first taught at Seminole High School, but several of her former students have reported that their government professors at colleges they attended could tell they had been Ms. Ward's students by how well they responded to questions in class. (George family.)

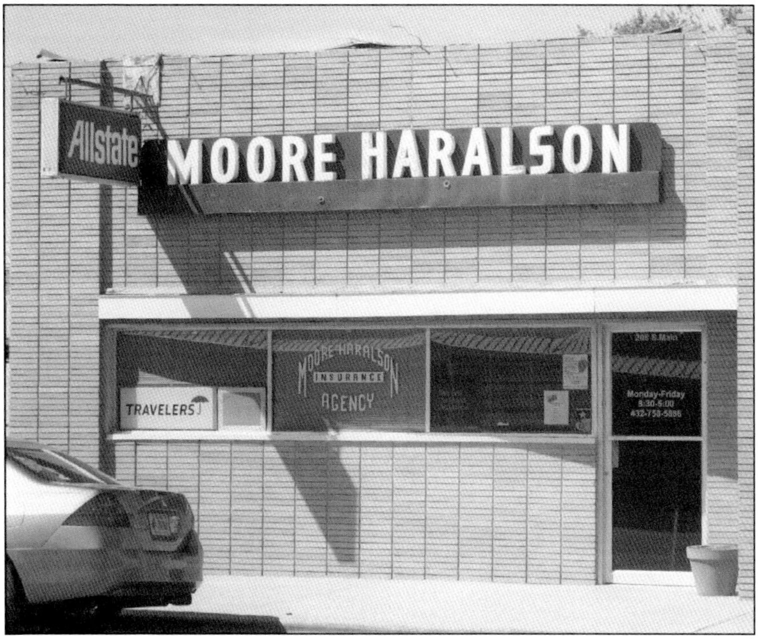

This photograph shows the Moore-Haralson Agency at 206 South Main Street as it appears today. Originally Cox Insurance Agency, it was founded in that location in 1913; it then became Cox & Moore, then Moore Insurance, and finally Moore-Haralson. It is the oldest continuously operated business in its original location in Seminole and Gaines County. (George family.)

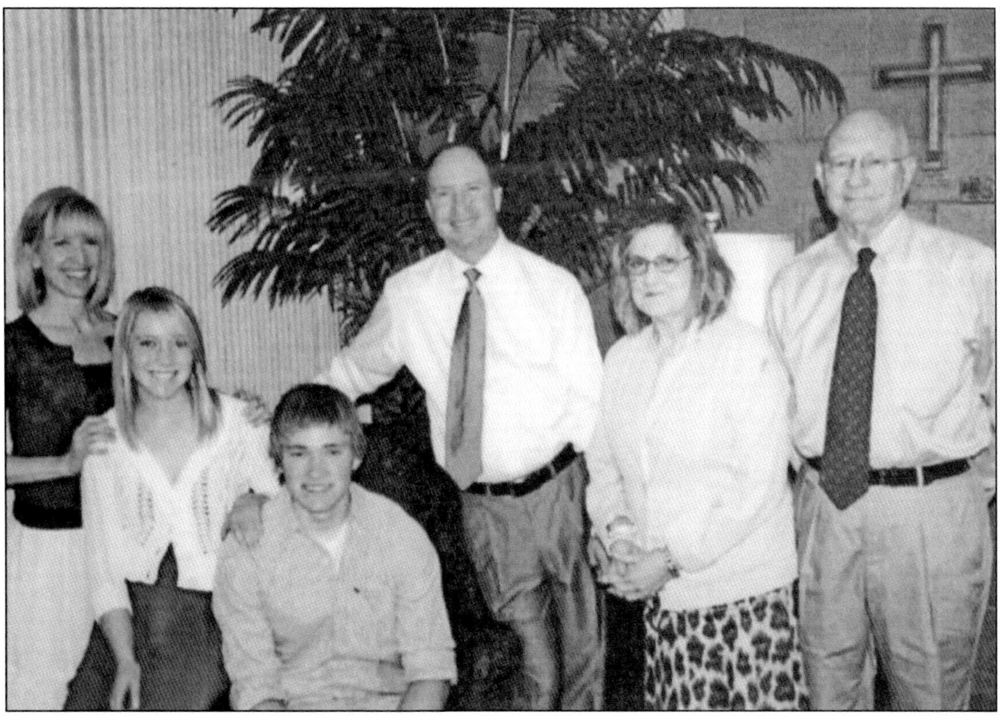

This informal Haralson family portrait was taken in the First Presbyterian Church's Fellowship Hall around 2008 or 2009. It shows, from left to right, Elaine, her children Hillary and Hunter, her husband Dennis, and Dennis's parents, Nancy and Carroll Haralson. (George family.)

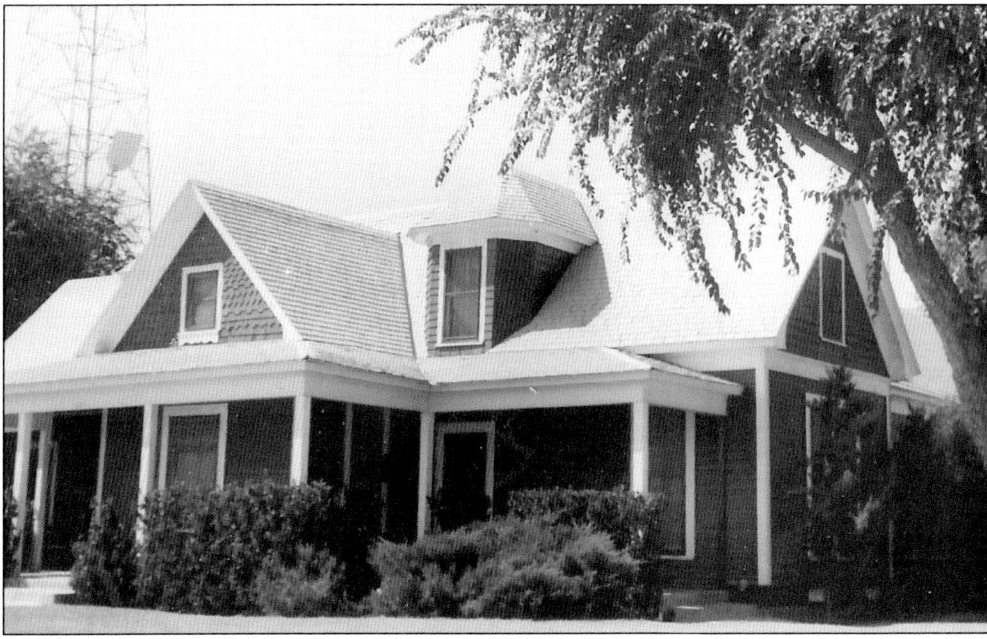

This historic home at Southwest Second Street and Avenue C was built by W.S. Dunn in 1907 and then sold to Ed Ramsey in 1909. After Ed's death, Mrs. Ramsey and her family lived on the first floor and took in boarders. R.W. Pittman, John Haney, B.B. Curry, and others, including the coauthor's mother, Alene McCrummen, lived here. In the 1950s, the Ramsey House was owned by Joe Dennis, who renovated the home. (Museum.)

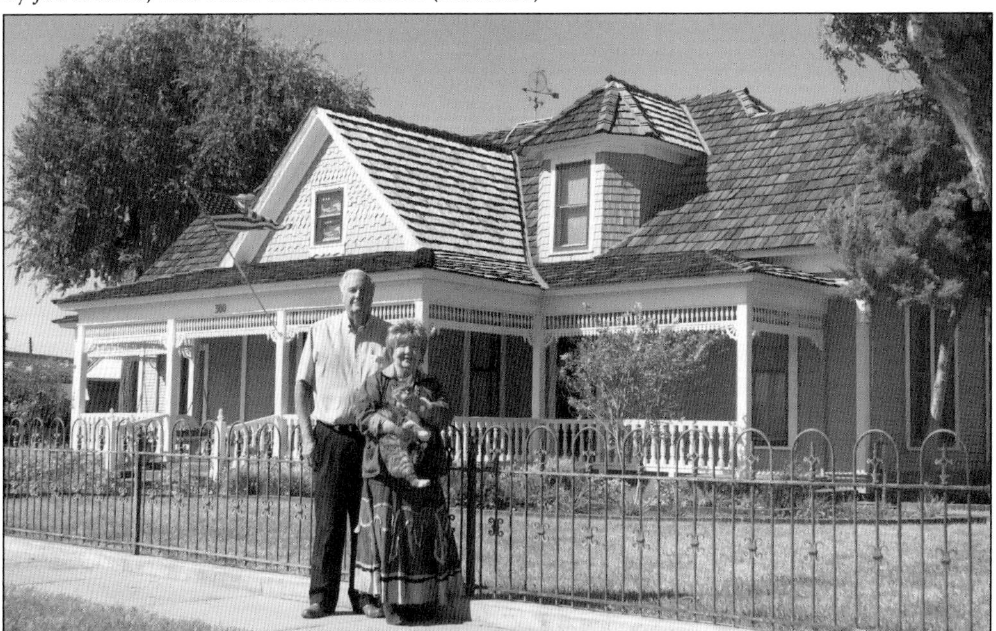

The Ramsey House, as it looks today, has been the home of Athen and Glenda Lowrie since they purchased it in 1982. They have done extensive renovations and improvements, including remarkable brickwork and landscaping that Athen did himself. Seen here are Athen, Glenda, and their cat Chocolate in what Glenda proudly calls the Lowrie House. (George family.)

Ysidro Lopez—"Sid" to all his friends and postal patrons—poses in this 1990 *Seminole Sentinel* picture showcasing the post office's newly purchased delivery trucks. Lopez moved to Seminole from Karne City, Texas, in 1965 when he was a sophomore in high school. Lopez's ready smile and eagerness to pitch in when needed make him a valuable asset at the post office and in Seminole. (*Sentinel.*)

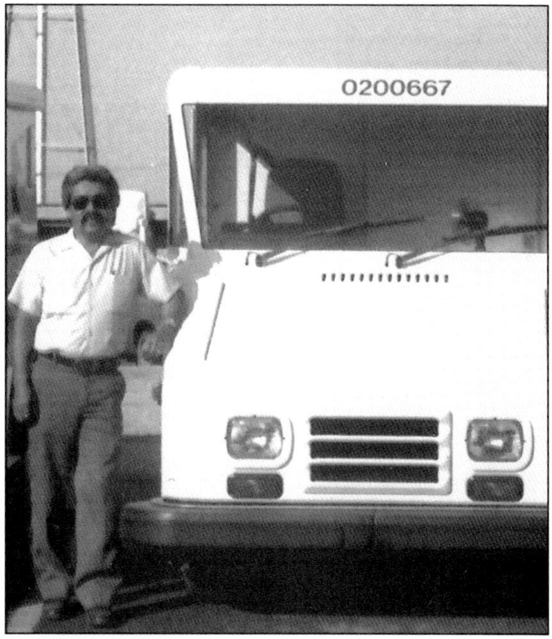

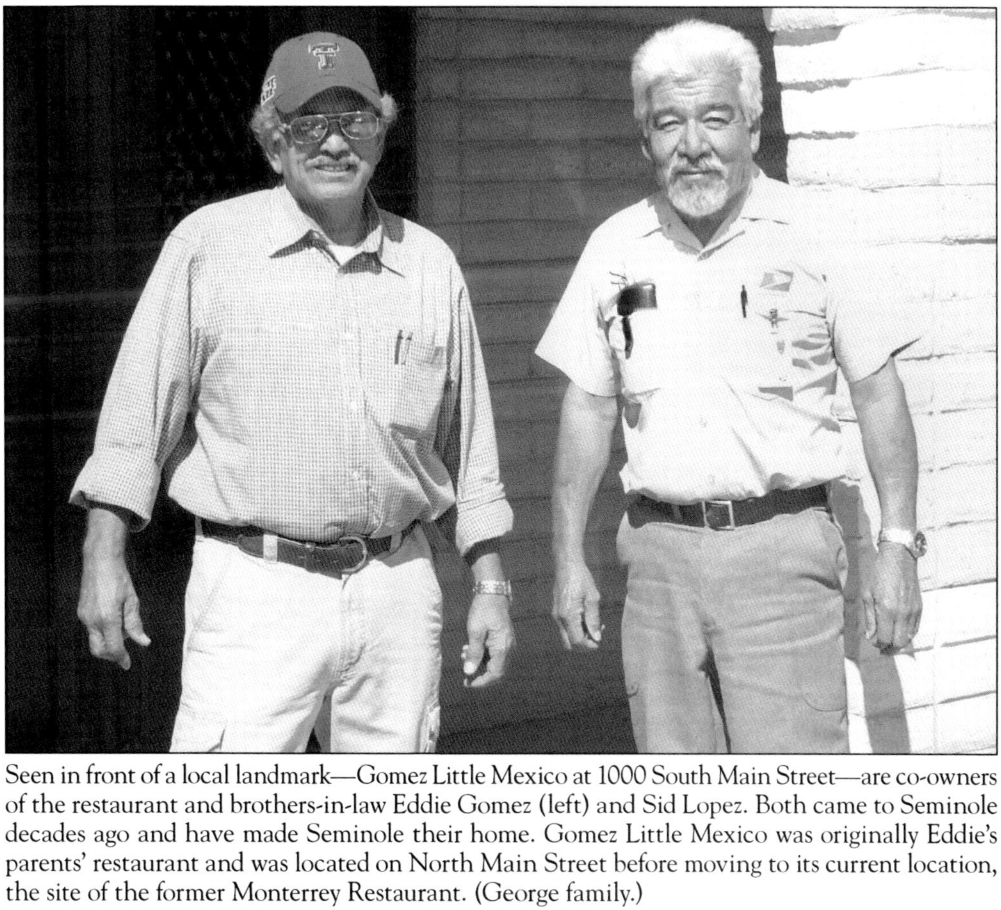

Seen in front of a local landmark—Gomez Little Mexico at 1000 South Main Street—are co-owners of the restaurant and brothers-in-law Eddie Gomez (left) and Sid Lopez. Both came to Seminole decades ago and have made Seminole their home. Gomez Little Mexico was originally Eddie's parents' restaurant and was located on North Main Street before moving to its current location, the site of the former Monterrey Restaurant. (George family.)

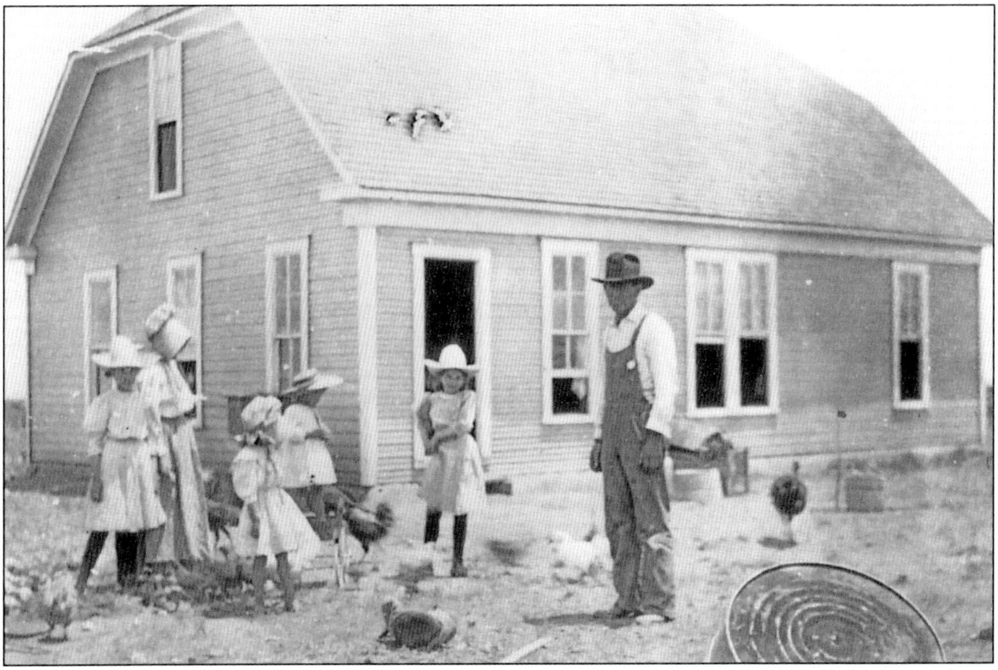

Pictured in another view of the original Cobb House just after it was completed in 1906 are, from left to right, Ora, Aurelia, Dorothy, Edna, Lois, and Dan Cobb. (Joyce Hargrove/Cobb family.)

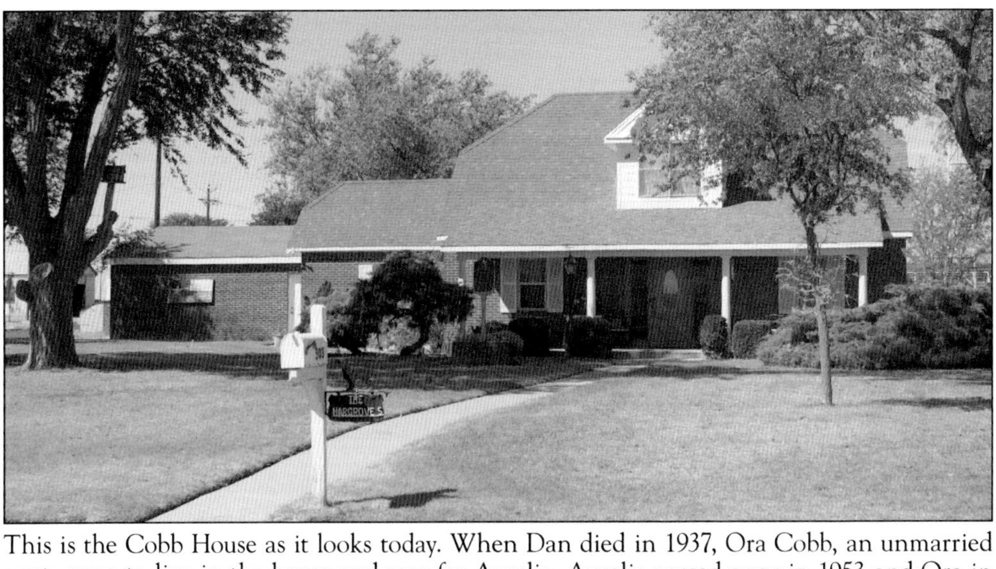

This is the Cobb House as it looks today. When Dan died in 1937, Ora Cobb, an unmarried aunt, came to live in the house and care for Aurelia. Aurelia passed away in 1953 and Ora in 1969. From then until 1993, when Charles and Joyce Hargrove bought the home, other Cobb family members lived there. The Hargroves have made additions and renovations to Charles's grandfather's creation, but the house is still a showcase. (George family.)

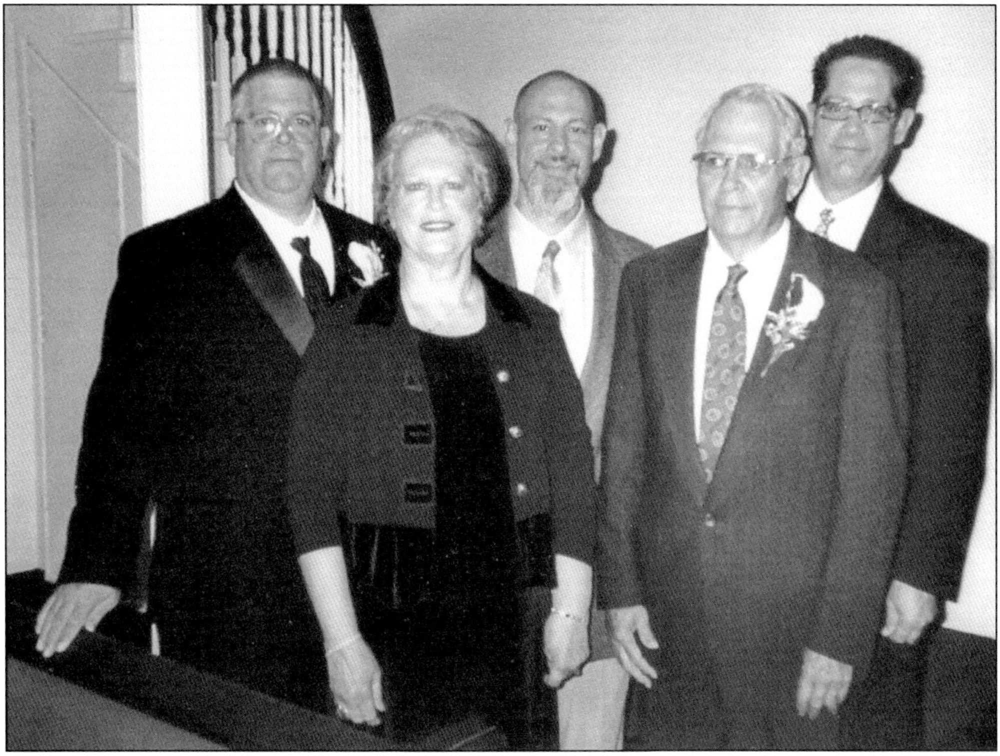

Pictured inside the Cobb House in this photograph are the Hargroves and their sons. From left to right are (first row) Joyce and Charles; (second row) sons Steve, Charles Jr., and David. Charles Sr., who grew up across the street from the Cobb House, remembers horseback riding where Wigwam Stadium is now, skinny-dipping in the municipal pool one night, and four years as a star athlete at Seminole High School (including a state championship). (Joyce Hargrove/Cobb family.)

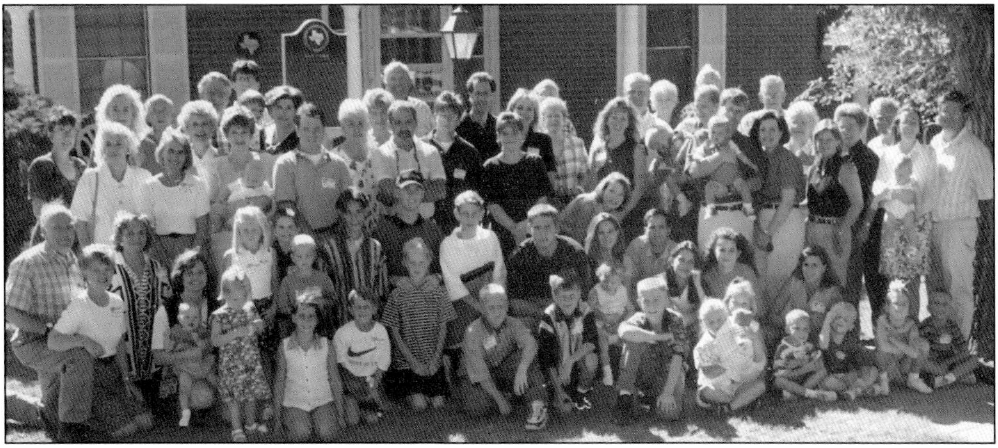

Pictured in 1996 are 77 descendants of Dan and Aurelia Cobb posing on the front lawn of the home Dan built. (Joyce Hargrove/Cobb family.)

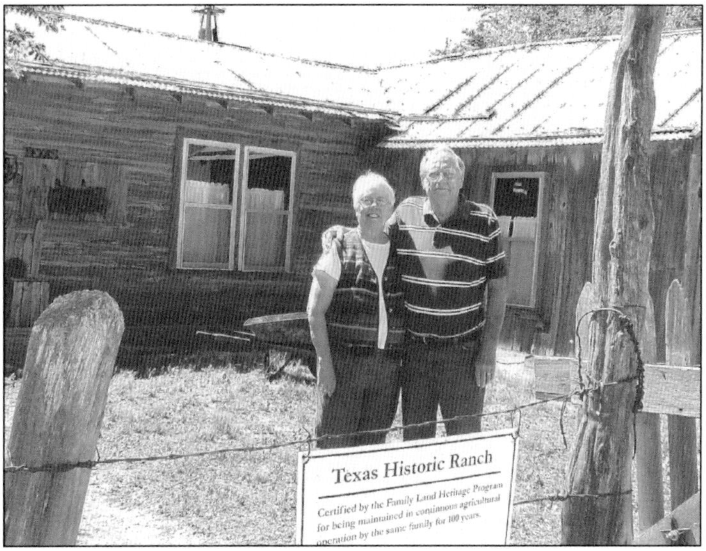

The J.B. Thompson Ranch was honored by the Texas Department of Agriculture Family Land Heritage Program in 2005. Seen in front of the last remaining house located on land homesteaded by J.B. Thompson in 1903 are Norma and Jack Mock. They spend their summers at the ranch where Jack grew up. Jack is the son of Fred and Ada Thompson Mock and the grandson of J.B. (Museum.)

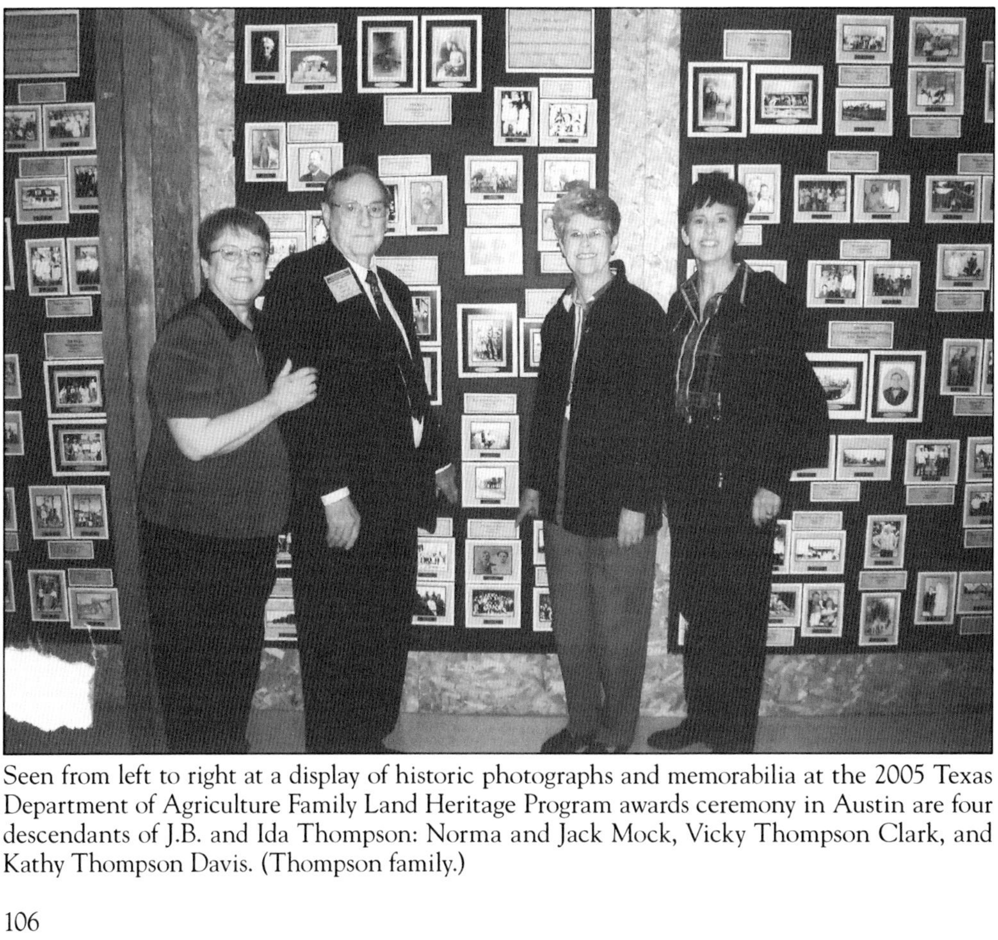

Seen from left to right at a display of historic photographs and memorabilia at the 2005 Texas Department of Agriculture Family Land Heritage Program awards ceremony in Austin are four descendants of J.B. and Ida Thompson: Norma and Jack Mock, Vicky Thompson Clark, and Kathy Thompson Davis. (Thompson family.)

This plaque hangs on the fence in front of the last remaining house on the Thompson Ranch, honoring more than 100 years of continuous ownership and operation by the Thompson family. The plaque is also visible in the photograph at the top of page 106. (Museum.)

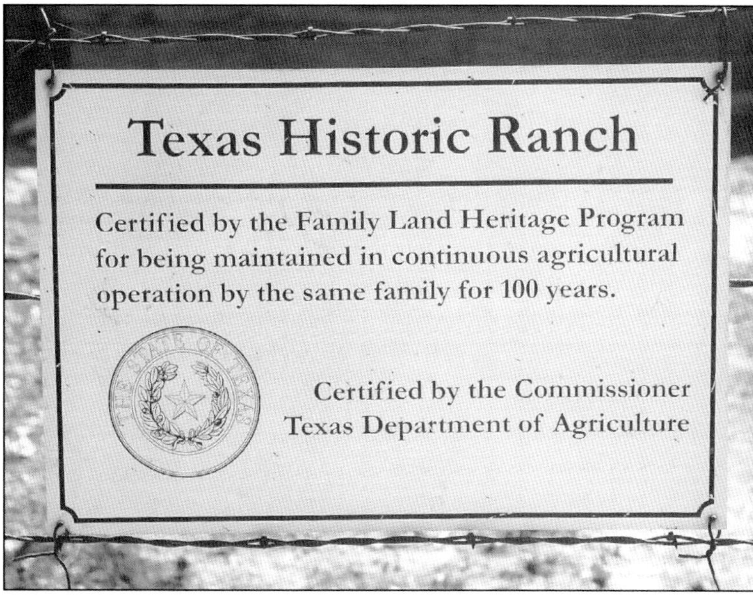

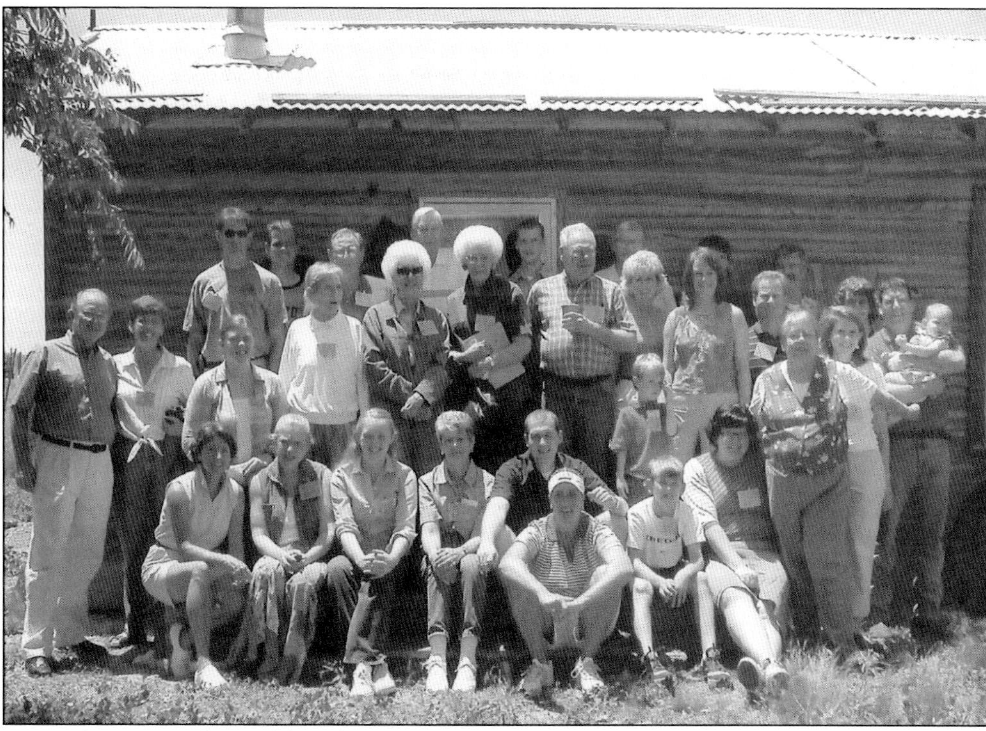

Pictured in 2003 in front of the Thompson Ranch house are descendants of J.B. and Ida Thompson. The image includes one great-nephew of Ida. The others are all descendants of Eunice Thompson Coker, Ada Thompson Mock, and John Thompson. (Thompson family.)

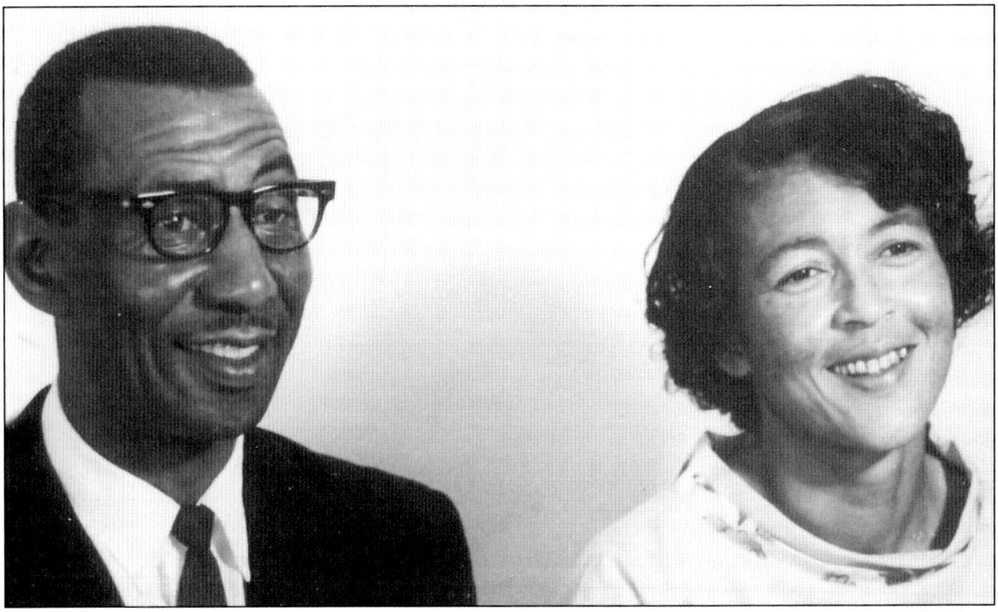

These photographs give just a hint of a remarkable couple and the remarkable family they raised—much of the time in Seminole. Above are Monroe and Betty Hill in 1968. Married in 1951, the Hills moved to Seminole in 1964. Monroe was a preacher for Mount Olive Baptist Church and later for the Morning Star House of Prayer. Many in Seminole knew him as "Preacher Hill." He also worked for Seminole public schools for many years. While raising 17 children, Betty also managed to go to college twice, receiving a degree both times. She worked as a nurse at Seminole Memorial Hospital from 1994 to 2001. Below is a picture of the Hill family in 1968, when 11 of their children lived at home. From left to right are (first row) DeAnna, David, Jackie, Joan, and Johnny; (second row) Debra, Donald, Betty (holding Dwight), Monroe (with Darla in his lap), and Janice. Their oldest son, James, was attending a school meeting and was not there for the portrait. (Both, Hill family.)

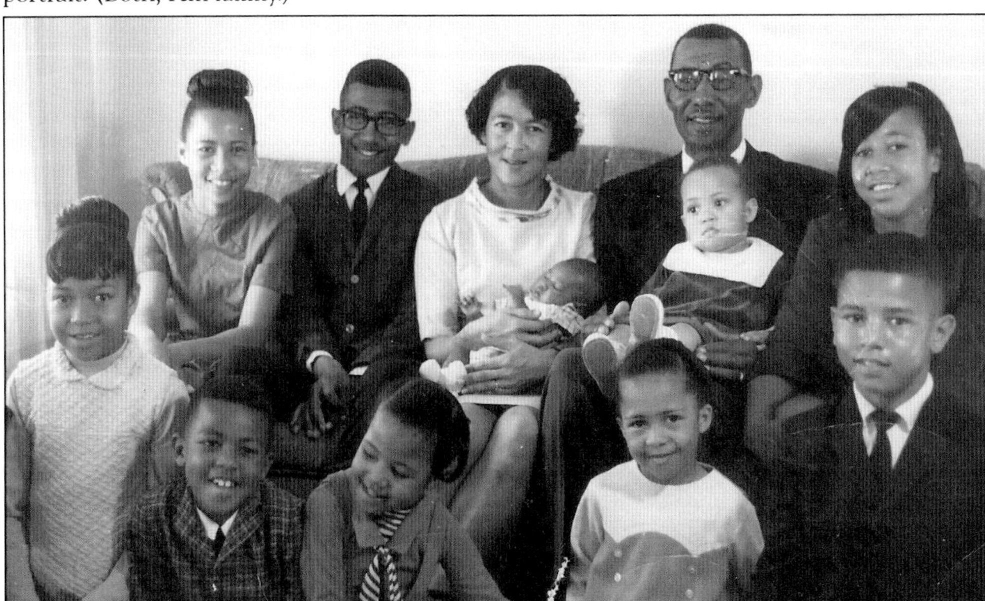

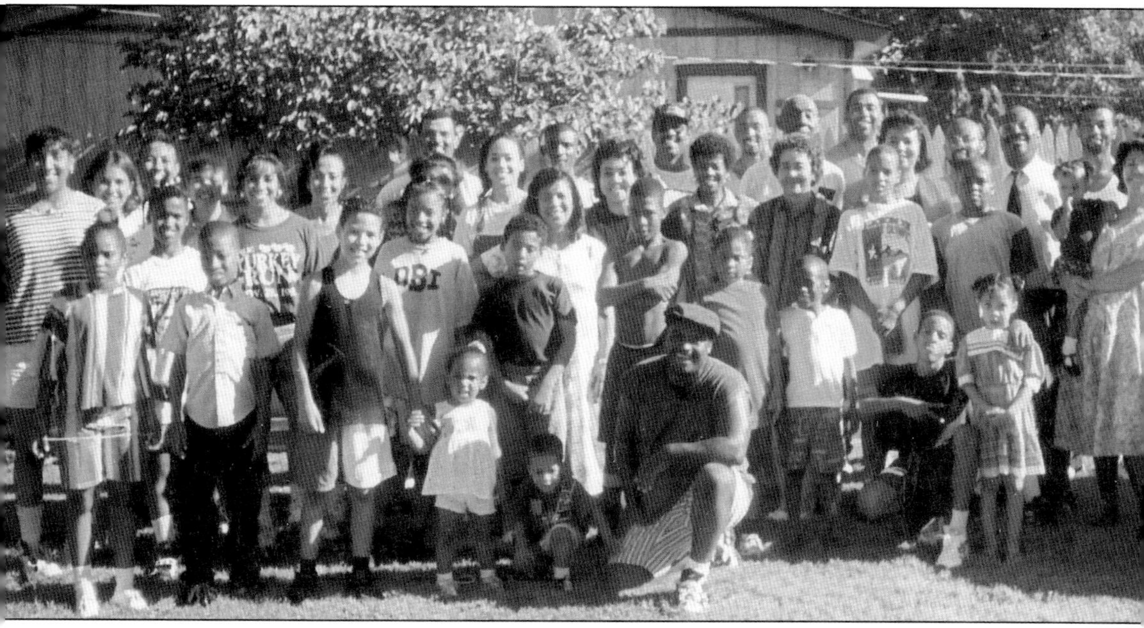

Above are the Hills gathered at the family home in 1996, one year before Monroe passed away. In 1981, the Hills were selected as Seminole's first "Family of the Year" because of "their love for God, love for each other and love for their fellow man," according to Marilyn Johnson of the selection committee. Today, the Hill children are scattered from Seminole to Hawaii but try to return to the family home for get-togethers whenever they can. (Hill family.)

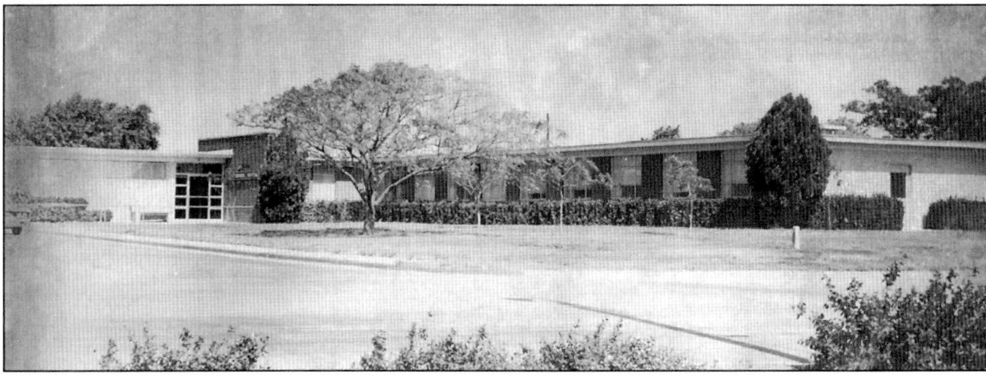

In 1952, when this photograph was taken, the modern brick structure seen here—Seminole Memorial Hospital—was a state-of-art-hospital and a structure that stood out on what was then the northwestern edge of town. The 28-bed facility had an X-ray, a surgery, a full laboratory, an emergency room, and an obstetrics department. Today, this building houses the Gaines County Library; the Gaines County Museum, Seminole Division; and various divisions of the Gaines County Health Department. (Auxiliary.)

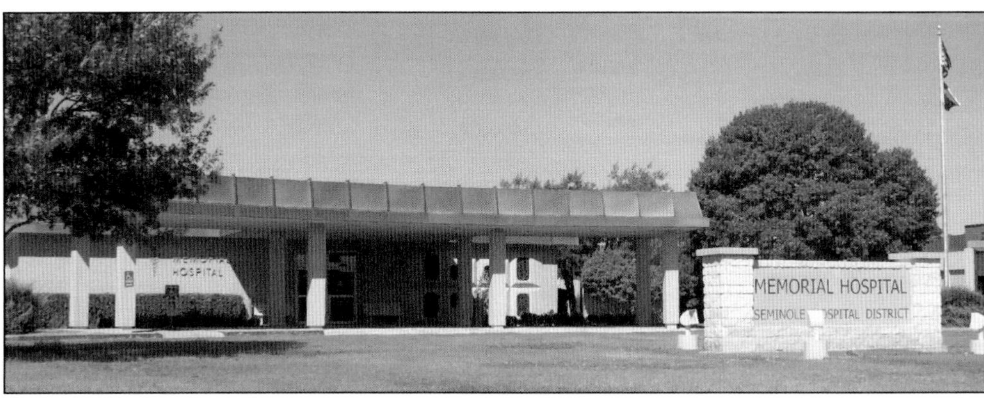

About one block north and half a block west of the "old" Memorial Hospital lies the current Seminole Memorial Hospital—also a modern, fully equipped medical center—with newly remodeled laboratory and radiology facilities, emergency room, chapel, obstetrics department, patient rooms, kitchen, and a wonderful physical therapy department. Attached to the northeast corner of the hospital is the M.S. and Meek Lane Doss Fitness Center, and on the west is the Memorial Health Center, Seminole's modern nursing and convalescent home. (George family.)

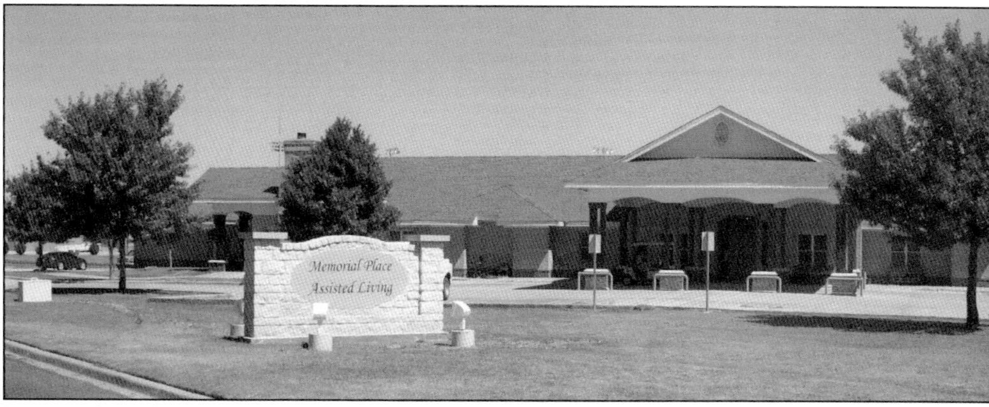

Just out along the Denver City Highway stands another branch of Seminole's health-care complex—Memorial Place Assisted Living. In this modern facility of private apartments, people can live virtually independently while at the same time receiving medical supervision and assistance with cooking, cleaning, and other household chores. (George family.)

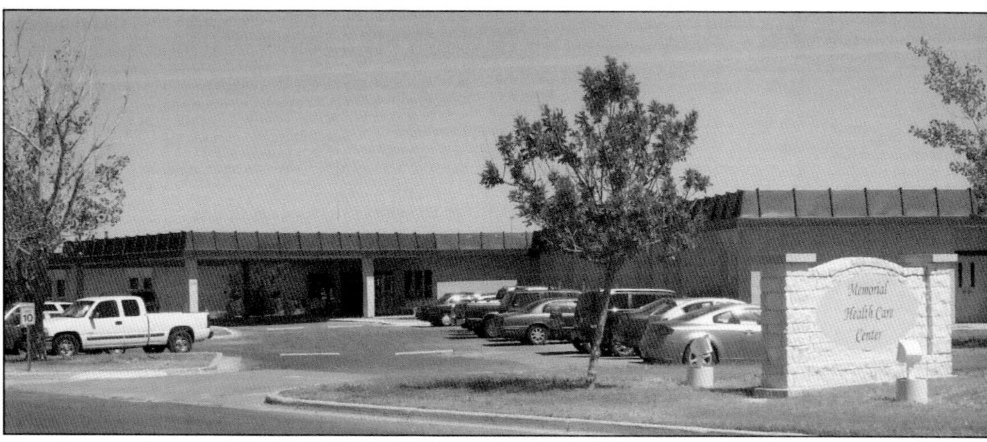

Seen here is the main entrance of Seminole's nursing and convalescent home, Memorial Health Care Center. The center has five wings of rooms that radiate out from a central nursing station and a large lobby with a flat-screen television, a grand piano, and plenty of space for visiting and other activities. Private and semiprivate rooms provide patients with as much health care as they may require. (George family.)

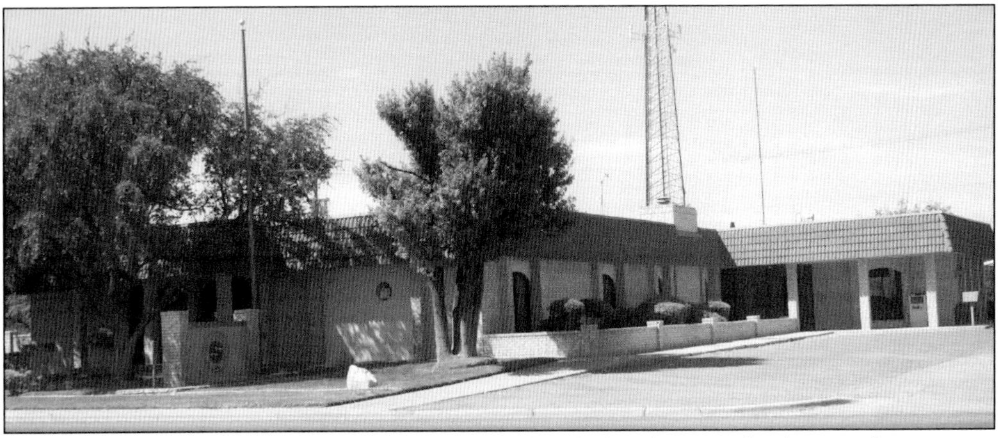

Located at 302 South Main Street, Seminole City Hall is the headquarters for the city administrator, the utility department, and the municipal court. Once occupied by First National Bank, the building became city hall in 2002. Before that, city hall had been at the old Seminole State Bank building at the corner of Main Street and Avenue A, across from the northwest corner of the courthouse square. (George family.)

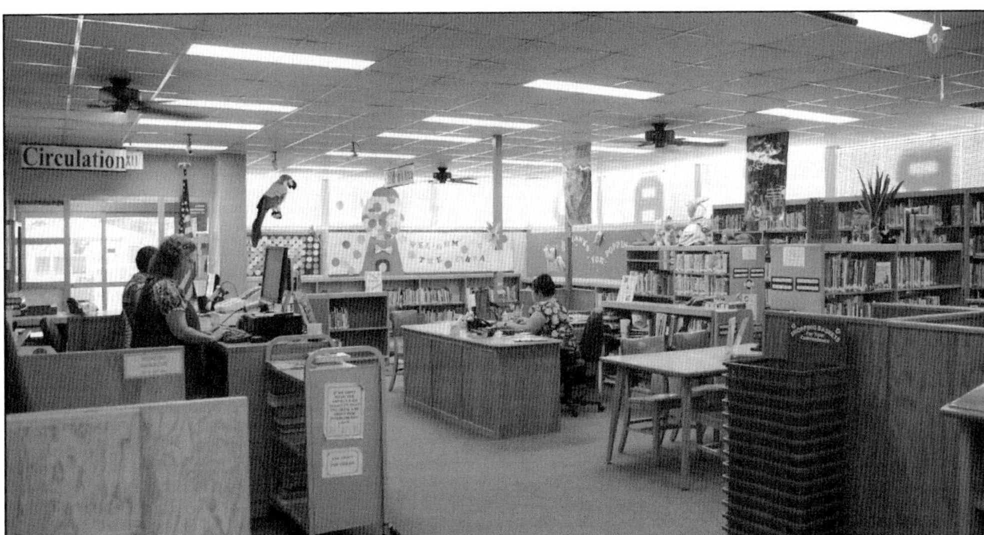

Located in the southwestern portion of the old Memorial Hospital building at 704 Hobbs Highway, the Gaines County Library offers many services to Gaines County residents and visitors. Numerous computer terminals, an impressive number of volumes for both children and adults, and a warm, welcoming atmosphere greet visitors. (George family.)

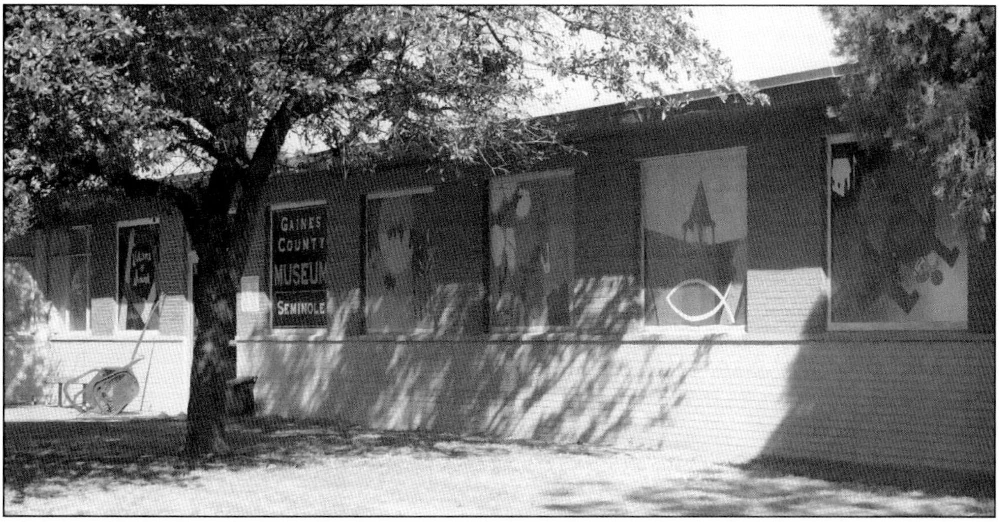

This view highlights the new murals adorning the front of the Gaines County Museum, Seminole Division. Through the efforts of Friends of the Museum (a group organized in 2009 to support the museum), the panels were painted by art students at Seminole High School and installed in 2011. The museum, which has undergone extensive improvements under director Roy Lynn Barnes, occupies the eastern portion of the old Seminole Memorial Hospital. (George family.)

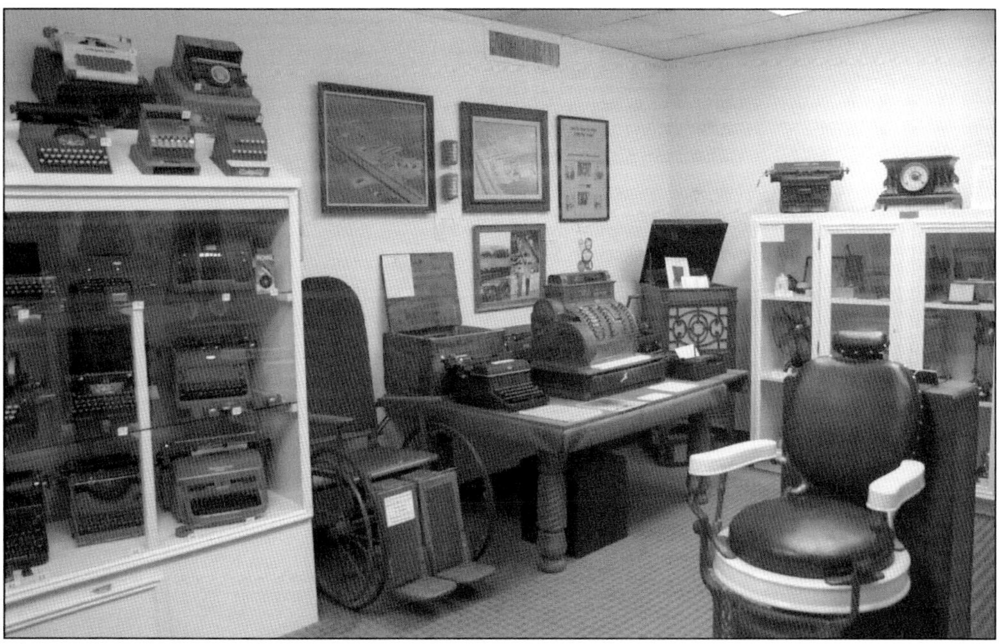

This room at the Seminole Museum contains typewriters and other office machines donated by Bea Barnes (including one that is older than the county), an early wheelchair, cash registers that may have been used in the early years of Cothes Drug, an Edison phonograph donated by Pauline Ogg (a descendant of the Dalmont family), a 100-year-old chair that once served both as a barber's chair and as a dentist's chair, and a mantle clock brought here over 100 years ago by J.S. and Cora George. (George family.)

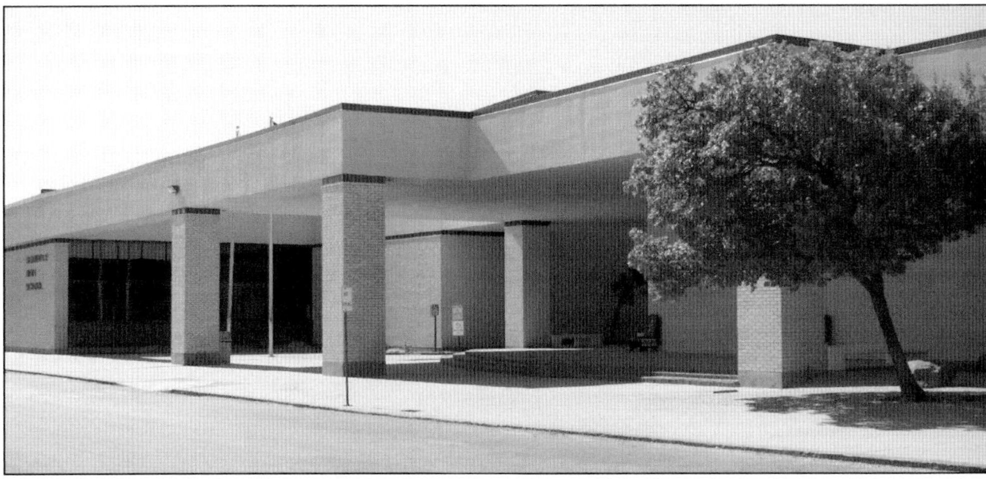

Seen here is the main entrance of the current Seminole High School (SHS), located on the Hobbs Highway. First completed and occupied by SHS students and faculty in 1980, this building has since been expanded. The school district has plans for further improvements, including a new auditorium, a new kitchen and cafeteria, and additional classrooms. (George family.)

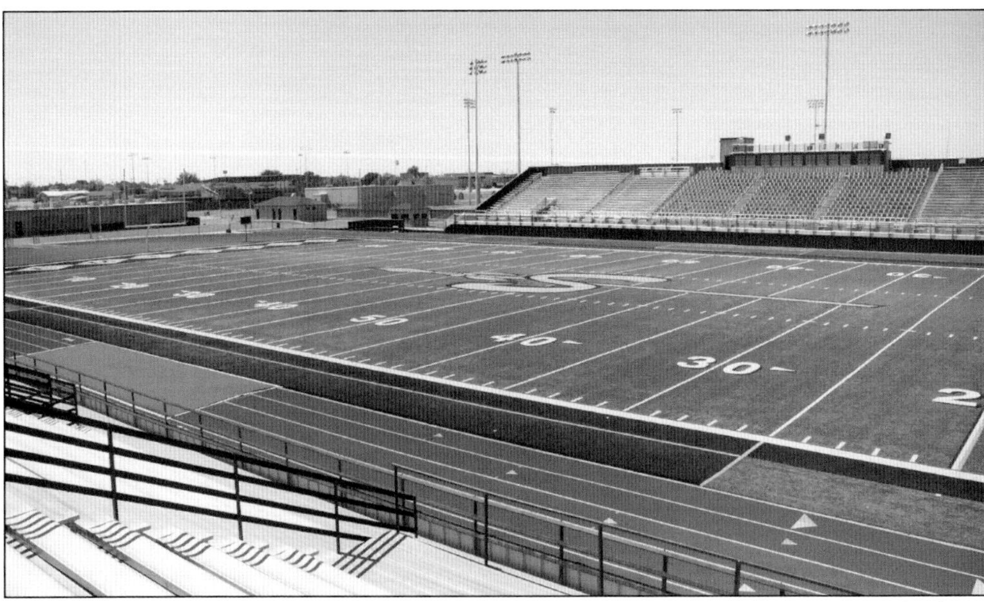

This is Wigwam Field, the scene of so many Friday-night football games, most of which are played before standing-room-only crowds. Located just northwest of the Seminole City Park, the ultramodern sports complex also features the Seminole Indian field house, indoor workout facilities, and, just west of the stadium, one of the best baseball fields in the region. (George family.)

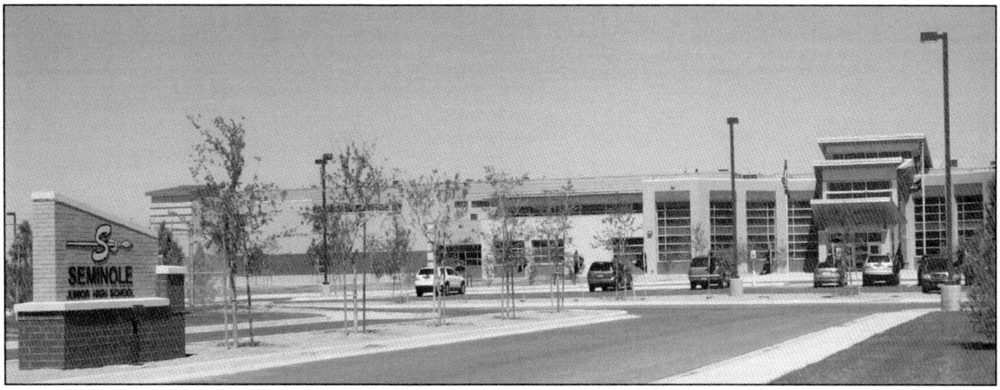

This is the newly constructed Seminole Junior High School, located on the northern edge of town. Completed in 2011, the complex serves over 500 sixth-, seventh-, and eighth-grade students with a faculty of over 62 teachers and aides. This ultramodern facility was part of a $110-million bond election passed by the citizens of Seminole, who are determined to provide area students the very best education possible. (George family.)

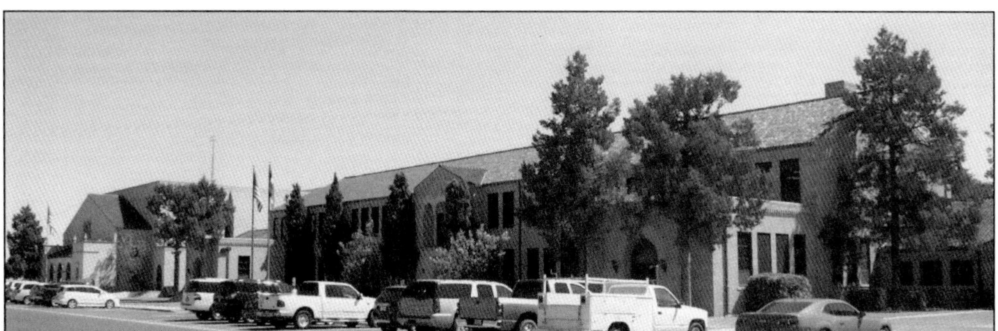

This building is the final result of construction begun back in 1948 (see page 66). After years as a high school and junior high, it will serve the students of Seminole Primary until their new building is complete. On the far left is the auditorium that was added some years later. At the other end of the building (not seen) is the large gymnasium that was also built later. (George family.)

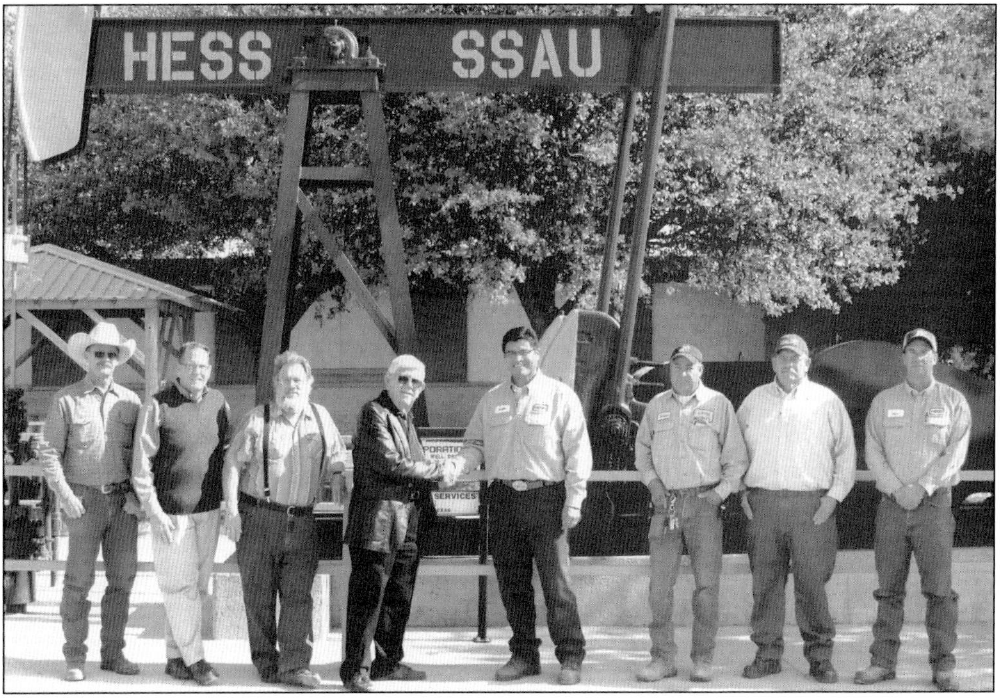

This historic pumpjack was donated by Hess Corporation and moved to the Gaines Museum, Seminole Division, by employees of Lufkin Industries to become part of the museum's complex in 2010. In the photograph are, from left to right, county commissioner Craig Belt, county judge Lance Celander, museum employee Gene Bering, museum director Roy Lynn Barnes, regional supervisor of the San Andres Unit of Amerada Hess Joaquin Martinez, Lufkin Industries employee Nick Lozano, Lufkin Industries general manager Frank Vallie, and Hess employee and pumpjack project liaison Rhea Wingo. (Museum.)

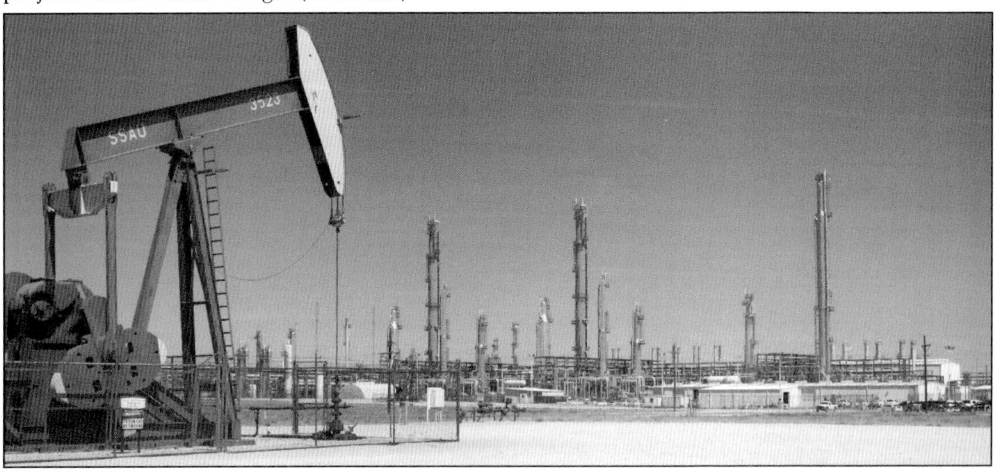

This view of the Hess Corporation Seminole Gas Processing Plant northwest of Seminole, often called the CO_2 gas plant, shows two aspects of the oil industry in Gaines County. The pumpjack on the left brings oil and natural gas to the surface. The gas plant in the distance processes carbon dioxide to be injected into stubborn oil formations deep underground. The carbon dioxide acts like detergent on a greasy pan, loosening the estimated six billion barrels of crude oil still underground and allowing it to be pumped to the surface. (George family.)

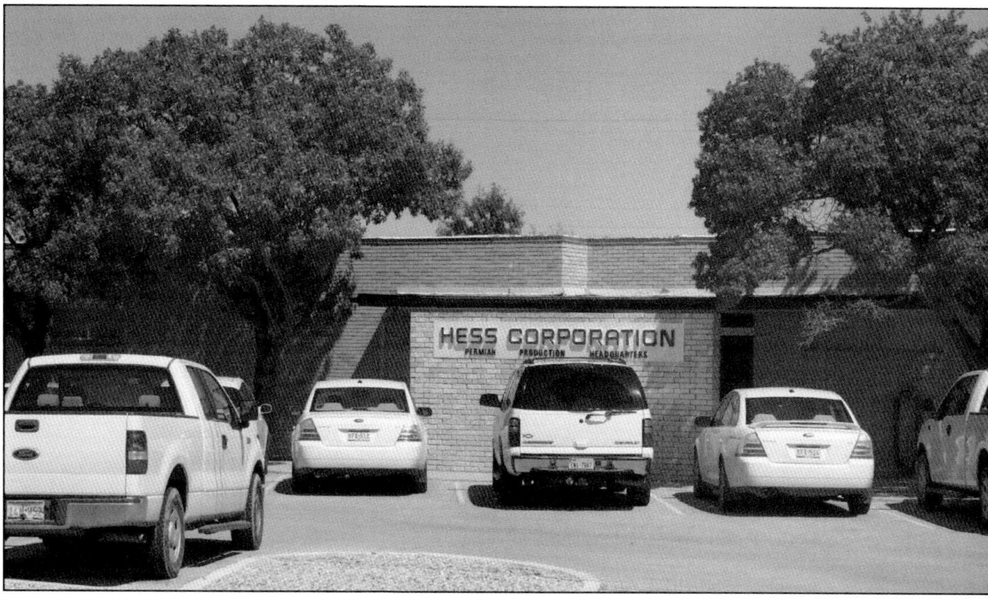

The offices of the San Andres Unit of Hess Corporation in Seminole take up almost a city block along the Hobbs Highway. Hess, along with numerous other oil companies and service industries, provides a major portion of the tax base for the county. They also provide jobs for local residents, recruit new families to the area, and are active in civic projects. (George family.)

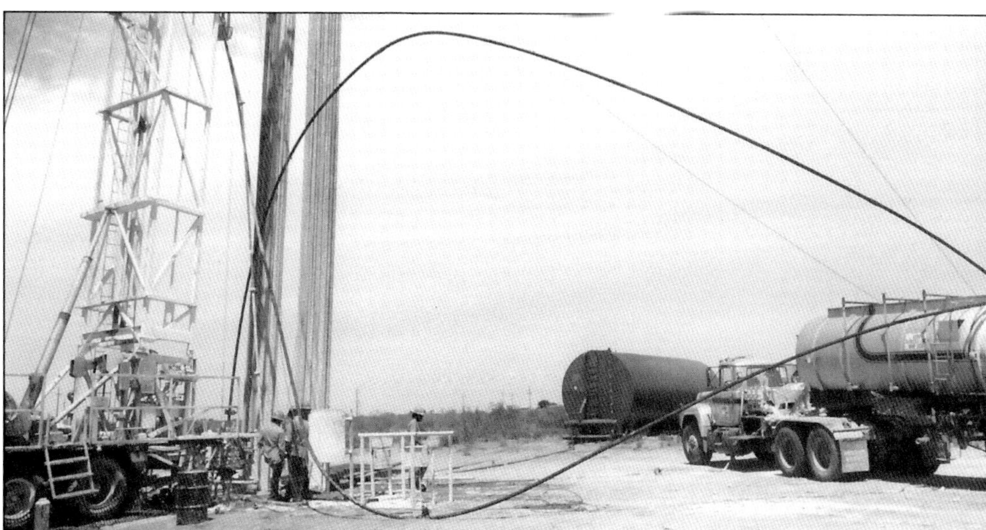

This photograph, taken in 1983, shows Amerada Hess equipment and employees working on one of their hundreds of wells across the county. (Hess.)

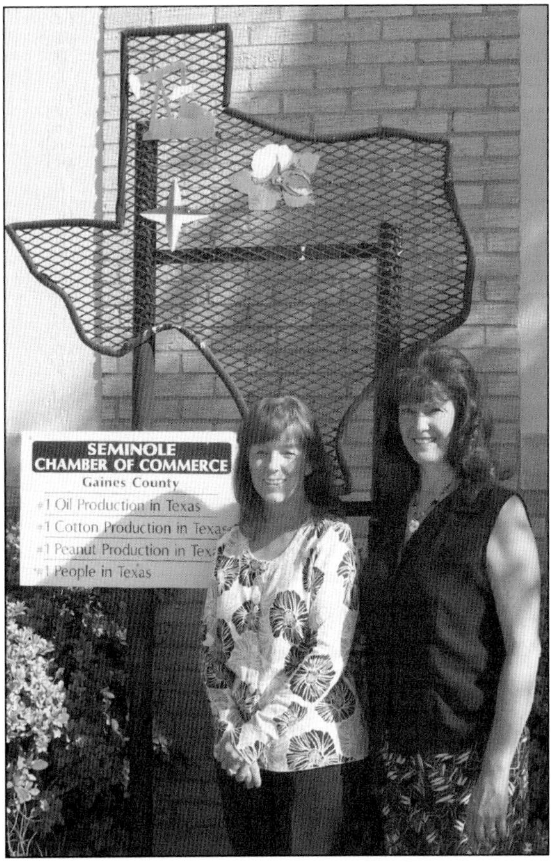

The Seminole Chamber of Commerce has been the city's best ally and advocate for a number of years. Pictured here, president Shelby Crow Concotelli (left) and her assistant Candy Boyer orchestrate dozens of events in Seminole each year, including the Great Comeback (an all-school, all-year reunion every three years), an annual Ag/Oil Appreciation Day, and special events such as the Centennial Celebration in 2005. The chamber is Seminole's ambassador to the world. (George family.)

Established by the Texas State Legislature in 1991, the Llano Estacado Underground Water Conservation District regulates underground water resources and promotes conservation in Gaines County. The district was headquartered in the basement of the courthouse until 2008, when this structure at 200 Southeast Avenue C was completed. (George family.)

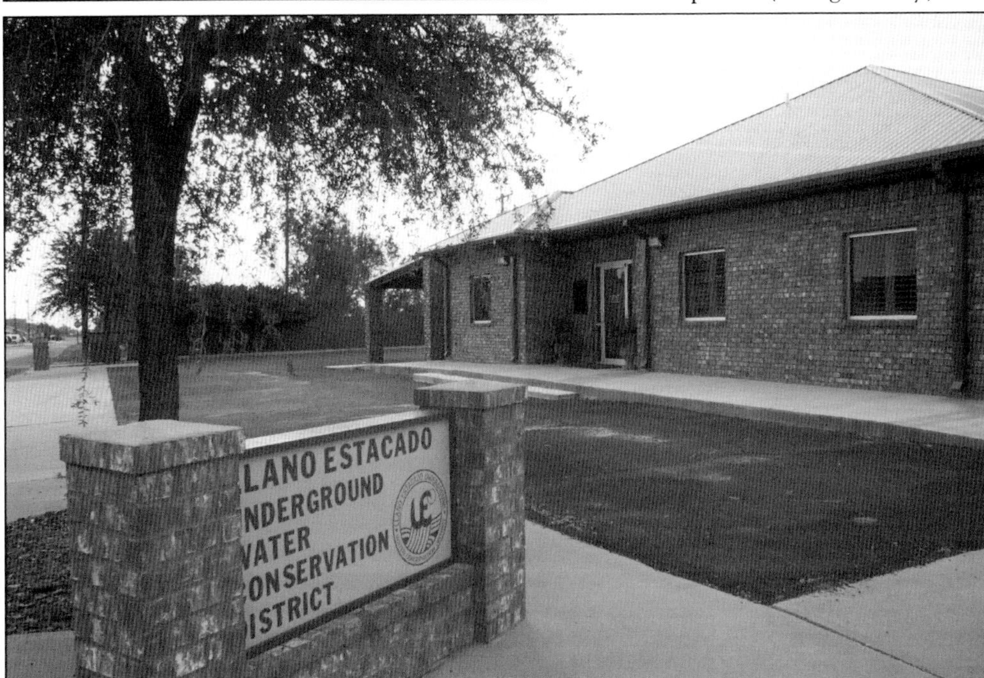

Besides oil, agriculture is also essential to the economy of Seminole and to Gaines County. Much of that comes from the production and processing of cotton. This 1991 *Sentinel* photograph shows a cotton stripper at work, pulling cotton bolls off the plants. From there, the cotton is compressed into modules that are trucked to gins around the county. (*Sentinel.*)

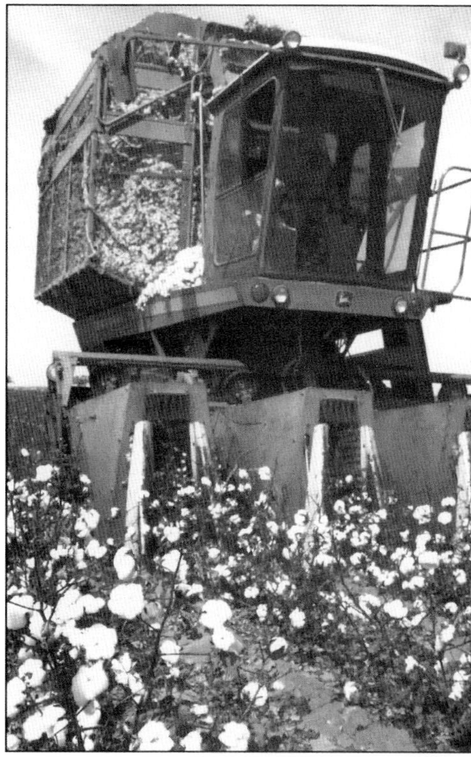

Shown in a photograph taken in 1991, the machinery in this cotton gin processes the cotton that has been harvested, removing the seeds and other trash so the cotton can be baled for shipment to textile mills. (*Sentinel.*)

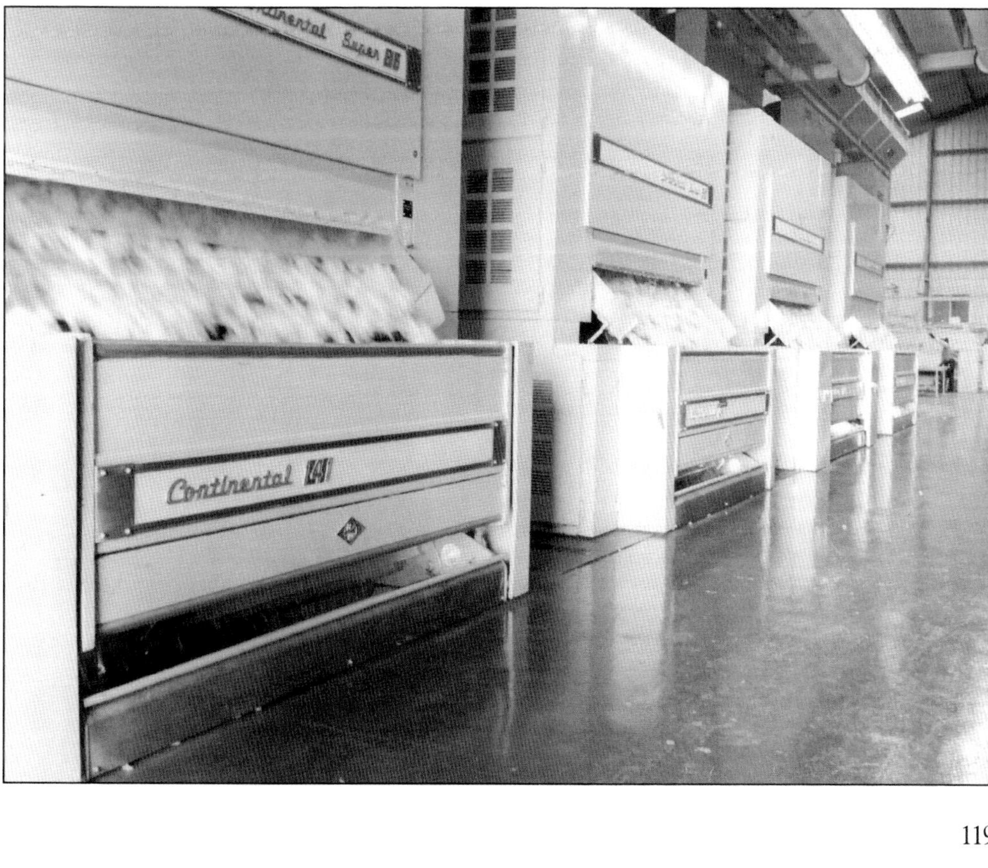

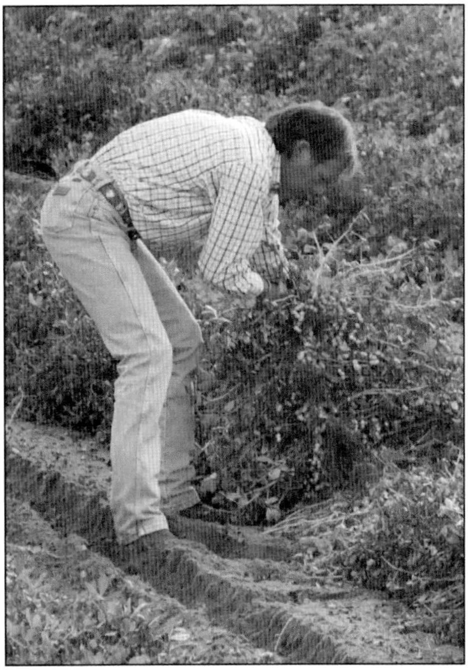

Peanuts are another essential Gaines County crop, with hundreds of acres in cultivation annually. In this photograph taken during the 2010 peanut harvest season, Jimbo Grissom, president of Western Peanut Growers' Association, inspects his crop after it has been dug and allowed to dry. The next step in the harvest is to gather the peanuts, separate them from the plants, and take them to processing plants, like Birdsong, Golden, or others, where they will be further dried, shelled, stored, and shipped for sale. (Chamber.)

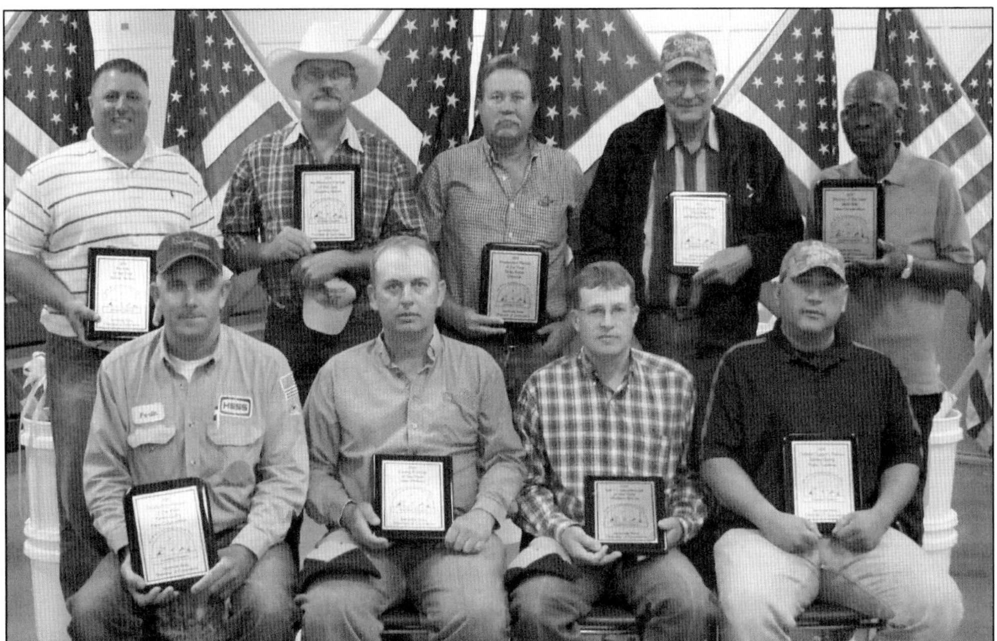

The 2011 Ag/Oil Appreciation Day awards include, from left to right, (first row) Ferlin Curtis, Co-Oilfield Production Person of the Year; John Friesen, Young Farmer of the Year; Weldon Shook, Ag Research and Education Award; and Robby Garza, Oilfield Support Person of the Year; (second row) Blaine Nichols, Farmer of the Year; Gregory Upton, Soil Conservationist of the Year; Ricky Bates, Co-Oilfield Production Person of the Year; Paul Bass, Oilman of the Year; and Matthew Bell Jr., Oilfield Retiree of the Year. Not pictured is Grady Billings, Peanut Farmer of the Year. (Chamber.)

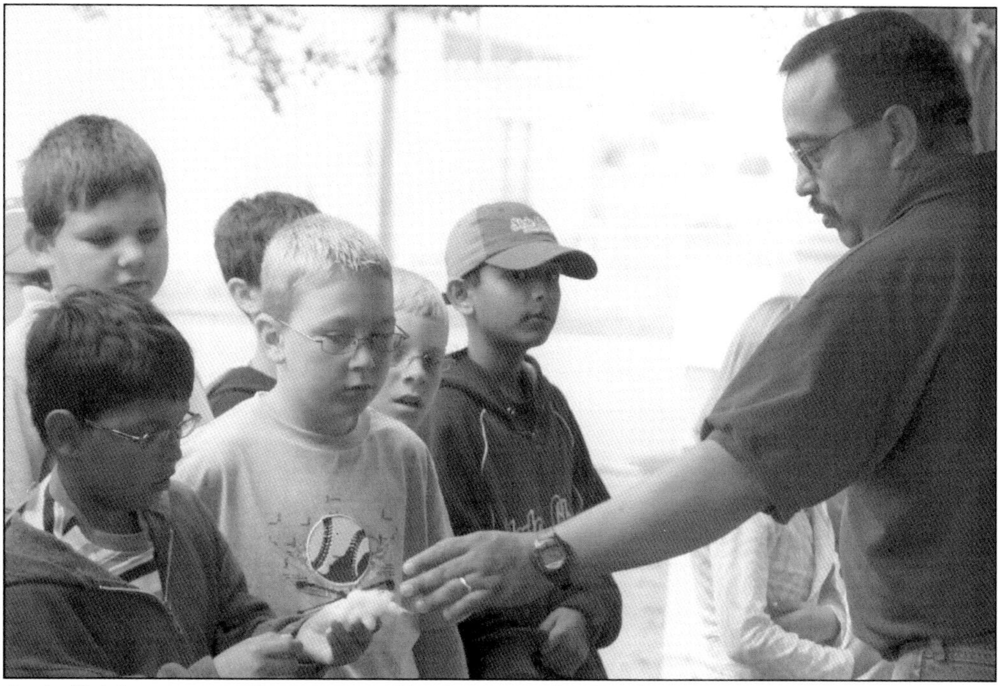

At Ag/Oil Appreciation Day, sponsored by the Seminole Chamber of Commerce, fifth-graders from all over Gaines County wander through exhibits that demonstrate the importance of agriculture and oil production for the county. Here, in a photograph taken during the 2007 event, students are given facts about the production of cotton, one of the county's primary crops. Gaines County has been number one in cotton production in Texas for many years. (Chamber.)

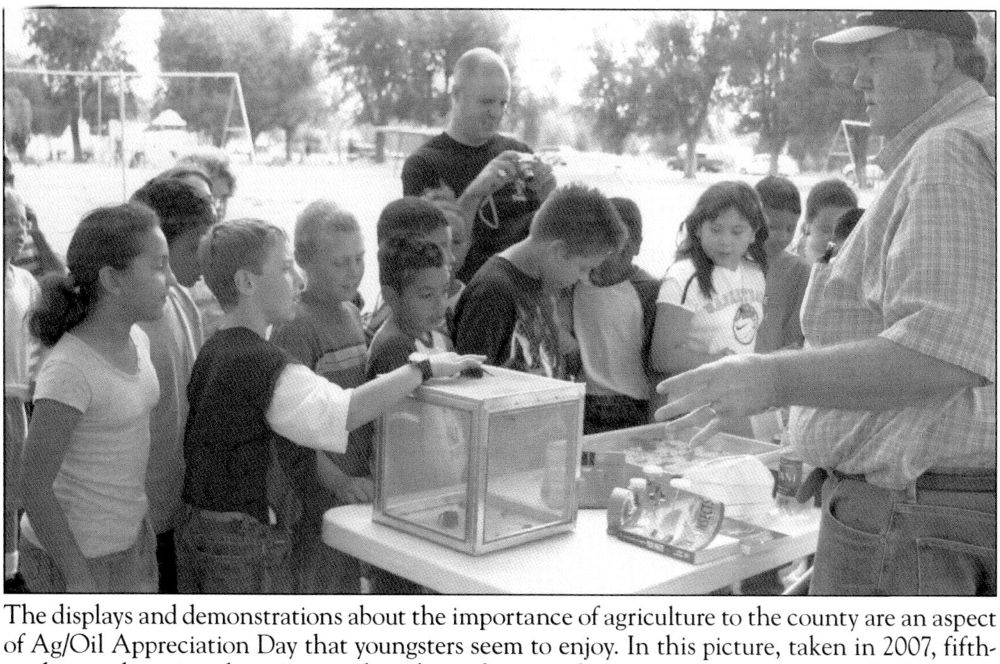

The displays and demonstrations about the importance of agriculture to the county are an aspect of Ag/Oil Appreciation Day that youngsters seem to enjoy. In this picture, taken in 2007, fifth-graders are learning about insects that plague farmers who grow cotton, peanuts, and other crops and how those pests are controlled. (Chamber.)

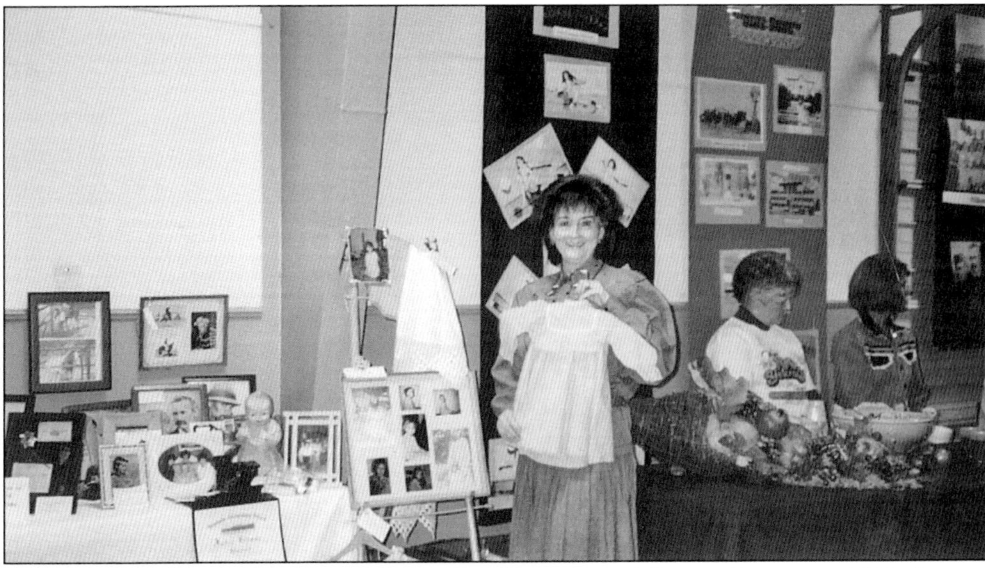

Because Seminole came into existence as the county seat of Gaines County in 1905, the year 2005 was not only the 100th birthday of the county but also the 100th birthday of the town. Displays at the Civic Building on Northeast Sixth Street summarized Seminole's 100-year history. Pictured here are, from left to right, Jackie Kay Martinez (a descendant of R.W. Pittman), county clerk Vicki Phillips, and district clerk Virginia Stewart. (Holbrooks family.)

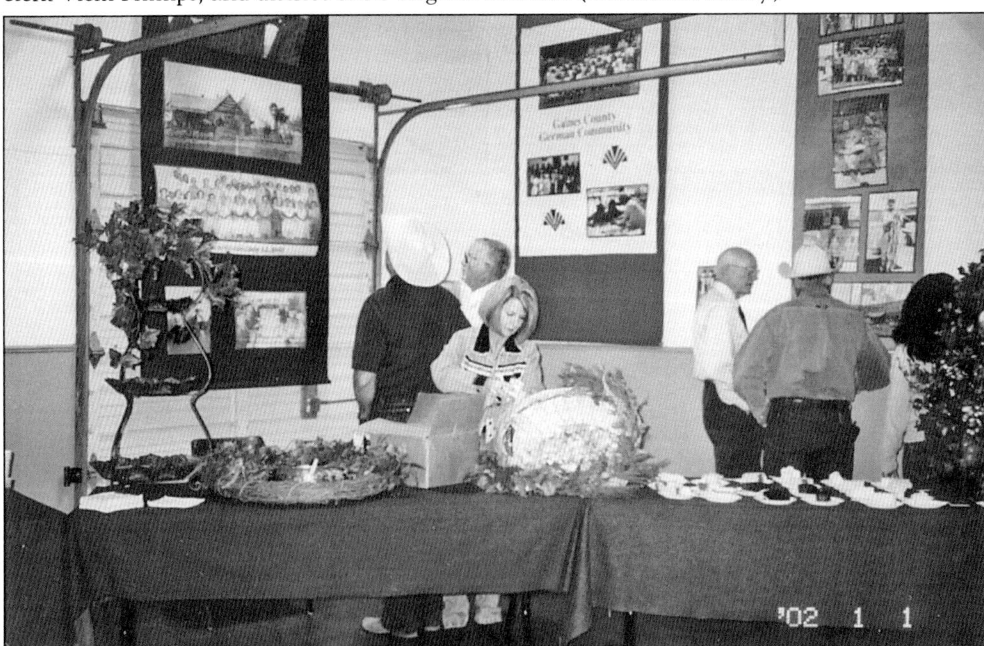

Pictured here are more of the vintage photographs and memorabilia from Seminole's 100 years of existence. These exhibits were also part of the Gaines County Civic Building's centennial display in 2005. In this shot, from left to right, former county judge Marcus Crow discusses photographs with an unidentified visitor while district clerk Virginia Stewart works on the table decoration. To the right, Carroll Haralson visits with two other unidentified visitors celebrating Seminole's past. (Holbrooks family.)

The Great Comeback is held every three years and is sponsored by the Seminole Chamber of Commerce for all graduates and former students of the Seminole schools. Hundreds gather to renew friendships and catch up on friends from all classes. In 2011, the Great Comeback was held in the former high school and junior high. Pictured here is chamber president Shelby Concotelli (left) speaking with Don Earl and his wife, Georgia. (*Sentinel.*)

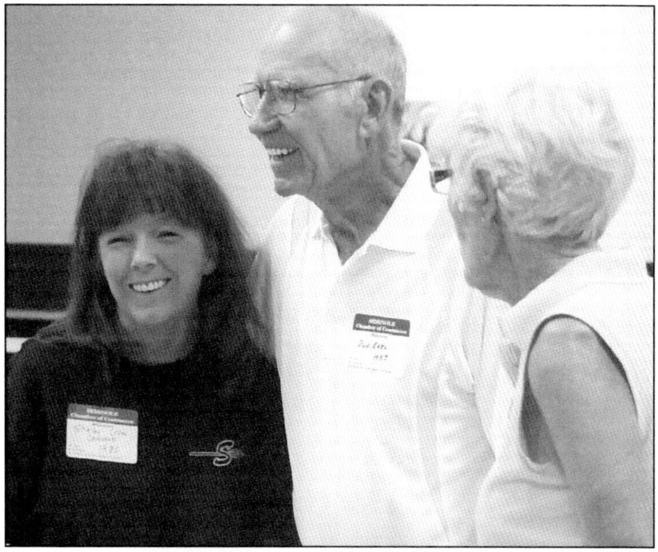

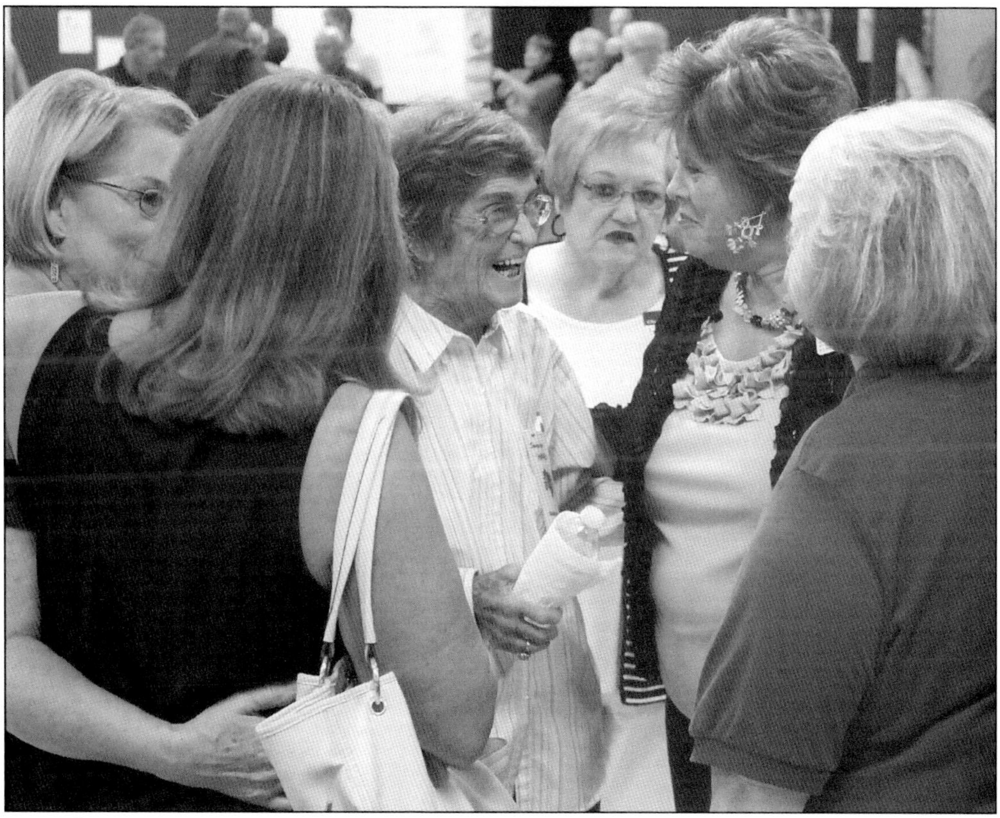

Lots of hugs, a few tears, tons of laughter, and more than a few jokes about waistlines and hairlines can be heard and seen each time the Seminole Chamber of Commerce hosts one of these Great Comebacks. This latest event took place on September 3, 2011. Pictured here are Sandra Ward (center, smiling) and several Seminole exes (one of them Judy Weems Ethridge, with large earrings directly in front of Ward) laughing about something they remembered about each other (or someone else!). (*Sentinel.*)

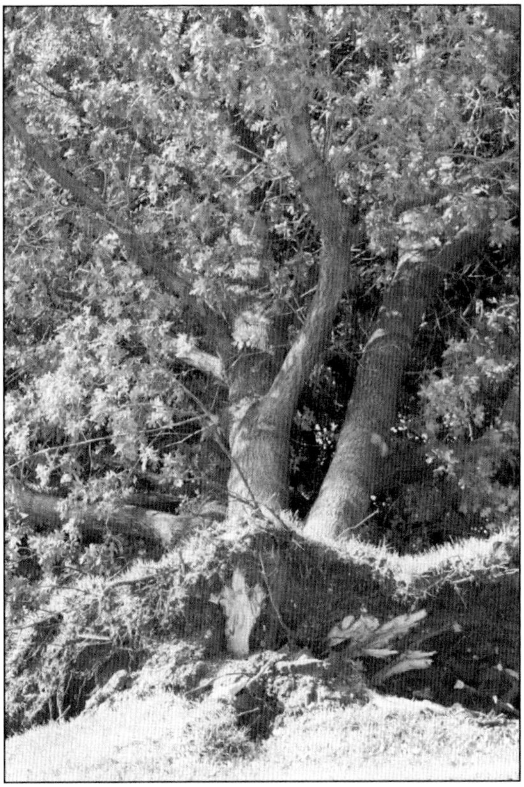

Former Seminole residents come home to see things that have not changed over the years and to marvel at those that have. This picture of an uprooted tree taken by the *Sentinel* on June 27, 2007, shows the results of one event that definitely changed a few things in Seminole—a severe storm known as a *derecho.* Taken from the Spanish word meaning "straight," a derecho is a widespread, long-lived, and violent straight-line wind usually associated with a fast-moving band of thunderstorms. (*Sentinel.*)

Seen in a snapshot taken by one of the coauthors early on the morning after the storm, June 27, 2007, is one of the most noticeable changes brought about on the night of June 26, 2007. Winds estimated at more than 120 miles per hour toppled the red-and-white communication tower that had stood over Seminole for decades. The tower lay across Southwest Avenue D, crushing a church's activity bus and the church's new sanctuary. (George family.)

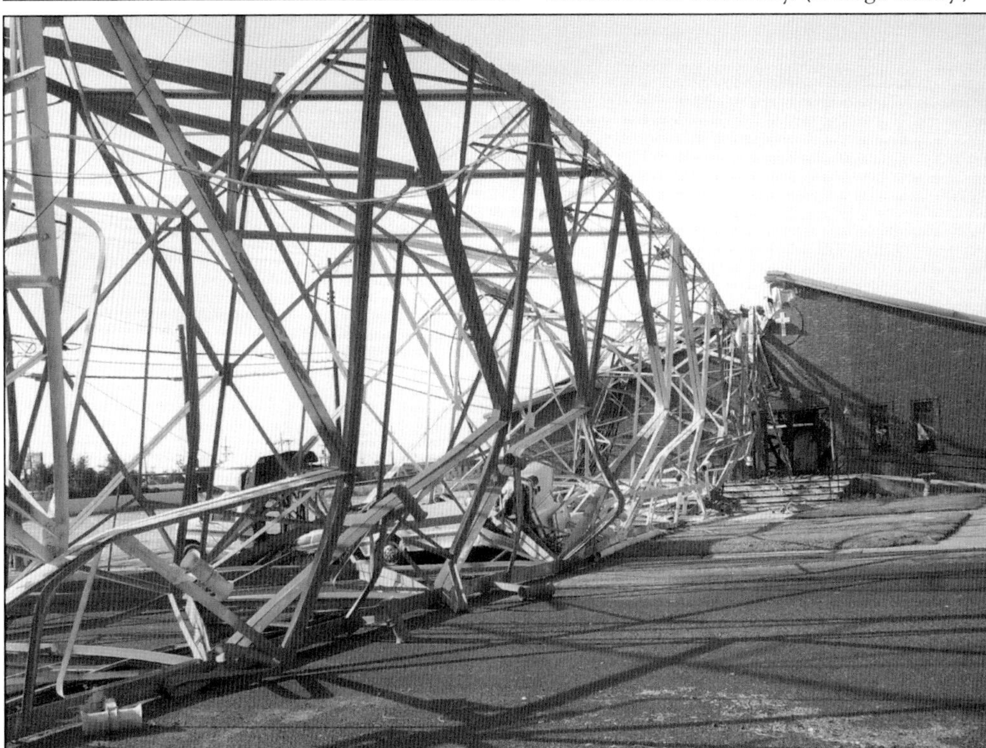

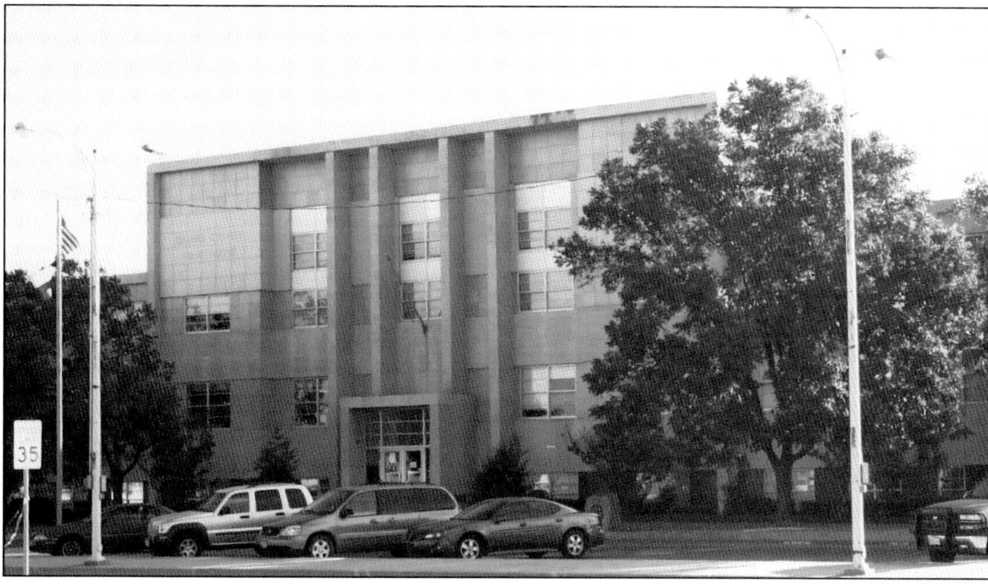

This is Seminole's courthouse before construction crews moved into town and surrounded it with chain-link fences, construction equipment, trucks, and storage units. The 1919 courthouse built by Dan Cobb was drastically remodeled, expanded, and modernized in 1955 after Seminole's Sesquicentennial Celebration. It was covered in concrete and limestone with carvings honoring ranching, farming, and oil on its west face. The current renovations should be completed in December 2011, and the courthouse will once again house Gaines County's officials. (*Sentinel.*)

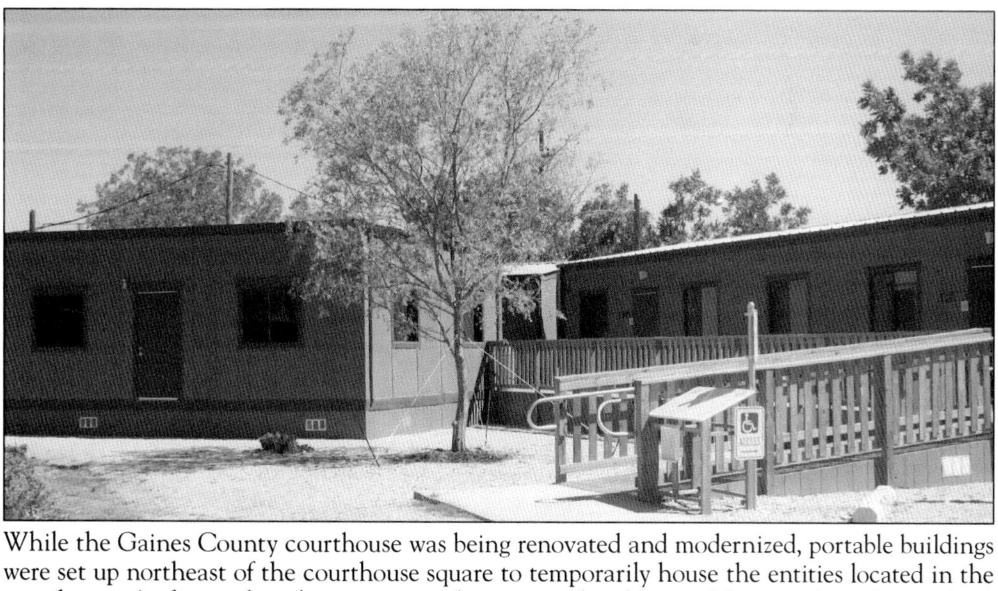

While the Gaines County courthouse was being renovated and modernized, portable buildings were set up northeast of the courthouse square to temporarily house the entities located in the courthouse. And even though a county employee recently told one of the coauthors that working in the temporary buildings was sort of like staying in a cabin on vacation, most county employees are eager to move back into the real courthouse. (George family.)

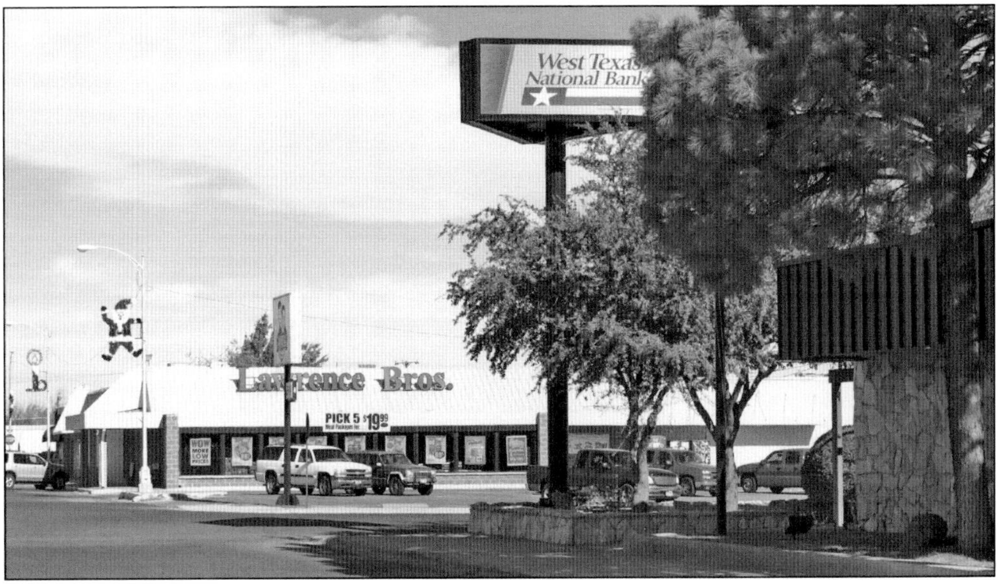

The following four pictures show downtown Seminole as it looks in 2011, with an extensive remodeling of the Gaines County Courthouse almost completed and a beautification project for the downtown area also well under way. This image shows businesses on the east side of the courthouse square. Diagonally across from the southeast corner of the courthouse—where the old county jail now headquarters the chamber of commerce—is one of Seminole's three banks, West Texas National Bank. Beyond that is one of the city's supermarkets, Lawrence Brothers IGA. In the distance is C&L Real Estate. (George family.)

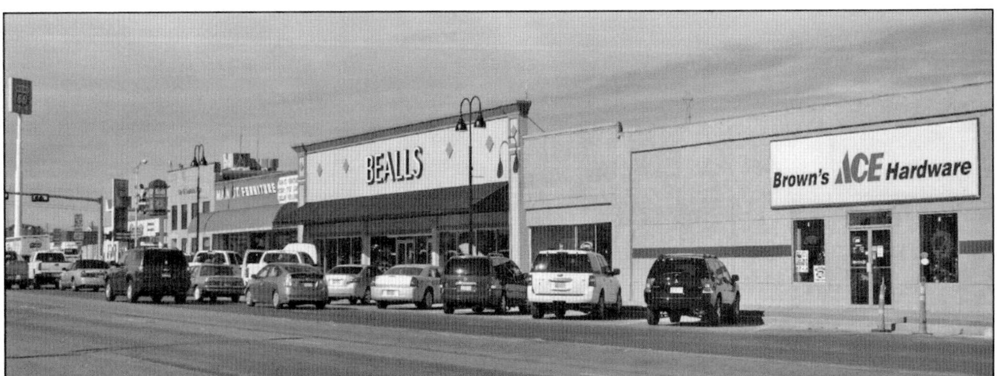

This view looks northwest along what is technically East Avenue A, but what most in Seminole either call the Hobbs highway or the Lamesa highway, depending on which way they are headed at the time. Visible here are Brown's Ace Hardware, Beall's Department Store, Main Street Furniture, and the old Seminole State Bank, which later served as Seminole City Hall. Beyond the traffic light is one of Seminole's newest businesses, Swift Stop gas station and convenience store. Also visible in this image are some of the improvements being made to the downtown area—new sidewalks, period lampposts, and decorative planters. (George family.)

This view, looking north along South Main Street directly across from the southwest corner of the courthouse, shows one of Seminole's antique shops as well as the new sidewalks, railings, and lampposts that are part of the city's beautification project slated to be complete by 2012. In the distance, in buildings that once housed dry goods shops, drugstores, cafés, barbershops, and grocery stores, are law offices, abstract offices, a nail salon, and Expressions, an upscale gift shop. (George family.)

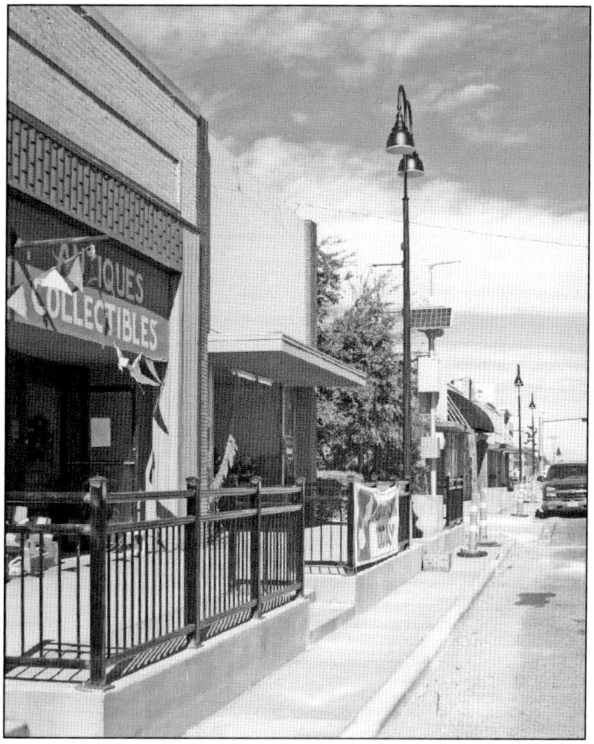

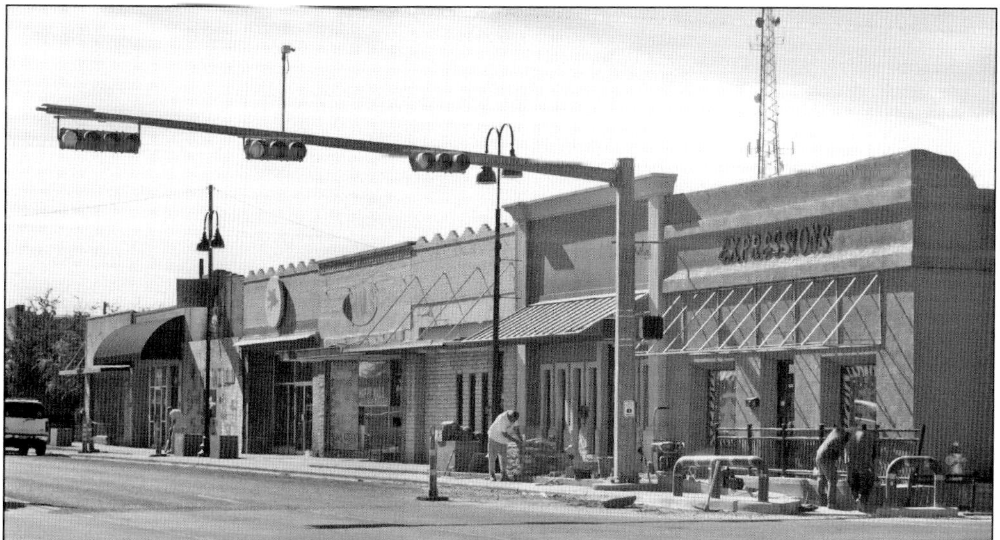

This photograph, taken looking toward the southwest from in front of the old city hall, shows workmen busy completing two stages of the beautification project. The workers on the right are installing metal railings similar to the ones seen in the picture above. The workers on the left are putting stone around concrete planters that will soon hold trees and other plants. New sidewalks are already in place, as are metal guardrails and period lampposts. On the corner of the Hobbs Highway and Main Street is Expressions, offering gifts for all occasions. Beyond that is the newly remodeled office of Permian Basin Abstract Company, the law office of James Caton, Happy Nails, and other businesses. (George family.)

Discover Thousands of Local History Books Featuring Millions of Vintage Images

Arcadia Publishing, the leading local history publisher in the United States, is committed to making history accessible and meaningful through publishing books that celebrate and preserve the heritage of America's people and places.

Find more books like this at
www.arcadiapublishing.com

Search for your hometown history, your old stomping grounds, and even your favorite sports team.

Consistent with our mission to preserve history on a local level, this book was printed in South Carolina on American-made paper and manufactured entirely in the United States. Products carrying the accredited Forest Stewardship Council (FSC) label are printed on 100 percent FSC-certified paper.

MADE IN THE USA